Heavenly Crochet Pleasures™

Publisher: Donna Robertson
Design Director: Fran Rohus
Production Director: Ange Van Arman

Editorial
Senior Editor: Jennifer Christiansen McClain
Editor: Sharon Lothrop
Associate Editors: Lyne Pickens, Trudy Atteberry, Jana Robertson

Photography
Photographers: Russell Chaffin, Keith Godfrey
Photo Stylist/Coordinator: Ruth Whitaker
Assistant Photo Stylist: Jan Jaynes

Book Design & Production
Betty Gibbs Radla

Production Assistants
Glenda Chamberlain, Jean Schrecengost

Product Design
Design Coordinator: Pam Prather

Business
CEO: John Robinson
Vice President/Marketing: Greg Deily
Vice President/M.I.S.: John Trotter

Credits

Sincerest thanks to all the designers, manufacturers and other professionals whose dedication has made this book possible. Special thanks to Quebecor Printing Book Group, Kingsport, TN.

Library of Congress Cataloging-in-Publication Data
ISBN: 1-57367-100-2
First Printing: 1997
Library of Congress Catalog Card Number: 97-68261
Published and Distributed by
The Needlecraft Shop, LLC, Big Sandy, Texas 75755
Printed in the United States of America.

Cover Model: Casey Moore

Dear Friends,

Each of us has our own version of paradise, but to most crocheters, heaven comes in the form of hooks, yarn, good patterns and plenty of people to lavish with the products of our labor. Our greatest pleasure is using our handiwork to bring warm hospitality to our homes or cuddly comfort to our children, as well as creating distinctive gifts that make memories of special occasions even more unforgettable. A crafter's halo really glows when showered with praise and thanks for another job well-done — that's why each chapter in this fun collection of new favorites is introduced by a guardian crochet angel.

Let Kitchen Angel fill that most important place in your home with a wholesome bliss that will keep everyone coming back for more. Nursery Angel watches over the precious cherubs in your life, showering them with blessed happiness and comfort, while Garden Angel spreads radiant sunshine all year long in the form of colorful floral designs. Their friends Holiday, Sewing and Kitty Angels also offer a divine selection of projects that will transport you to new heights of *Heavenly Crochet Pleasures*.

If you desire a truly out-of-this-world crochet experience, then this book is for you.

Happy Crocheting,

Jennifer

Contents

Baby Snuggles

Grandma's Favorites

Fashions & Comforts

Grandma's Garden

Heartfelt Hospitality

Holiday Happiness

General Instructions

Baby Snuggles

Create a haven of serene comfort
for your little cherub where warmth
and love abound when you surround
them with delightful handmade toys
and wearables. Cuddly, colorful designs
for any occasion lend magic to those
early years and live on in latter days
as treasured mementos.

Nursery Angel

DESIGNED BY ESTELLA WHITFORD

SIZE
8½" tall.

MATERIALS
Worsted-weight yarn — 3½ oz. tan, 2 oz. glitter white, small amount each lt. blue, pink and black; 6" piece wired metallic gold braid; polyester fiberfill; tapestry needle; G crochet hook or size needed to obtain gauge.

GAUGE
4 sc sts = 1"; 4 sc rows = 1".

SKILL LEVEL
★★ Average

BEAR ANGEL
Head & Body
NOTE: Do not join rnds unless otherwise stated. Mark first st of each rnd.

Rnd 1: Starting at **Head,** with tan, ch 2, 6 sc in 2nd ch from hook (6 sc).

Rnd 2: 2 sc in each st around (12).

Rnd 3: (Sc in next st, 2 sc in next st) around (18).

Rnd 4: (Sc in each of next 2 sts, 2 sc in next st) around (24).

Rnds 5-7: Sc in each st around.

Rnd 8: (Sc in each of next 2 sts, sc next 2 sts tog) around (18).

Rnd 9: (Sc next 2 sts tog) around (9).

Rnd 10: 2 sc in each st around (18).

Rnd 11: (Sc in each of next 2 sts, 2 sc in next st) around (24).

Rnds 12-17: Sc in each st around.

Rnd 18: (Sc in each of next 2 sts, sc next 2 sts tog) around (18). Stuff.

Rnd 19: (Sc next 2 sts tog) around (9).

Rnd 20: Sc in first st, (sc next 2 sts tog) around, join with sl st in first sc, leaving 8" for sewing, fasten off (5).

Arm (make 2)
Rnd 1: Starting at **paw,** with tan, ch 2, 6 sc in 2nd ch from hook (6 sc).

Rnd 2: (Sc in next st, 2 sc in next st) around (9).

Rnds 3-10: Sc in each st around. At end of last rnd, join with sl st in first sc, leaving 10" for sewing, fasten off. Stuff.

Flatten last rnd and sew Arms over rnds 11-13 on each side of Body.

Leg (make 2)
Rnd 1: Starting at **foot,** with tan, ch 2, 6 sc in 2nd ch from hook (6 sc).

Rnd 2: (Sc in next st, 2 sc in next st) around (9).

Rnds 3-16: Sc in each st around. At end of last rnd, join with sl st in first sc, leaving 10" for sewing, fasten off. Stuff.

For **foot shaping,** with tan, tack 3 sts of rnd 2 to sts of rnd 6.

Sew Legs to bottom of Body with each foot facing forward.

Ear (make 2)
Rnd 1: With tan, ch 2, 6 sc in 2nd ch from hook (6 sc).

Rnd 2: (Sc in next st, 2 sc in next st) around (9).

Rnd 3: Sc in each st around, join with sl st in first sc, leaving 8" for sewing, fasten off.

Flatten and sew Ears to top of Head ⅝" apart.

With black, using French Knot (see page 159), embroider eyes over rnd 3 of Head ¼" apart. With black, using Satin Stitch (see page 159), embroider nose centered below eyes; using Straight Stitch (see page 158), embroider mouthline below nose.

For **halo,** twist ends of wired gold braid together. Place over one Ear and tack to back of Head.

SKIRT
Row 1: With glitter white, ch 26, sc in 2nd ch from hook, sc in each ch across, turn (25 sc).

Row 2: Ch 3, dc in same st, 2 dc in each st across, turn (50 dc).

Row 3: Ch 3, dc in each st across, turn.

Row 4: Ch 3, skip next st, (dc, ch 2, dc) in next st, *skip next 2 sts, (dc, ch 2, dc) in next st; repeat from * across to last 2 sts, skip next st, dc in last st, turn.

Row 5: Ch 3, (dc, ch 2, dc) in each ch-2 sp across with dc in last st, fasten off.

Place around Bear's Body, overlapping to fit. Tack in place.

WING (make 2)
Row 1: With glitter white, ch 4, sc in 2nd ch from hook, sc in each ch across, turn (3 sc).

Rows 2-5: Ch 1, 2 sc in first st, sc in each st across

with 2 sc in last st, turn, ending with 11 sts in last row.

Row 6: Ch 1, sc in each st across, turn.

Row 7: Ch 1, sc first 2 sts tog, sc in each st across to last 2 sts, sc last 2 sts tog, turn (9).

Row 8: Ch 1, sc in each st across, turn.

Rows 9-12: Repeat rows 7 and 8 alternately, ending with 5 sts in last row.

Rnd 13: Working around outer edge, ch 1, sc first 2 sts tog, sc in next st, sc last 2 sts tog, sc in end of each row across; working in starting ch on opposite side of row 1, sc in first ch, 3 sc in next ch, sc in last ch; sc in end of each row across, join with sl st in first sc, fasten off.

Sew first 3 sts of rnd 13 on both Wings together. Sew center of Wings to back of Bear, gathering slightly.

For **hanger,** tie desired length glitter white to back of Head above Wings.

BLANKET
Strip A (make 2)

Row 1: With pink, ch 6, sc in 2nd ch from hook, sc in each ch across, turn (5 sc).

Rows 2-4: Ch 1, sc in each st across, turn. At end of last row, fasten off.

Row 5: Join lt. blue with sc in first st, sc in each st across, turn.

Rows 6-8: Repeat rows 2-4.

Row 9: With pink, repeat row 5.

Rows 10-12: Repeat rows 2-4.

Row 13: Repeat row 5.

Rows 14-16: Repeat rows 2-4.

Strip B (make one)

Reversing colors, work same as Strip A.

Sew long edges of Strips together creating a patchwork design by placing Strip B between both Strips A.

For **knot,** cut one strand 3" long; tie in knot around center st of one blue square on Blanket. Trim ends to ½". Repeat on remaining blue squares.

For **border,** working around entire outer edge, join glitter white with sl st in any st, ch 3, dc in each st and in end of each row around with 3 dc in each corner st, join with sl st in top of ch-3, fasten off. Tack Blanket between Bear's paws as shown in photo.❖

Pink Ice Layette

DESIGNED BY CAROL SMITH

SIZE & GAUGE FOR SWEATER, HAT & BOOTIES

Newborn, F hook, 9 dc = 2"; 5 dc rows = 2".
6 mos., G hook, 4 dc = 1"; 9 dc rows = 4".

SIZE & GAUGE FOR AFGHAN

Afghan is 30½" square. Each Motif is 3" across.

MATERIALS FOR SWEATER, HAT & BOOTIES

Baby sport pompadour yarn — 7 oz. pink/white variegated; baby pompadour — 6 oz. pink; 5 yds. pink ¼" ribbon; 5 pink ⅜" heart-shaped buttons; pink sewing thread; sewing and tapestry needles; crochet hook needed to obtain size and gauge given above.

MATERIALS FOR AFGHAN

Baby sport pompadour yarn — 9 oz. pink/white variegated; baby pompadour — 7 oz. pink; G crochet hook needed to obtain gauge.

SKILL LEVEL

★★ Average

SWEATER

FIRST ROW
First Motif

Rnd 1: With variegated, ch 6, sl st in first ch to form ring, ch 3, 2 dc in ring, ch 2, (3 dc in ring, ch 2) 7 times, join with sl st in top of ch-3 (8 3-dc groups, 8 ch-2 sps).

NOTE: For **shell,** (3 dc, ch 2, 3 dc) in next st or ch sp.

Rnd 2: Sl st in each of next 2 sts, sl st in next ch sp, ch 1, sc in same sp, shell in next ch sp, (sc in next ch sp, shell in next ch sp) around, join with sl st in first sc, fasten off (4 sc, 4 shells).

Rnd 3: Join pink with sc in any dc on rnd 1, ch 3, (sc in next dc, ch 3) around, join, fasten off.

Rnd 4: Join pink with sc in first dc of any shell on rnd 2, ch 3; skipping each sc and ch sp, (sc in next dc, ch 3) around, join, fasten off (24 sc, 24 ch-3 sps).

Second Motif

Rnds 1-3: Repeat same rnds of First Motif.

NOTE: For **joining ch-3 sp,** ch 1, sc in corresponding ch-3 sp on other Motif, ch 1.

Rnd 4: Join pink with sc in first dc of any shell on rnd 2; skipping each sc and ch sp, (ch 3, sc in next dc) 2 times; joining to side of last Motif (see Joining

Diagram), work joining ch-3 sp, *sc in next dc, (ch 3, sc in next dc) 2 times, work joining ch-3 sp; repeat from *, (sc in next dc on this Motif, ch 3) around, join, fasten off.

Repeat Second Motif 6 more times for a total of 8 Motifs.

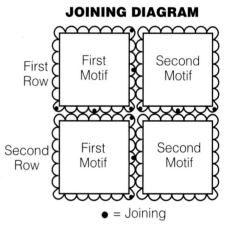

JOINING DIAGRAM

First Row — First Motif / Second Motif
Second Row — First Motif / Second Motif

● = Joining

SECOND ROW
First Motif

Joining to bottom of First Motif on last row, work same as First Row Second Motif.

Second Motif

Rnds 1-3: Repeat same rnds of First Motif on First Row.

Rnd 4: Join pink with sc in first dc of any shell on rnd 2; skipping each sc and ch sp, (ch 3, sc in next dc) 2 times; joining to bottom of next Motif on First Row, work joining ch-3 sp, [*sc in next dc, (ch 3, sc in next dc) 2 times, work joining ch-3 sp; repeat from *]; joining to side of last Motif made on this row; repeat between [ ], (sc in next dc on this Motif, ch 3) around, join, fasten off.

Repeat Second Motif 6 more times for a total of 8 Motifs.

BODICE

Row 1: Working across top edge of First Row, join variegated with sl st in first corner ch sp, ch 3, 2 dc in each of next 2 ch sps, dc in next ch sp, 2 dc in each of next 2 ch sps, (skip next corner ch sp, dc in next joining sc, skip next corner ch sp, 2 dc in each of next 2 ch sps, dc in next ch sp, 2 dc in each of next 2 ch sps) 7

Continued on page 12

times, dc in last corner ch sp, turn (81 dc).

Rows 2-3: Ch 3, dc in each st across, turn.

Row 4: For **left front,** ch 3, dc in next 15 sts leaving remaining sts unworked, turn (16).

Rows 5-9: Ch 3, dc in each st across, turn.

Row 10: For **neck shaping,** sl st in first 10 sts, ch 3, dc in last 6 sts, turn (7).

Row 11: Ch 1, sc in each of first 2 sts, hdc in each of next 2 sts, dc in each of last 3 sts, turn, fasten off.

Row 4: For **armhole opening,** skip next 8 sts on row 3; for **back,** join with sl st in next st, ch 3, dc in next 32 sts leaving remaining sts unworked, turn (33 dc).

Rows 5-9: Ch 3, dc in each st across, turn.

Row 10: Ch 3, dc in next 8 sts, ch 3, skip next st, sc in next 13 sts, ch 3, skip next st, dc in last 9 sts, turn (31 dc, 2 ch-3 sps).

Row 11: Ch 1, sc in each of first 3 sts, hdc in each of next 2 sts, dc in next 4 sts, ch 3, skip next ch-3 sp, sl st in next 13 sts, ch 3, skip next ch-3 sp, dc in next 4 sts, hdc in each of next 2 sts, sc in each of last 3 sts, turn, fasten off.

Row 4: For **armhole opening,** skip next 8 sts on row 3; for **right front,** join with sl st in next st, ch 3, dc in last 15 sts, turn (16 dc).

Rows 5-9: Ch 3, dc in each st across, turn.

Row 10: For **neck shaping,** ch 3, dc in next 6 sts leaving remaining sts unworked, turn (7).

Row 11: Ch 3, dc in each of next 2 sts, hdc in each of next 2 sts, sc in each of last 2 sts, turn, fasten off.

Matching sts, sew shoulder seams.

SLEEVE (make 2)

Row 1: With variegated, ch 6, 2 dc in 4th ch from hook, 3 dc in each of last 2 chs, turn (9 dc).

Rows 2-5: Ch 3, 2 dc in same st, dc in each st across with 3 dc in last st, turn, ending with 25 dc in last row.

Rows 6-7: Ch 3, dc in each st across, turn.

Rnd 8: Working in rnds, ch 3, dc in each st around; for **armhole opening,** ch 8, join with sl st in top of ch-3, **turn** (25 dc, 8 chs).

Rnd 9: Ch 3, skip first 2 chs, dc in next 5 chs, skip next ch, dc in each st around, join, **turn** (30 dc).

Rnds 10-12: Ch 3, dc in each st around, join.

Rnd 13: Ch 1, sc in first st, skip next 2 sts, shell in next st, skip next 2 sts, (sc in next st, skip next 2 sts, shell in next st, skip next 2 sts) around, join with sl st in first sc, **do not** turn (5 sc, 5 shells).

Rnd 14: Ch 3, 2 dc in same st, sc in ch sp of next shell, (shell in next sc, sc in ch sp of next shell) around,

3 dc in same st as first st, ch 2, join with sl st in top of ch-3, fasten off.

Rnd 15: Working in front of sts, join pink with sc in first dc of first shell on rnd 13; skipping each sc and ch sp, ch 3, (sc in next dc, ch 3) around; join with sl st in first sc, fasten off.

Rnd 16: Working in dc of rnd 14, repeat rnd 15.

Matching center of row 1 to shoulder seam, sew Sleeves to armhole openings.

RIGHT FRONT & NECK RUFFLE

Row 1: Working in ch sps, sts and in ends of rows across right front edge and neck opening of Sweater, join variegated with sc in bottom corner ch sp, *shell in next ch sp, skip next ch sp, sc in next ch sp, skip next ch sp, shell in next ch sp*, skip next corner ch sp, sc in next joining sc, skip next corner ch sp; repeat between **, sc in next corner ch sp, skip next row on Bodice, shell in next row, (sc in top of next row, skip next row, shell in next row) 2 times, skip next row; working across neck edge, evenly space 47 dc across, turn.

Row 2: Working in **front lps** only of last 47 sts made, ch 3, skip first st, shell in next st, skip next 2 sts, (sc in next st, skip next 2 sts, shell in next st, skip next 2 sts) 7 times, sl st in last st, fasten off.

Row 3: Join pink with sc in first dc of first shell on row 1, skipping ch sps and sc, (ch 3, sc in next dc) across to neck edge; working in remaining **front lps** of next 47 sts, ch 3, sc in next dc, ch 3, skip next dc, sc in next dc, *(ch 3, sc in next st) 2 times, ch 3, skip next st, sc in next st; repeat from * across, **turn;** working in dc only of row 2, (ch 3, sc in next dc) across, fasten off.

Tack tip of each shell across neck edge to Bodice.

LEFT FRONT EDGING

Working in ch sps of Motifs across left front, join variegated with sc in first corner ch sp of First Motif on First Row at waist edge, *shell in next ch sp, skip next ch sp, sc in next ch sp, skip next ch sp, shell in next ch sp*, skip next corner ch sp, sc in next joining sc, skip next corner ch sp; repeat between **, sc in next corner ch sp, fasten off.

FINISHING

1: Cut 3 pieces ribbon each 8" long. Tie each piece into a bow. Sew one button to center of each bow. Sew buttons evenly spaced to left front Bodice as shown in photo. Use sps between sts on right front

Bodice for buttonholes.

2: Weave 24" piece ribbon through every 1 or 2 sts on row 1 of Bodice; fold ends to wrong side; cut off excess; sew ends in place.

3: Starting at top of one Sleeve, weave 18" piece of ribbon through every 2 sts on rnd 12; tie ends into bow. Repeat on other Sleeve.

BOOTIE (make 2)

Rnd 1: Ch 4, sl st in first ch to form ring, ch 3, 16 dc in ring, join with sl st in top of ch-3, **turn** (17 dc).

Rnds 2-4: Ch 3, dc in each st around, join, **turn.**

Rows 5-9: Working in rows; for **ankle opening,** ch 3, dc in each st across, **turn.** At end of last row, fasten off.

Fold last row in half to form heel, sew together.

Rnd 10: Working around ankle opening in ends of rows; for **cuff,** join with sc in end of any row, 2 sc in same row, 3 sc in end of each row around, join with sl st in first sc (30).

Rnd 11: Ch 1, sc in first st, skip next 2 sts, shell in next st, skip next 2 sts, (sc in next st, skip next 2 sts, shell in next st, skip next 2 sts) around, join with sl st in first sc, **do not** turn (5 sc, 5 shells).

Rnd 12: Ch 3, 2 dc in same st, sc in ch sp of next shell, (shell in next sc, sc in ch sp of next shell) around, 3 dc in same st as first st, ch 2, join with sl st in top of ch-3, fasten off.

Rnd 13: Working in front of sts, join pink with sc in first dc of first shell on rnd 11; skipping each sc and ch sp, ch 3, (sc in next dc, ch 3) around; join with sl st in in first sc, fasten off.

Rnd 14: Working in dc of rnd 12, repeat rnd 13.

Starting at center front, weave 18" piece of ribbon through ends of rows around ankle opening, tie into bow.

BONNET

FIRST MOTIF

Work same as Sweater's First Row First Motif on page 10.

SECOND MOTIF

Work same as Sweater's First Row Second Motif.

Repeat Second Motif 2 more times for a total of 4 Motifs.

CROWN

Row 1: Working across one long edge of Motifs, join variegated with sl st in first corner ch sp, ch 3, 2 dc in each of next 2 ch sps, dc in next ch sp, 2 dc in each of next 2 ch sps, (skip next corner ch sp, dc in next joining sc, skip next corner ch sp, 2 dc in each of next 2 ch sps, dc in next ch sp, 2 dc in each of next 2 ch sps) 3 times, dc in last corner ch sp, turn (41 dc).

Row 2: Ch 3, dc in each st across, turn.

Row 3: Ch 3, dc in next 13 sts, (yo, insert hook in next st, yo, draw lp through, yo, draw through 2 lps on hook) 12 times, yo, draw through all 13 lps on hook, dc in last 15 sts, turn (30).

Row 4: Ch 3, dc in next 10 sts, (yo, insert hook in next st, yo, draw lp through, yo, draw through 2 lps on hook) 8 times, yo, draw through all 9 lps on hook, dc in last 11 sts, turn (23). Leaving long end for sewing, fasten off.

Fold last row in half; matching sts, sew together.

EDGING

Working across bottom straight edge, join variegated with sl st in first corner ch sp on Motif, ch 3, *2 dc in each of next 2 ch sps, dc in next ch sp, 2 dc in each of next 2 ch sps, dc in next corner ch sp*, 2 dc in end of next 8 rows, dc in next corner ch sp on Motif; repeat between **, fasten off.

FINISHING

1: Weave 18" piece of ribbon through every 1 or 2 sts on Edging, pull ends even.

2: Cut 2 pieces of ribbon each 8" long. Tie each piece into a bow. Sew one button to center of each bow. Sew bows to bottom corners of Bonnet.

AFGHAN

FIRST ROW
First Motif

Work same as Sweater's First Row First Motif on page 10.

Second Motif

Work same as Sweater's First Row Second Motif.

Repeat Second Motif 8 more times for a total of 10 Motifs.

SECOND ROW
First Motif

Work same as Sweater's Second Row First

Continued on page 24

Petite Ripples

DESIGNED BY ELLEN ANDERSON

SIZE
31" x 37½".

MATERIALS
Pompadour baby yarn — 11 oz. multicolor, 3½ oz. each lavender and white; E and F crochet hooks or sizes needed to obtain gauges.

GAUGES
E hook, 6 dc = 1"; 3 dc rows = 1¼".
F hook, 5 sc = 1"; 12 ripple rows = 3½".

SKILL LEVEL
★★ Average

CENTER STRIP (make 2)
Row 1: With F hook and lavender, ch 170, dc in back bar (see illustration) of 4th ch from hook, dc in back bar of each ch across, turn (168 dc).

BACK BAR OF CHAIN

NOTES: For **popcorn (pc),** 5 dc in next st, drop lp from hook, insert hook in first st of 5-dc group, draw dropped lp through, ch 1.

Use E hook unless otherwise stated.

Front of row 2 is right side of work.

Row 2: Ch 3, dc in each of next 2 sts, pc in next st, (dc in next 6 sts, pc in next st) across to last 3 sts, dc in each of last 3 sts, turn (144 dc, 24 pc).

Row 3: Ch 3, dc in each st across, turn, fasten off (168 dc).

Row 4: Working this row in **back lps** only, join white with sc in first st, *[hdc in next st, dc in next st, tr in next st, dc in next st, hdc in next st], sc in each of next 2 sts; repeat from * across to last 6 sts; repeat between [ ], sc in last st, **do not** turn, fasten off.

Row 5: Working this row in **back lps** only, with F hook and multicolor, join with sc in first st, sc in each of next 2 sts, 3 sc in next st, (sc in next 6 sts, 3 sc in next st) across to last 3 sts, sc in each of last 3 sts, turn (216 sc).

Rows 6-16: Working these rows in **back lps** only, ch 1, skip first st, sc in each of next 3 sts, 3 sc in next st, (sc in each of next 3 sts, skip next 2 sts, sc in each of next 3 sts, 3 sc in next st) across to last 4 sts, sc in each of next 2 sts, skip next st, sc in last st, turn. At end of last row, fasten off.

Row 17: Working this row in **back lps** only, join white with sl st in first st, ch 4, skip next st, dc in next st, hdc in next st, sc in next st, hdc in next st, dc in next st, *tr in next st, skip next 2 sts, tr in next st, dc in next st, hdc in next st, sc in next st, hdc in next st, dc in next st; repeat from * across to last 2 sts, skip next st, tr in last st, **do not** turn, fasten off (168 sts).

Row 18: Working in starting ch on opposite side of row 1, with right side of pc on row 2 facing you, repeat row 4.

Rows 19-31: Repeat rows 5-17.

END STRIP (make 2)
Rows 1-30: Repeat same rows of Center Strip.

POPCORN STRIP (make 3)
Rows 1-3: Repeat same rows of Center Strip.

STRIP ASSEMBLY DIAGRAM

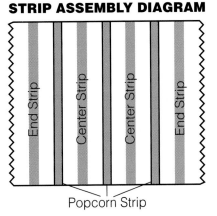

End Strip · Center Strip · Center Strip · End Strip

Popcorn Strip

ASSEMBLY
Working in **back lps** only, with white, sew Strips together according to Strip Assembly Diagram, with right side of all pc facing up.❖

Baby Fans

DESIGNED BY ELLEN ANDERSON

SIZE
36" square.

MATERIALS
Pompadour baby yarn — 15 oz. white; 5 yds. of 3/16" satin ribbon; F crochet hook or size needed to obtain gauge.

GAUGE
9 dc = 2"; 5 dc rows = 2".

SKILL LEVEL
★★ Average

AFGHAN

Rnd 1: Ch 4, sl st in first ch to form ring, ch 3, 2 dc in ring, (ch 2, 3 dc in ring) 3 times; to **join,** hdc in top of ch-3 (12 dc, 4 ch sps).

Rnds 2-37: Ch 3, dc around joining hdc, hdc in each st around with (2 dc, ch 2, 2 dc) in each corner ch sp, 2 dc around joining hdc of last rnd, join as before, ending with 147 dc across each side between ch sps in last rnd.

Rnd 38: Ch 3, dc around joining hdc, ch 1, skip next st, (dc in next st, ch 1, skip next st) around to next ch sp, *(2 dc, ch 2, 2 dc) in next ch sp, ch 1, skip next st, (dc in next st, ch 1, skip next st) around to next ch sp; repeat from * around, 2 dc around joining hdc of last rnd, join.

Rnd 39: Ch 3, dc around joining hdc, dc in each ch and in each st around with, (2 dc, ch 2, 2 dc) in each corner ch sp, 2 dc around joining hdc of last rnd, ch 2, join with sl st in top of ch-3 (155 dc across each side between ch sps).

Rnd 40: Sl st in each of next 2 sts, ch 1, sc in same st, ch 3, skip next 2 sts, sc in next st, ch 5, skip next 3 sts, sc in next st, [*(ch 3, skip next 2 sts, sc in next st) 2 times, ch 5, skip next 3 sts, sc in next st; repeat from * across to 5 sts before next ch sp, ch 3, skip next 2 sts, sc in next st, ch 3, skip next 2 sts, (sc, ch 5, sc) in next ch sp]; repeat

between [ ] 3 more times, ch 3, skip last 2 sts, join with sl st in first sc.

Rnd 41: Sl st in first ch-3 sp, ch 1, sc in same sp, *[(9 dc in next ch-5 sp, sc in next ch-3 sp, ch 3, sc in next ch-3 sp) across to next corner ch-5 sp, 11 dc in next corner ch-5 sp, sc in next ch-3 sp, ch 3], sc in next ch-3 sp; repeat from * 2 more times; repeat between [ ], join.

Rnd 42: Sl st in next dc, ch 4, dc in next dc, (ch 1, dc in next dc) 7 times, sc in next ch-3 sp, [*dc in next dc, (ch 1, dc in next dc) 8 times, sc in next ch-3 sp; repeat from * across to next corner 11-dc group, dc in next dc, (ch 1, dc in next dc) 10 times, sc in next ch-3 sp]; repeat between [ ] around, join with sl st in 3rd ch of ch-4.

NOTES: For **small decrease (sm dec),** yo 2 times, insert hook in same ch-1 sp, yo, draw lp through, (yo draw through 2 lps on hook) 2 times, yo 2 times, insert hook in next ch-1 sp, yo, draw lp through, (yo, draw through 2 lps on hook) 2 times, yo, draw through all 3 lps on hook.

For **large decrease (lg dec),** yo 2 times, insert hook in same ch-1 sp, yo, draw lp through, (yo, draw through 2 lps on hook) 2 times, *yo 2 times, insert hook in next ch-1 sp, yo, draw lp through, (yo, draw through 2 lps on hook) 2 times; repeat from * 2 more times, yo, draw through all 5 lps on hook

Rnd 43: Sl st in first ch-1 sp, ch 3, tr in next ch-1 sp, ◊[ch 3, (sm dec, ch 3) 5 times, *lg dec, ch 3, (sm dec, ch 3) 5 times; repeat from * around to ch sp before next corner, lg dec, ch 3, (sm dec, ch 3) 7 times], lg dec; repeat from ◊ 2 more times; repeat between [ ], sm dec, join with sl st in top of ch-3.

Rnd 44: Skip next tr, sl st in next ch-3 sp, ch 1, (2 sc, ch 3, 2 sc) in same sp and in each ch-3 sp around, join with sl st in first sc, fasten off.

Cut ribbon into 4 pieces each 45" long. Weave each piece through ch-1 sps across each side of rnd 38; tie ends into bow on each corner.❖

Circus Pillow

DESIGNED BY SANDRA MILLER MAXFIELD

SIZE
18" square.

MATERIALS
Worsted-weight yarn — 9 oz. each red and yellow, 3½ oz. each white and gray, small amount each pink and black; 1 yd. gold ⅜" trim; grey sewing thread; ¾" yellow pom-pom; 18" square pillow form; hot glue gun; sewing and tapestry needles; H crochet hook or size needed to obtain gauge.

GAUGE
13 dc = 4"; 7 dc rows = 4".

SKILL LEVEL
★★ Average

FRONT
Row 1: With red, ch 58, dc in 4th ch from hook, dc in each ch across, turn, fasten off (56 dc).

NOTES: When changing colors (see page 159), always drop all colors to same side of work. Do not carry dropped colors across to next section of same color. Use a separate ball of yarn for each color section. Fasten off colors when no longer needed.

Work graph from left to right on odd rows and from right to left on even rows.

Each square on graph equals 2 dc.

First ch-3 counts as first dc.

Row 2: For row 2 of graph, ch 3, dc in next st changing to yellow, dc in next 4 sts changing to red in last st made, (dc in next 4 sts changing to yellow in last st made, dc in next 4 sts changing to red in last st made) across to last 2 sts, dc in each of last 2 sts, turn.

Rows 3-30: Ch 3, dc in each st across changing colors according to graph, turn. At end of last row, fasten off.

BACK
Rows 1-5: Repeat same rows of Front.

Rows 6-29: Repeat rows 2-5 of Front consecutively.

Row 30: Ch 3, dc in each st across, **do not** turn or fasten off.

Rnd 31: For **edging,** holding Front and Back wrong sides together with Front facing you and pillow form between, matching sts, working through both thicknesses, ch 1, sc in end of each row and in each st around with 3 sc in each corner st, join with sl st in first sc, fasten off.

SMALL TASSEL
Cut 3 strands each red and yellow each 4" long. Tie separate strand red tightly around middle of all strands held together; fold strands in half. Tie 4" strand red around strands ½" from top of fold; secure and hide ends inside Tassel. Trim all ends evenly.

Glue 1½" piece of trim around Tassel ¼" from top of fold. Glue Tassel below blanket on elephant as shown in photo.

LARGE TASSEL
Cut 18 strands each red and yellow each 9" long. Tie separate strand red tightly around middle of all strands held together; fold strands in half. Wrap 11" strand red around strands 1" from top of fold, covering ½"; secure and hide ends inside Tassel. Trim all ends evenly.

Glue 2½" piece of trim around Tassel 1" from top of fold. Tie Tassel to each corner of Pillow.

FINISHING
Glue pom-pom to tip of hat on elephant.

Cut 12" piece from trim. With sewing thread and needle, sew trim around blanket on elephant as shown in photo. Cut 5" piece from trim. Sew to neck of elephant as shown.❖

CIRCUS PILLOW GRAPH

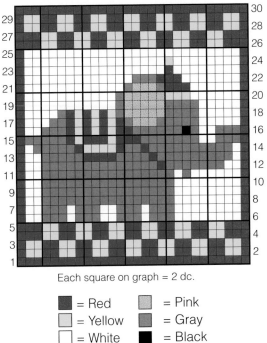

Each square on graph = 2 dc.

■ = Red   ▨ = Pink
▨ = Yellow   ▦ = Gray
□ = White   ■ = Black

All in White

DESIGNED BY CAROL SMITH

SIZES & GAUGE
Newborn, E hook, 21 hdc = 4"; 9 hdc rows = 2".
6 mos., F hook, 19 hdc = 4"; 4 hdc rows = 1".
12 mos., G hook, 17 hdc = 4"; 7 hdc rows = 2".

MATERIALS
Baby pompadour yarn — 11 oz. for newborn, 13 oz. for 6 mos., 15 oz. for 12 mos. white; 3 yds. pink ¼" satin ribbon; 54 pink with pearl centers ¾" wide x 1" long satin ribbon bows; 3 white ⁷⁄₁₆" flat buttons; pink and white sewing thread; sewing and tapestry needles; crochet hook needed to obtain size and gauge given above.

SKILL LEVEL
★★ Average

DRESS
Skirt
NOTES: For **beginning half shell (beg half shell)**, ch 3, 4 dc in next ch sp.

For **shell,** 9 dc in next st or ch sp.

For **ending half shell (end half shell),** 5 dc in last ch sp.

For **beginning V-st (beg V-st),** ch 5, dc in same st.

For **V-stitch (V-st),** (dc, ch 2, dc) in next st.

Row 1: Ch 94, sc in 2nd ch from hook, (skip next ch, shell in next ch, skip next ch, sc in next ch) across, turn (24 sc, 23 shells).

Row 2: Beg V-st, (ch 5, skip next shell, V-st in next sc) across, turn (24 V-sts, 23 ch-5 sps).

Row 3: Beg half shell; working over next ch sp, sc in center dc of next shell on row before last, (shell in ch sp of next V-st on last row; working over next ch sp, sc in center dc of next shell on row before last) across to last V-st, end half shell, turn.

Row 4: Ch 1, sc in first st, ch 3, V-st in next sc, (ch 5, skip next shell, V-st in next sc) across to last half shell, ch 3, sc in last, st, turn.

Row 5: Ch 1, sc in first st, shell in next V-st; (working over next ch-5 sp, sc in center dc of next shell on row before last, shell in next V-st) across to last st, sc in last st, turn.

Rows 6-25: Repeat rows 2-5 consecutively. At end of last row, fasten off.

Bodice
Row 1: Working in starting ch on opposite side of row 1, with wrong side of row 1 facing you, join with sl st in first ch, ch 2, skip next ch-1 sp, hdc in next ch, (hdc in next ch-1 sp, hdc in next ch) across, turn (92 hdc).

Rows 2-4: Ch 2, hdc in each st across, turn.

Row 5: For **right back,** ch 2, hdc in next 24 sts leaving remaining sts unworked, turn (25).

Row 6: Ch 2, hdc in each st across, turn.

Row 7: Ch 2, hdc in each st across to last 2 sts, hdc last 2 sts tog, turn (24).

Rows 8-11: Repeat rows 6 and 7 alternately, ending with 22 sts in last row.

Row 12: Ch 2, hdc in next 10 sts, hdc next 2 sts tog leaving remaining sts unworked, turn (12).

Row 13: Ch 3, dc in each of next 2 sts, hdc in each of next 3 sts, sc in each of next 3 sts, sl st in next st leaving last 2 sts unworked, **do not** turn, fasten off (9 sts).

Row 5: For **armhole opening,** skip next 3 sts on row 4; for **front,** join with sl st in next st, ch 2, hdc in next 35 sts leaving remaining sts unworked, turn (36 hdc).

Row 6: Ch 2, hdc in each st across, turn.

Row 7: Ch 2, skip next st, hdc in each st across to last 2 sts, hdc last 2 sts tog, turn (34).

Rows 8-11: Repeat rows 6 and 7 alternately, ending with 30 sts in last row.

Row 12: For **left shoulder,** ch 2, skip next st, hdc in next 7 sts, hdc last 2 sts tog leaving remaining sts unworked, turn (9).

Row 13: Ch 3, dc in each of next 2 sts, hdc in each of next 3 sts, sc in last of last 3 sts, turn, fasten off.

Row 12: For **neck,** skip next 8 sts on row 11; for **right shoulder,** join with sl st in next st, ch 2, skip next st, hdc in next 7 sts, hdc last 2 sts tog, turn (9).

Row 13: Ch 1, sc in each of first 3 sts, hdc in each of next 3 sts, dc in each of last 3 sts, fasten off.

Row 5: For **armhole opening,** skip next 3 sts on row 4; for **left back,** join with sl st in next st, ch 2, hdc in each st across, turn (25 hdc).

Row 6: Ch 2, hdc in each st across, turn.

Row 7: Ch 2, skip next st, hdc in each st across, turn (24).

Rows 8-11: Repeat rows 6 and 7 alternately, ending with 22 sts in last row.

Row 12: Sl st in first 10 sts, ch 2, skip next st, hdc in each st across, turn (12).

Continued on page 24

Mint Doll Dress

DESIGNED BY BEVERLY MEWHORTER

SIZE
Fits 10" baby doll.

MATERIALS
Pompadour baby yarn — 4 oz. mint; 5 yds. mint ⅛" satin ribbon; tapestry needle; E crochet hook or size needed to obtain gauge.

GAUGE
6 sc = 1"; 2 shell rows and 2 sc rows = 1½".

SKILL LEVEL
★★ Average

DRESS
NOTE: Front of row 1 is wrong side of work.

Row 1: Starting at **neck**, ch 31, sc in 2nd ch from hook, sc in each ch across, turn (30 sc).

Row 2: Ch 1, sc in each st across, turn.

Row 3: Ch 1, 2 sc in each st across, turn (60).

Row 4: Ch 1, sc in each st across, turn.

Row 5: Ch 1, sc in first 10 sts; for **armhole**, ch 12, skip next 12 sts; sc in next 16 sts; for **armhole**, ch 12, skip next 12 sts; sc in last 10 sts, turn (36 sc, 24 chs).

Row 6: Ch 1, sc in each st and in each ch across, turn (60 sc).

Row 7: Ch 1, sc in each st across, turn.

Row 8: Ch 1, sc in first st, (ch 3, sc in next st) across, turn (59 ch-3 sps).

Row 9: Ch 1, sc in first ch-3 sp, (ch 1, sc in next ch-3 sp) across, turn.

NOTES: For **shell**, (dc, ch 1, dc, ch 1, dc) in next st.

For **beginning shell (beg shell)**, ch 4, (dc, ch 1, dc) in same st.

Row 10: Ch 1, sc in first sc, (shell in next sc, sc in next sc) across, turn.

Row 11: Beg shell, (sc in 2nd dc of next shell, shell in next sc) across, turn.

Row 12: Ch 1, sc in 2nd dc of first shell, (shell in next sc, sc in 2nd dc of next shell) across, turn.

Rows 13-30: Repeat rows 11 and 12 alternately. At end of last row, fasten off.

Neck Edging
Row 1: Working in starting ch on opposite side of row 1, with wrong side facing you, join with sc in first ch, sc in each ch across with 2 sc in last ch, turn (31 sc).

Row 2: Ch 1, sc in first st, shell in next st, (skip next st, sc in next st, skip next st, shell in next st) across to last st, sc in last st, fasten off.

Sleeves
Rnd 1: Working around armhole, join with sc in 6th ch on underarm, sc in next 6 chs, sc in end of next st on row 4, sc in next 12 sts, sc in end of next st on row 4, sc in last 5 chs, join with sl st in first sc (26 sc).

Rnd 2: Ch 1, 2 sc in each st around, join (52).

Rnds 3-4: Ch 1, sc in each st around, join.

Rnd 5: Ch 1, sc in first st, (sc next 2 sts tog, sc in next st) around, join (35).

Rnd 6: Ch 1, sc in first st, (sc next 2 sts tog) around, join (18).

Rnd 7: Ch 1, sc in first st, ch 3, (sc in next st, ch 3) around, join.

Rnd 8: Sl st in first ch-3 sp, ch 1, sc in same sp, shell in next ch-3 sp, (sc in next ch-3 sp, shell in next ch-3 sp) around, join, fasten off.

Repeat in other armhole.

Finishing
1: Sew ends of rows 12-30 on Dress together.

2: Cut 6 pieces ribbon each 8" long. Tie each piece into bow around sts of row 28 evenly spaced around bottom of Dress as shown in photo.

3: Cut 2 pieces ribbon each 15" long. Weave one piece through sts of row 1 and other piece through ch-3 sps of row 8. Place Dress on doll. Pull ribbon ends to gather Dress around body, ties ends of each ribbon into a bow at back.

4: Cut 2 pieces ribbon each 10" long. Weave through sts of rnd 6 on each Sleeve. Pull to gather, tie ends into a bow. Tie 8" piece ribbon into a bow around st on row 8 at center front of Dress.

BOOTIE (make 2)
Rnd 1: Starting at **sole**, ch 11, sc in 2nd ch from hook, sc in each ch across with 2 sc in last ch; working on opposite side of ch, sc in each ch across, join with sl st in first sc (20 sc).

Rnd 2: Ch 1, sc in each st around, join.

Rnd 3: Working this rnd in **back lps** only, ch 1, sc in each st around, join.

Rnd 4: Ch 1, sc in each st around, join.

Rnd 5: Ch 1, sc in first st, ch 3, (sc in next st, ch 3) around, join.

Continued on page 24

Mint Doll Dress

Continued from page 22

Rnd 6: Sl st in first ch sp, ch 1, sc in same sp, shell in next ch sp, (sc in next ch sp, shell in next ch sp) around, join, fasten off.

Weave 12" piece ribbon through ch-3 sps of rnd 5. Place Bootie on doll's foot, pull ribbon to gather; tie ends into a bow.

DIAPER

Row 1: For **front,** starting at **crotch,** ch 6, sc in 2nd ch from hook, sc in each ch across, turn (5 sc).

Rows 2-5: Ch 1, sc in each st across, turn.

Rows 6-7: Ch 1, sc in first st, (2 sc in next st, sc in next st) across, turn (7, 10).

Row 8: Ch 1, sc in each of first 2 sts, (2 sc in next st, sc in next st) across, turn (14).

Rows 9-11: Ch 1, sc in each st across, turn.

Row 12: Ch 3, sl st in each st across to last st, ch 3, sl st in last st, fasten off.

Row 13: For **back,** working in starting ch on opposite side of row 1, join with sc in first ch, sc in each ch across, turn (5 sc).

Rows 14-15: Ch 1, sc in each st across, turn.

Rows 16-18: Repeat rows 6-8.

Rows 19-25: Ch 1, sc in each st across, turn.

Row 26: Ch 3, sc in each st across to last st, ch 3, sc in last st, **do not** turn; for **first ruffle,** working in ends of rows, skip first row, sc in next row, shell in next row, (skip next row, sc in next row, shell in next row) 7 times, sc in last row, sl st in base of ch-3 on front, fasten off.

For **2nd ruffle,** working in ends of rows on opposite side of Diaper, join with sl st in end of row 11 on front, sc in next row, shell in next row, (skip next row, sc in next row, shell in next row) 7 times, sc in last row, sl st in base of ch-3 on back, fasten off.

Cut 2 pieces ribbon each 8" long. Place Diaper on doll. Insert one ribbon piece through ch-3 sps of front and back on one side of Diaper; tie ends into a bow. Repeat on other side.

HEADBAND

Rnd 1: Ch 36, sl st in first ch to form ring, ch 1, sc in first ch, ch 3, (sc in next ch, ch 3) around, join with sl st in first sc, fasten off.

Rnd 2: Working in starting ch on opposite side of rnd 1, join with sc in first ch, ch 3, (sc in next ch, ch 3) around, join, fasten off.

Tie 18" piece ribbon into a double bow; tack to Headband. Place Headband on doll's head.❖

Pink Ice Layette

Continued from page 13

Motif on page 10.

Second Motif

Work same as Sweater's Second Row Second Motif.

Repeat Second Motif 8 more times for a total of 10 Motifs.

Repeat Second Row 8 more times for a total of 10 rows.

Edging

Working around outer edge, join variegated with sc in any ch sp, ch 3, (sc in next ch sp, ch 3) around, join with sl st in first sc, fasten off.❖

All in White

Continued from page 21

Row 13: Sl st in each of first 3 sts, ch 1, sc in each of next 3 sts, hdc in each of next 3 sts, dc in each of last 3 sts, fasten off (9 sts).

Sew rows 4-25 of Skirt together. Sew shoulder seams.

Collar

Row 1: Working across neck opening, with right side of work facing you, join with sc in first st on left back shoulder, evenly space 42 more sc across to right back, turn (43 sc).

Row 2: Ch 1, sc in first st, (skip next 2 sts, shell in next st, skip next 2 sts, sc in next st) across, turn (8 sc, 7 shells).

Rows 3-4: Repeat rows 2 and 3 of Skirt. At end of last row, fasten off.

Tack Collar to Bodice.

Sleeve (make 2)

Row 1: Ch 14, sc in 2nd ch from hook, (skip next ch, shell in next ch, skip next ch, sc in next ch) across, turn (4 sc, 3 shells).

Rows 2-11: Repeat rows 2-5 of Skirt consecutively, ending with row 3. At end of last row, fasten off.

Matching center of row 1 on Sleeve to shoulder seam, sew Sleeve to ends of rows on each side of armhole opening.

Finishing

1: Sew buttons evenly spaced down right back opening using sps between sts on left back for buttonholes.

2: Weave 1 yd. of ribbon through every 2 sts on row 2 of Bodice. Fold ends to wrong side, trim excess; sew in place.

3: Sew one bow between shells on last row of Collar, each Sleeve and Skirt as shown in photo.

BOOTIE (make 2)

Rnd 1: Ch 5, sl st in first ch to form ring, ch 2, 17 hdc in ring, join with sl st in top of ch-2, **turn** (18 hdc).

Rnd 2: Ch 2, hdc in next st, 2 hdc in next st, (hdc in each of next 2 sts, 2 hdc in next st) around, join, **turn** (24).

Rnds 3-6: Ch 2, hdc in each st around, join, **turn.**

Rows 7-14: Working in rows; for **ankle opening,** ch 2, hdc in each st across, turn. At end of last row, fasten off.

Fold last row in half to form heel, sew together.

Rnd 15: Working in ends of rows for **cuff,** join with sl st in any row, ch 2, evenly space 29 more hdc around, join with sl st in top of ch-2 (30).

Rnd 16: Ch 3, 4 dc in same st, skip next 2 sts, sc in next st, skip next 2 sts, (shell in next st, skip next 2 sts, sc in next st, skip next 2 sts) around, 4 dc in same st as first st, join with sl st in top of ch-3 (5 shells, 5 sc).

Rnd 17: Ch 1, sc in first st, ch 3, V-st in next sc, ch 3, (sc in center dc of next shell, ch 3, V-st in next sc, ch 3) around, join with sl st in first sc.

Rnd 18: Ch 1, sc in first st, shell in next V-st, (sc in next sc, shell in next V-st) around, join.

Rnd 19: Beg V-st, ch 2, sc in center dc of next shell, ch 2, (V-st in next sc, ch 2, sc in center dc of next shell, ch 2) around, join with sl st in 3rd ch of ch-5.

Rnd 20: Sl st in first ch sp, ch 3, 8 dc in same sp, sc in next sc, (shell in next V-st, sc in next sc) around, join with sl st in top of ch-3, fasten off.

Finishing

1: Starting at center front, weave 18" piece of ribbon through ends of rows around ankle opening; tie ends into a bow.

2: Sew one bow between each shell on rnd 18.

BONNET

Row 1: Ch 5, sl st in first ch to form ring, ch 7, hdc in 3rd ch from hook, hdc in next 4 chs, 10 hdc in ring; working on opposite side of ch 7, hdc in last 6 chs, turn (22 hdc).

Row 2: Ch 2, hdc in next 5 sts, 2 hdc in each of next 10 sts, hdc in last 6 sts, turn (32).

Row 3: Ch 2, hdc in each st across, turn.

Row 4: Ch 2, hdc in next 10 sts, 2 hdc in next st, (hdc in next st, 2 hdc in next st) 4 times, hdc in last 12 sts, turn (37).

Row 5: Ch 2, hdc in next 13 sts, 2 hdc in next st, (hdc in each of next 2 sts, 2 hdc in next st) 3 times, hdc in last 13 sts, turn (41).

Row 6: Ch 1, sc in first st, *(skip next 2 sts, shell in next st, skip next 2 sts, sc in next st) 2 times*, (skip next st, shell in next st, skip next st, sc in next st) 4 times; repeat between **, turn (9 sc, 8 shells).

Rows 7-20: Repeat rows 2-5 of Dress Skirt consecutively, ending with row 3. At end of last row, **do not** turn or fasten off.

Row 21: Working in ends of rows, ch 2, 2 hdc in first row, 2 hdc in next row, (skip next 2 rows, 2 hdc in each of next 2 rows) 3 times, 2 hdc in next row, (hdc next 2 rows tog) 5 times, 2 hdc in each of next 3 rows, (skip next 2 rows, 2 hdc in each of next 2 rows) 3 times, turn.

Row 22: Ch 2, hdc in each st across, turn.

Row 23: Ch 1, sc in each st across, fasten off.

Finishing

1: Weave remaining ribbon through every 2 sts on row 22, pulling ends even.

2: Sew one bow between each shell on row 20.❖

Grandma's Favorites

Forever etched in some of our fondest
memories are the welcoming sights and
scintillating smells of Grandma's house.
Recapture those heartwarming times
with a medley of touchable creations
filled with graceful charm, just
like Grandma herself.

Sewing Angel

DESIGNED BY ESTELLA WHITFORD

SIZE
9" tall.

MATERIALS
Worsted-weight yarn — 3½ oz. peach, 3 oz. each spruce and glitter white, small amount each black, dk. green, gray, red and off-white; size 10 bedspread cotton — scrap of metallic gold; black embroidery floss; 10" white 4" wide pre-gathered lace; 2" square scrap cotton fabric; 2 white ½" buttons; metallic gold novelty eyeglasses; 1⅜" scissors charm; 4 straight pins; 6" piece wired metallic gold braid; white sewing thread; polyester fiberfill; sewing and tapestry needles; G crochet hook or size needed to obtain gauge.

GAUGE
4 sc sts = 1"; 4 sc rows = 1"

SKILL LEVEL
★★ Average

ANGEL
Head & Body
NOTE: Do not join rnds unless otherwise stated. Mark first st of each rnd.

Rnd 1: Starting at **Head,** with peach, ch 2, 6 sc in 2nd ch from hook (6 sc).

Rnd 2: 2 sc in each st around (12).

Rnd 3: (Sc in next st, 2 sc in next st) around (18).

Rnd 4: (Sc in each of next 2 sts, 2 sc in next st) around (24).

Rnds 5-7: Sc in each st around.

Rnd 8: (Sc in each of next 2 sts, sc next 2 sts tog) around (18).

Rnd 9: (Sc next 2 sts tog) around (9).

Rnd 10: 2 sc in each st around (18).

Rnd 11: (Sc in each of next 2 sts, 2 sc in next st) around (24).

Rnds 12-17: Sc in each st around.

Rnd 18: (Sc in each of next 2 sts, sc next 2 sts tog) around (18). Stuff.

Rnd 19: (Sc next 2 sts tog) around (9).

Rnd 20: Sc in next st, (sc next 2 sts tog) around, join with sl st in first sc, leaving 8" for sewing, fasten off (5).

Arm (make 2)
Rnd 1: Starting at **hand,** with peach, ch 2, 6 sc in 2nd ch from hook (6 sc).

Rnd 2: (Sc in next st, 2 sc in next st) around (9).

Rnds 3-10: Sc in each st around. At end of last rnd, join with sl st in first sc, leaving 10" for sewing, fasten off. Stuff.

Sew Arms over rnds 11-13 on each side of Body.

Leg (make 2)
Rnd 1: Starting at **shoe,** with black, ch 2, 6 sc in 2nd ch from hook (6 sc).

Rnd 2: (Sc in next st, 2 sc in next st) around (9).

Rnds 3-6: Sc in each st around. At end of last rnd, join with sl st in first sc, fasten off.

Rnd 7: Join peach with sc in first st, sc in each st around.

Rnds 8-16: Sc in each st around. At end of last rnd, join with sl st in first sc, leaving 10" for sewing,, fasten off. Stuff.

For **shoe shaping,** with black, tack 3 sts of rnd 2 to sts of rnd 6. For **shoe strap,** with black, ch 9, fasten off. Sew ends of strap to each side of shoe.

With off-white, using French Knot (see page 159), embroider button over end of strap on outside of Leg.

Sew Legs to bottom of Body with each shoe facing forward.

BLOUSE
Row 1: Starting at **neckline,** with glitter white, ch 23, sc in 2nd ch from hook, sc in each ch across, turn (22 sc).

Row 2: Ch 1, sc in each st across, turn.

Row 3: Ch 1, sc in first 4 sts; for **armhole,** ch 5, skip next 3 sts; sc in next 8 sts; for **armhole,** ch 5, skip next 3 sts; sc in last 4 sts, turn (16 sc, 10 chs).

Row 4: Ch 1, sc in each st and in each ch across, turn (26 sc).

Row 5: Ch 1, sc in each of first 2 sts, (2 sc in next st, sc in each of next 2 sts) across, turn (34).

Rows 6-9: Ch 1, sc in each st across, turn. At end of last row, **do not** turn.

Rnd 10: Working in rnds, ch 1, sc in end of each row across; working in starting ch on opposite side of row 1, sc in first ch, ch 3, sc in next ch, (ch 3, skip next ch, sc in next ch) across; sc in end of each row across, sc in each st across, join with sl st in first sc, fasten off.

Sleeves

Rnd 1: Working around armhole, join glitter white with sc in center ch at underarm, sc in same ch, 2 sc in each ch and in each st around, join with sl st in first sc (16 sc).

Rnds 2-3: Ch 1, sc in each st around, join. At end of last rnd, fasten off.

Repeat in other armhole.

Place Blouse on Doll, sew ends of rows 4-9 together in front. For **slip,** sew bound edge of lace around bottom of Blouse.

JUMPER

Row 1: Starting at **bib,** with spruce, ch 7, sc in 2nd ch from hook, sc in each ch across, turn (6 sc).

Row 2: Ch 1, 2 sc in first st, sc in each st across with 2 sc in last st, turn (8).

Row 3: Ch 1, sc in each st across, turn.

Rows 4-5: Repeat row 2 (10, 12). At end of last row, **do not** turn, ch 17, sl st in first sc.

Rnd 6: Working in rnds, ch 1, sc in each st and in each ch around, join with sl st in first sc (29).

Rnd 7: Ch 1, sc in each st around, join.

Rnd 8: Ch 3, dc in same st, 2 dc in each st around, join with sl st in top of ch-3 (58 dc).

NOTE: When changing colors (see page 159), work over dropped color. Carry across to next section of same color.

Rnd 9: Ch 3, dc in each st around changing to glitter white in last st made, join.

Rnd 10: Ch 3, dc in each of next 3 sts changing to spruce in last st made, dc in next 4 sts changing to glitter white in last st made, (dc in next 4 sts changing to spruce in last st made, dc in next 4 sts changing to glitter white in last st made) around to last 2 sts, dc in each of last 2 sts changing to spruce in last st made, join.

Rnd 11: Ch 3, dc in each of next 3 sts changing to glitter white in last st made, dc in next 4 sts changing to spruce in last st made, (dc in next 4 sts changing to glitter white in last st made, dc in next 4 sts changing to spruce in last st made) around to last 2 sts, dc in each of last 2 sts, join, fasten off.

Rnd 12: Join glitter white with sl st in first st, ch 3, 5 dc in same st, skip next 3 sts, (6 dc in next st, skip next 2 sts) around, join, fasten off.

Pocket

Row 1: Starting at **bottom,** with spruce, ch 5, sc in 2nd ch from hook, sc in each ch across, turn (4 sc).

Rows 2-3: Ch 1, sc in each st across, turn. At end of last row, fasten off.

Row 4: Join glitter white with sc in first st, sc in each st across, fasten off.

Sew Pocket over rnds 8 and 9 of Junper on left side as shown in photo.

For **strap,** with spruce, ch 23, sc in 2nd ch from hook, sc in each ch across, fasten off.

Sew ends of strap to top corners of Jumper, sew middle to center back of Jumper. Sew one button over each end of strap. Place fabric square inside Pocket. Place Jumper on doll.

PINCUSHION

Rnd 1: Starting at **top,** with red, ch 2, 6 sc in 2nd ch from hook (6 sc).

Rnd 2: 2 sc in each st around (12).

Rnd 3: (Sc in next st, 2 sc in next st) around (18).

Rnds 4-5: Sc in each st around.

Rnd 6: (Sc in next st, sc next 2 sts tog) around (12).

Rnd 7: (Sc next 2 sts tog) around, join with sl st in first sc, leaving 8" for sewing, fasten off. Stuff. Sew opening closed.

With dk. green, using Straight Stitch (see page 158), embroider 5 long stitches around Pincushion.

Leaves

Rnd 1: With dk. green, ch 2, 6 sc in 2nd ch from hook (6 sc).

Rnd 2: Ch 2, (sl st in next st, ch 2) around, join with sl st in joining sl st of last rnd, fasten off. Sew to top of Pincushion.

Insert end of 3" strand metallic crochet cotton through one ch-2 sp on side of Leaves and through top of scissors charm, tie ends into a knot.

WING (make 2)

Row 1: With glitter white, ch 4, sc in 2nd ch from hook, sc in each ch across, turn (3 sc).

Rows 2-5: Ch 1, 2 sc in first st, sc in each st across with 2 sc in last st, turn, ending with 11 sts in last row.

Row 6: Ch 1, sc in each st across, turn.

Row 7: Ch 1, sc first 2 sts tog, sc in each st across to last 2 sts, sc last 2 sts tog, turn (9).

Row 8: Ch 1, sc in each st across, turn.

Continued on page 57

Theater Gown

DESIGNED BY SANDRA MILLER MAXFIELD

SIZE
Fits 11½" fashion doll.

MATERIALS
Size 10 bedspread cotton — 350 yds. jade, 150 yds. white, 12 yds. purple and 10 yds. pink; size 30 crochet cotton — 250 yds. white; 14" piece of cord elastic; 55 white 2-mm pearl beads; 8 small snaps; 9" square piece cardboard; polyester fiberfill; dried beans; craft glue or hot glue gun; white and jade sewing thread; sewing, beading and tapestry needles; No. 11, No. 7 and No. 0 steel crochet hooks or sizes needed to obtain gauges.

GAUGES
With **No. 0 hook** and 2 strands size 10 bedspread cotton held tog, 5 sts = 1"; 4 dc rows = 1½". With **No. 7 hook** and one strand size 10 bedspread cotton, 8 sts = 1"; 11 sc rows = 1". With **No. 11 hook** and one strand size 30 crochet cotton, 4 sts = ⅜".

SKILL LEVEL
★★ Average

PILLOW FORM
Inner Circle
   NOTES: Do not join rnds unless otherwise stated. Mark first st of each rnd.
   When changing colors (see page 159), work over dropped color and carry across to next section of same color.
   Rnd 1: With No. 0 hook and 2 strands white bedspread cotton held tog, ch 2, 6 sc in 2nd ch from hook (6 sc).
   Rnd 2: 2 sc in each st around (12).
   Rnd 3: (Sc in next st, 2 sc in next st) around (18).
   Rnd 4: (Sc in each of next 2 sts, 2 sc in next st) around (24).
   Rnd 5: Sc in each st around.
   Rnd 6: (Sc in each of next 3 sts, 2 sc in next st) around, join with sl st in first sc, fasten off.
   Using crocheted piece as pattern, cut 2 circles from cardboard ⅛" smaller around outer edge.

Inner Tube Base
   Rnds 1-6: Work same rnds as Inner Circle. At end of last rnd, **do not** fasten off.
   Rnd 7: Working this rnd in **back lps** only, ch 2, hdc in each st around, join with sl st in top of ch-2 (30 hdc).
   Rnds 8-9: Ch 2, hdc in each st around, join.
   Rnd 10: Place one cardboard circle in bottom of Inner Tube Base; matching sts, sl st last rnds of Inner Circle and Inner Tube Base tog, filling with dried beans and inserting other cardboard circle on top of beans before closing, **do not** fasten off.

Inner Tube
   Rnd 1: Working in **back lps** only of sl sts, ch 3, dc in each st around, join with sl st in top of ch-3 (30 dc).
   Rnds 2-11: Ch 3, dc in each st around, join.
   Rnd 12: Working this rnd in **back lps** only, ch 3, dc in each st around, join.
   Rnd 13: Ch 3, dc in each st around, join.
   Rnd 14: With No. 7 hook and one strand white bedspread cotton, (ch 3, skip next st, dc in next st) 14 times, ch 3, dc in last st, fasten off.
   For Drawstring, with No. 7 hook and one strand white bedspread cotton, ch 120, fasten off. Weave Drawstring through sts of row 14 on Inner Tube.

Skirt
   Rnd 1: With open end of Tube facing you, working in remaining **front lps** of rnd 11, with No. 0 hook and 2 strands white bedspread cotton held tog, join with sl st in center back st, ch 3, dc in each st around, join (30 dc).
   Rnds 2-8: Ch 3, dc in each st around, join.
   Rnd 9: Ch 3, dc in next 4 sts, 2 dc in next st, (dc in next 5 sts, 2 dc in next st) around, join (35).
   Rnd 10: Ch 3, dc in each st around, join.
   Rnd 11: Ch 3, dc in next 5 sts, 2 dc in next st, (dc in next 6 sts, 2 dc in next st) around, join (40).
   Rnd 12: Ch 3, dc in each st around, join.
   Rnd 13: Ch 3, dc in next 6 sts, 2 dc in next st, (dc in next 7 sts, 2 dc in next st) around, join (45).
   Rnd 14: Ch 3, dc in each st around, join.
   Rnd 15: Ch 3, dc in next 7 sts, 2 dc in next st, (dc in next 8 sts, 2 dc in next st) around, join (50).
   Rnd 16: Working this rnd in **back lps** only, ch 4, skip next st, (dc in next st, ch 1, skip next st) around, join with sl st in 3rd ch of ch-4, fasten off.
   Weave 11" piece of cord elastic through top of sts on last rnd, overlap ends about ½" and securely sew ends together.

Continued on page 32

Theater Gown

Continued from page 30

Cut 3¾" circle from cardboard. Place doll in Tube, stretching top edge up to just below doll's waist and tie ends of drawstring at back into a bow. Stuff lower back half of Skirt behind Tube being careful not to over stuff; front half of Inner Tube Base should be touching the front of Skirt; then place cardboard circle in bottom of Pillow Form, covering fiberfill.

GOWN
Skirt
Row 1: With No. 7 hook and jade, ch 27, sc in 2nd ch from hook, sc in each ch across, turn (26 sc).

Row 2: Ch 1, sc in each of first 2 sts, 2 sc in next st, sc in next st, 2 sc in next st, (sc in each of next 2 sts, 2 sc in next st, sc in next st, 2 sc in next st) 4 times, sc in last st, turn (36).

Rows 3-4: Ch 1, sc in each st across, turn.

Row 5: Ch 1, sc in first 5 sts, 2 sc in next st, (sc in next 5 sts, 2 sc in next st) 5 times, turn (42).

Row 6: Ch 1, sc in each st across, turn.

Row 7: Ch 1, 2 sc in first st, sc in next 6 sts, (2 sc in next st, sc in next 6 sts) 5 times, turn (48).

Row 8: Ch 1, 2 sc in first st, sc in next 7 sts, (2 sc in next st, sc in next 7 sts) 5 times, turn (54).

Row 9: Ch 1, 2 sc in first st, sc in next 8 sts, (2 sc in next st, sc in next 8 sts) 5 times, turn (60).

Rows 10-12: Ch 1, sc in each st across, turn.

Row 13: Ch 1, sc in first 19 sts, 2 sc in next st, sc in next 20 sts, 2 sc in next st, sc in last 19 sts, turn (62).

Rows 14-15: Ch 1, sc in each st across, turn.

Row 16: Ch 1, sc in first 20 sts, 2 sc in next st, sc in next 20 sts, 2 sc in next st, sc in last 20 sts, turn (64).

Rows 17-18: Ch 1, sc in each st across, turn.

Row 19: Ch 1, sc in first 21 sts, 2 sc in next st, sc in next 20 sts, 2 sc in next st, sc in last 21 sts, turn (66).

Rows 20-21: Ch 1, sc in each st across, turn

Row 22: Ch 1, sc in first 22 sts, 2 sc in next st, sc in next 20 sts, 2 sc in next st, sc in last 22 sts, turn (68).

Rows 23-24: Ch 1, sc in each st across, turn.

Row 25: Ch 1, sc in first 23 sts, 2 sc in next st, sc in next 20 sts, 2 sc in next st, sc in last 23 sts, turn (70).

Rows 26-27: Ch 1, sc in each st across, turn.

Row 28: Ch 1, sc in first 24 sts, 2 sc in next st, sc in next 20 sts, 2 sc in next st, sc in last 24 sts, turn (72).

Rows 29-30: Ch 1, sc in each st across, turn.

Row 31: Ch 1, sc in first 25 sts, 2 sc in next st, sc in next 20 sts, 2 sc in next st, sc in last 25 sts, turn (74).

Rows 32-33: Ch 1, sc in each st across, turn.

Row 34: Ch 1, sc in first 26 sts, 2 sc in next st, sc in next 20 sts, 2 sc in next st, sc in last 26 sts, turn (76).

Rows 35-36: Ch 1, sc in each st across, turn.

Row 37: Ch 1, sc in first 27 sts, 2 sc in next st, sc in next 20 sts, 2 sc in next st, sc in last 27 sts, turn (78).

Row 38: Ch 1, sc in each st across, turn.

Row 39: Ch 1, sc in first 28 sts, 2 sc in next st, sc in next 20 sts, 2 sc in next st, sc in last 28 sts, turn (80).

Row 40: Ch 1, sc in each st across, turn.

Row 41: Ch 1, sc in first 29 sts, 2 sc in next st, sc in next 20 sts, 2 sc in next st, sc in last 29 sts, turn (82).

Row 42: Ch 1, sc in each st across, turn.

Rnd 43: Working in rnds, ch 1, sc in first 6 sts, (2 sc in next st, sc in next 13 sts) 5 times, 2 sc in next st, sc in last 5 sts, join with sl st in first sc, **turn** (88).

Rnd 44: Ch 1, sc in each st around, join, **turn.**

Rnd 45: Ch 1, sc in first 6 sts, 2 sc in next st, (sc in next 14 sts, 2 sc in next st) 5 times, sc in last 6 sts, join, **turn** (94).

Rnds 46-47: Ch 1, sc in each st around, join, **turn.**

Rnd 48: Ch 1, sc in first 7 sts, 2 sc in next st, (sc in next 15 sts, 2 sc in next st) 5 times, sc in last 6 sts, join, **turn** (100).

Rnds 49-50: Ch 1, sc in each st around, join, **turn.**

Rnd 51: Ch 1, sc in first 7 sts, 2 sc in next st, (sc in next 16 sts, 2 sc in next st) 5 times, sc in last 7 sts, join, **turn** (106).

Rnds 52-53: Ch 1, sc in each st around, join, **turn.**

Rnd 54: Ch 1, sc in first 8 sts, 2 sc in next st, (sc in next 17 sts, 2 sc in next st) 5 times, sc in last 7 sts, join, **turn** (112).

Rnds 55-56: Ch 1, sc in each st around, join, **turn.**

Rnd 57: Ch 1, sc in first 8 sts, 2 sc in next st, (sc in next 18 sts, 2 sc in next st) 5 times, sc in last 8 sts, join, **turn** (118).

Rnds 58-59: Ch 1, sc in each st around, join, **turn.**

Rnd 60: Ch 1, sc in first 9 sts, 2 sc in next st, (sc in next 19 sts, 2 sc in next st) 5 times, sc in last 8 sts, join, **turn** (124).

Rnds 61-63: Ch 1, sc in each st around, join, **turn.**

Rnd 64: Ch 1, sc in first 9 sts, 2 sc in next st, (sc in next 20 sts, 2 sc in next st) 5 times, sc in last 9 sts, **turn** (130).

Rnd 65: Ch 1, sc in each st around, join, fasten off.

Skirt Placket
Row 1: Working in ends of rows across left edge of back opening on Skirt, with No. 7 hook and jade, join with sc in end of first row at bottom of opening, sc in each row across to waist line, turn.

Row 2: Ch 1, sc in each st across, fasten off.
Sew four snaps evenly spaced down back opening.

Underskirt

Rnd 1: With No. 7 hook and jade, ch 70, sl st in first ch to form ring, ch 3, dc in same ch, dc in next 9 chs, (2 dc in next ch, dc in next 9 chs) around, join with sl st in top of ch-3 (77 dc).

Rnd 2: Ch 3, dc in each st around, join.

Rnd 3: Ch 3, dc in same st, dc in next 10 sts, (2 dc in next st, dc in next 10 sts) around, join (84).

Rnd 4: Repeat rnd 2.

Rnd 5: Ch 3, dc in same st, dc in next 11 sts, (2 dc in next st, dc in next 11 sts) around, join (96).

Rnd 6: Repeat rnd 2.

Rnd 7: Ch 3, dc in same st, dc in next 23 sts, (2 dc in next st, dc in next 23 sts) around, join (100).

Rnd 8: Repeat rnd 2.

Rnd 9: Ch 3, dc in same st, dc in next 24 sts, (2 dc in next st, dc in next 24 sts) around, join (104).

Rnd 10: Repeat rnd 2.

Rnds 11-14: Ch 3, dc in same st, dc in each st around, join. At end of last rnd, fasten off.

Skirt Lace

Row 1: With No. 7 hook and white size 30 crochet cotton, ch 71, sc in 2nd ch from hook, sc in each ch across, turn (70 sc).

Row 2: Ch 1, sc in first st, (ch 3, sc in next st) across, turn (69 ch-3 sps).

Rows 3-5: Ch 3, sc in first ch sp, (ch 3, sc in next ch sp) across, turn.

Row 6: Ch 3, sc in first ch sp, (ch 3, sc in next ch sp) across, turn.

Rows 7-17: Ch 4, sc in first ch sp, (ch 4, sc in next ch sp) across, turn.

Row 18: Ch 1, (2 sc, ch 2, 2 sc) in each ch sp across, fasten off.

Sew top edge of Skirt Lace to top of rnd 2 on Underskirt. Place Underskirt over Pillow Form with bottom edge just touching the floor; tack or glue top edge in place.

Bodice

Row 1: With No. 7 hook and jade, ch 33, sc in 2nd ch from hook, sc in each of next 3 chs, 2 sc in next ch, sc in next 10 chs, skip next 2 chs, sc in next 10 chs, 2 sc in next ch, sc in last 4 chs, turn (32 sc).

Row 2: Ch 1, sc in each of first 3 sts, 2 sc in each of next 2 sts, sc in next 10 sts, skip next 2 sts, sc in next 10 sts, 2 sc in each of next 2 sts, sc in each of last 3 sts, turn (34).

Row 3: Ch 1, sc in each of first 3 sts, 2 sc in next st, sc in next st, 2 sc in next st, sc in next 10 sts, skip next 2 sts, sc in next 10 sts, 2 sc in next st, sc in next st, 2 sc in next st, sc in each of last 3 sts, turn (36).

Rows 4-8: Ch 1, sc in first 6 sts, 2 sc in next st, sc in next 10 sts, skip next 2 sts, sc in next 10 sts, 2 sc in next st, sc in last 6 sts, turn (36).

Row 9: Ch 1, sc in each st across, turn.

Rows 10-13: Ch 1, 2 sc in first st, sc in each st across, turn, ending with 40 sc in last row.

Row 14: Ch 1, sc in each of first 2 sts, 2 sc in next st, sc in next 13 sts, skip next st, 10 dc in next st, skip next st, sc in next 13 sts, 2 sc in next st, sc in each of last 2 sts, turn (56 sts).

Row 15: Ch 1, sc in first 16 sts, skip next st, dc in next 9 sts, skip next st, sc in each of next 2 sts, skip next st, dc in next 9 sts, skip next st, sc in last 16 sts, turn (52).

Row 16: Ch 1, sc in first 15 sts, skip next st, sc in next 9 sts, skip next 2 sts, sc in next 9 sts, skip next st, sc in last 15 sts, turn (48).

Row 17: Ch 1, sc in each st across, turn.

Row 18: Ch 1, sc in first 9 sts; for **shoulder strap,** ch 12; skip next 6 sts, sc in next 18 sts; for **shoulder strap,** ch 12; skip next 6 sts, sc in last 9 sts, turn

Row 19: Ch 1, sc in each st and in each ch across, **do not** turn, fasten off.

Row 20: For **collar,** working this row in **back lps** only, join with sl st in first st, ch 1, sc in each st across, turn (60 sc).

Row 21: Ch 1, sc in first 8 sts, sc next 2 sts tog, (sc in next 8 sts, sc next 2 sts tog) across, turn (54).

Row 22: Working this row in **back lps** only, ch 1 (sc in next 7 sts, sc next 2 sts tog) across, fasten off (48).

Row 23: For **lace edging,** with No. 11 hook and white size 30 crochet cotton, working in remaining lps of row 1 on bottom edge of Bodice, with wrong side facing you, join with sc in first st, sc in same st, sc in each st across, turn (33).

Row 24: Ch 1, sc in first st, (ch 3, skip next st, sc in next st) across, fasten off.

Back Placket

Row 1: Working in ends of rows on left back of Bodice, with No. 7 hook and jade, join with sl st in end of row 1, ch 1, sc in each row across to neck edge, turn (22 sc).

Row 2: Ch 1, sc in each st across, fasten off.

Sew four snaps evenly spaced down back opening of Bodice.

Continued on page 34

Lower Bodice Ruffle

Row 1: Working in remaining lps of row 21 on Bodice, with No. 11 hook and white size 30 crochet cotton, join with sc in first st, sc in each st across, turn (54).

Row 2: Ch 1, sc in first st, (ch 3, sc in next st) across, turn.

Row 3: Ch 3, sc in first ch sp, (ch 3, sc in next ch sp) across, turn.

Row 4: Ch 3, sc in first ch sp, (ch 3, sc in next ch sp) across, turn.

Row 5: Ch 1, (3 sc in next ch sp, sc in next sc) across, fasten off.

Upper Bodice Ruffle

Working in remaining lps of row 19, work same as Lower Bodice Ruffle.

Sleeve (make 2)

Foundation: With No. 7 hook and jade, ch 20, sl st in first ch to form ring.

Row 1: Working in foundation to form the cap of Sleeve, sc in next 4 chs, sl st in next ch, turn (5 sts).

Row 2: Ch 1, sc in first sl st, sc in next 4 sc, sl st in next ch on foundation, turn (6).

Row 3: Ch 1, sc in first sl st, sc in next 5 sc, sl st in next ch on foundation, turn (7).

Row 4: Ch 1, sc in first sl st, sc in next 6 sc, sl st in next ch on foundation, turn (8).

Row 5: Ch 1, sc in first sl st, sc in next 7 sc, sl st in next ch on foundation, turn (9).

Row 6: Ch 1, sc in first sl st, sc in next 8 sc, sl st in next ch on foundation, turn (10).

Rnd 7: Working in rnds, ch 1, sc in next sl st, sc in next 9 sc, sc in next ch on foundation, sc in next 9 chs, **do not** join or turn.

Rnd 8: Sc in first 10 sts, skip next st, sc in last 9 sts (19).

Rnd 9: Skip first sc, sc in last 18 sts.

Rnd 10: Sc in each st around.

Rnd 11: Sc in each st around skipping one st at center of underarm (17).

Rnd 12: Sc in each st around.

Rnd 13: Sc in each st around skipping one st at center of underarm (16).

Rnds 14-19: Sc in each st around. At end of last rnd, join with sl st in first sc, fasten off.

Rnd 20: For **bottom portion of Sleeve,** with No. 7 hook and white size 30 crochet cotton, join with sc in first st, sc in each st around, join (17).

Rnd 21: Ch 1, sc in first st, (ch 3, sc in next st) around; to **join,** ch 2, dc in first sc.

Rnds 22-33: Ch 1, sc around joining dc, (ch 3, sc in next ch sp) around, join as before.

Rnds 34-35: Ch 1, sc around joining dc, (ch 4, sc in next ch sp) around, join.

Rnd 36: Ch 1, sc around joining dc, sc in each ch sp around, join with sl st in first sc (17).

Rnd 37: Ch 1, sc in each st around, join, fasten off.

Rnd 38: For **cuff,** with No. 7 hook and purple, join with sc in first st, sc in each st around, join.

Rnd 39: Ch 1, sc in each st around, join, fasten off.

Arm Band (make 2)

With No. 7 hook and purple, ch 20, sc in 2nd ch from hook, (ch 2, sl st in 2nd ch from hook, skip one ch on beginning ch, sc in next ch) across, fasten off.

Sew Arm Band over rnds 19 and 20 of Sleeve.

Roses (make 5)

With No. 11 hook and purple, ch 18, sc in 6ch ch from hook, (ch 3, skip next ch, sc in next ch) across, fasten off.

Roll into a coil; tack together at bottom.

Rosebuds (make 12 pink, 1 purple)

With No. 11 hook, ch 10, sc in 6th ch from hook, (ch 3, skip next ch, sc in next ch) across, fasten off.

Roll into a coil; tack together at bottom.

Leaf (make 24)

With No. 11 hook and jade, ch 4, sc in 2nd ch from hook, sc in each of last 2 chs, fasten off.

3-tiered Jabot (make 2)

Row 1: With No. 11 hook and white size 30 crochet cotton, ch 5, sc in 2nd ch from hook, sc in each ch across, turn (4 sc).

Row 2: Ch 1, sc in each st across, turn.

Row 3: Working this row in **back lps** only, ch 1, sc in each st across, turn.

Rows 4-5: Repeat rows 2 and 3.

Row 6: For **lower ruffle,** (sc, ch 4, sc) in first st, (ch 4, sc in next st) 2 times, (ch 4, sc, ch 4, sc) in last st, turn.

Rows 7-11: Ch 4, sc in first ch sp, (ch 4, sc in next ch sp) across, turn. At end of last row, fasten off.

3-Tiered Jabot Middle Ruffle
Row 1: Working in remaining lps of row 4 on Jabot, with No. 11 hook and white size 30 crochet cotton, join with sc in first st, ch 4, sc in same st, (ch 4, sc in next st) across, turn.

Rows 2-5: Ch 4, sc in first ch sp, (ch 4, sc in next ch sp) across, turn. At end of last row fasten off.

3-Tiered Jabot Top Ruffle
Row 1: Working in remaining lps of row 2 on Jabot, with No. 11 hook and white size 30 crochet cotton, join with sc in first st, ch 4, sc in same st, (ch 4, sc in next st) across, turn.

Rows 2-4: Ch 4, sc in first ch sp, (ch 4, sc in next ch sp) across, turn. At end of last row, fasten off.

2-Tiered Jabot (make 2)
Rows 1-3: Repeat same rows of 3-Tiered Jabot.

Row 4: For **lower ruffle,** (sc, ch 4, sc) in first st, (ch 4, sc in next st) 2 times, (ch 4, sc, ch 4, sc) in last st, turn.

Rows 5-8: Ch 4, sc in first ch sp, (ch 4, sc in next ch sp) across, turn. At end of last row, fasten off.

2-Tiered Jabot Top Ruffle
Work same as 3-Tiered Jabot Top Ruffle.

RETICULE
Rnd 1: With No. 7 hook and jade, ch 10, sc in 2nd ch from hook, sc in next 7 chs, 3 sc in last ch; working on opposite side of starting ch, sc in next 7 chs, 2 sc in last ch, **do not** join (20 sc).

Rnds 2-9: Sc in each st around.

Rnd 10: Sc in each st around, sc in next st, sl st in next st. (At side edge.)

Row 11: Working in rows, for **flap,** sc in first 10 sts leaving remaining sts unworked, turn (10 sc).

Row 12: Ch 1, skip first st, sc in next 7 sts, skip next st, sc in last st, turn (8).

Row 13: Ch 1, skip first st, sc in next 5 sts, skip next st, sc in last st, turn (6).

Row 14: Ch 1, skip first st, sc in each of next 3 sts, skip next st, sc in last st, turn (4).

Row 15: Ch 1, skip first st, sc in next st, skip next st, sc in last st, turn (2).

Row 16: Ch 1, skip first st, sc in last st, fasten off.

For **handle,** join jade with sl st in rnd 10 at edge of flap, ch 24, sl st in rnd 10 at opposite edge of flap, fasten off.

Reticule Trim
Rnd 1: With No. 11 hook and white size 30 crochet cotton, ch 4, sl st in first ch to form ring, ch 1, sc in ring, ch 3, (sc in ring, ch 3) 4 times, join with sl st in first sc (5 ch sps).

Rnd 2: Sl st in first ch sp, ch 1, (sc, ch 3, sc, ch 3) in same sp, (sc, ch 3, sc, ch 3) in each ch sp around, join (10 ch sps).

Rnds 3-5: Sl st in first ch sp, ch 1, sc in same sp, ch 3, (sc in next ch sp, ch 3) around, join. At end of last rnd, fasten off.

Place Trim over bottom of Reticule, pulling top edge of Trim up even with rnd 9. Spacing ch sps evenly around Reticule, tack top edge of Trim in place.

Thread 55 pearl beads onto white sewing thread. Starting at bottom of Reticule, sew one bead to each sc st around Trim and one to center top of each ch-3 sp on last rnd of Trim.

For **tassel,** wrap jade around two fingers 10 times. Slide lps off fingers and tie together at one end using separate strand of jade. Clip lps at other end. Wrap separate strand of jade around all lps ¼" from folded end. Trim ends. Sew tassel to center bottom of Reticule.

FINISHING
1: Draw up front of Skirt and tack in three places as shown in photo, forming pleats. Sew one 3-Tiered Jabot to center front tuck and one 2-Tiered Jabot to each side tuck as shown.

2: Glue one purple Rose, two pink Rosebuds and four Leaves over each Jabot as shown.

3: Place Bodice on doll. Glue one pink Rosebud and two Leaves over each Arm Band as shown.

4: Tack remaining Jabot to center front of Bodice just below top of Top Ruffle. Glue one purple Rose, two pink Rosebuds and four Leaves over top of Jabot.

5: Glue remaining Rose, Rosebuds and Leaves together for hair ornament.

6: Style doll's hair as desired. Pin ornament in hair.❖

Starfire Doily

DESIGNED BY HAZEL HENRY

SIZE
7" across.

MATERIALS
Size 20 crochet cotton — 50 yds. each natural, blue and pink; No. 10 steel crochet hook or size needed to obtain gauge.

GAUGE
Rnds 1-5 = 2⅛" across.

SKILL LEVEL
★★ Average

DOILY

Rnd 1: With natural, ch 6, sl st in first ch to form ring, ch 1, 12 sc in ring, join with sl st in first sc (12 sc).

Rnd 2: Ch 1, sc in first st, (ch 3, sc in next st) around; to **join**, ch 1, hdc in first sc (12 ch-3 sps).

Rnd 3: Ch 1, sc around joining hdc, (ch 5, sc in next ch-3 sp) around; to **join,** ch 2, dc in first sc (12 ch-5 sps).

Rnd 4: Ch 1, sc around joining dc, ch 5, (sc in next ch-5 sp, ch 5) around, join with sl st in first sc.

NOTES: For **beginning shell (beg shell),** ch 4, (tr, ch 3, 2 tr) in same ch sp.

For **shell,** (2 tr, ch 3, 2 tr) in next ch sp.

Rnd 5: Sl st in each of next 2 chs, beg shell, ch 3, (sc, ch 3, sc) in next ch-5 sp, ch 3, *shell in next ch-5 sp, ch 3, (sc, ch 3, sc) in next ch-5 sp, ch 3; repeat from * around, join with sl st in top of ch-4, fasten off (18 ch-3 sps, 6 shells).

Rnd 6: Join blue with sl st in any ch-3 sp between 2 sc, beg shell, *[ch 5, skip next ch-3 sp, (sc, ch 3, sc) in ch sp of next shell, ch 5, skip next ch-3 sp], shell in next ch-3 sp; repeat from * 4 more times; repeat between [ ], join (12 ch-5 sps, 6 shells, 6 ch-3 sps).

Rnd 7: Sl st in next st, sl st in next ch sp, beg shell, *[ch 5, sc in next ch-5 sp, ch 7, skip next ch-3 sp, sc in next ch-5 sp, ch 5], shell in next shell; repeat from * 4 more times; repeat between [ ], join.

Rnd 8: Sl st in next st, sl st in next ch sp, beg shell, *[ch 9, skip next ch-5 sp, (sc, ch 3, sc) in next ch-7 lp, ch 9, skip next ch-5 sp], shell in next shell; repeat from * 4 more times; repeat between [ ], join, fasten off.

Rnd 9: Join pink with sl st in any ch-3 sp between 2 sc, ch 4, (tr, ch 2, 2 tr, ch 2, 2 tr) in same sp, *[ch 8, skip next ch-9 lp, shell in next shell, ch 8, skip next ch-9 lp], (2 tr, ch 2, 2 tr, ch 2, 2 tr) in next ch-3 sp; repeat from * 4 more times; repeat between [ ], join.

Rnd 10: Sl st in next st, sl st in next ch sp, ch 4, (tr, ch 2, 2 tr) in same sp, *[ch 2, (2 tr, ch 2, 2 tr) in next ch-2 sp, ch 8, skip next ch-8 lp, shell in next shell, ch 8, skip next ch-8 lp], (2 tr, ch 2, 2 tr) in next ch-2 sp; repeat from * 4 more times; repeat between [ ], join.

Rnd 11: Sl st in next st, sl st in next ch sp, ch 4, (tr, ch 2, 2 tr) in same sp, (2 tr, ch 2, 2 tr) in each of next 2 ch-2 sps, *[ch 8, skip next ch-8 lp, shell in next shell, ch 8, skip next ch-8 lp], (2 tr, ch 2, 2 tr) in each of next 3 ch-2 sps; repeat from * 4 more times; repeat between [ ], join, fasten off.

Rnd 12: Join natural with sl st in any shell, ch 4, (tr, ch 3, 2 tr, ch 3, 2 tr) in same sp, *[ch 8, skip next ch-8 lp, (2 tr, ch 2, 2 tr) in next ch-2 sp, ◊ch 2, (2 tr, ch 2, 2 tr) in next ch-2 sp; repeat from ◊ one more time, ch 8, skip next ch-8 lp], (2 tr, ch 3, 2 tr, ch 3, 2 tr) in next shell; repeat from * 4 more times; repeat between [ ], join.

NOTE: For **picot,** ch 6, sl st in 5th ch from hook.

Rnd 13: Sl st in next st, sl st in next ch-3 sp, ch 4, (tr, picot, ch 1, 2 tr) in same sp, (2 tr, picot, ch 1, 2 tr) in next ch-3 sp, *[ch 8, skip next ch-8 lp, sc in each of next 2 tr, (2 sc in next ch-3 sp, sc in each of next 2 tr) 2 times, picot, ch 1, skip next ch-2 sp, sc in each of next 2 tr, (2 sc in next ch-2 sp, sc in each of next 2 tr) 2 times, ch 8, skip next ch-8 lp], (2 tr, picot, ch 1, 2 tr) in each of next 2 ch-3 sps; repeat from * 4 more times; repeat between [ ], join, fasten off.❖

Garden Tea Gown

DESIGNED BY SANDRA MILLER MAXFIELD

SIZE
Fits 11½" fashion doll.

MATERIALS
Size 10 bedspread cotton — 350 yds. beige, 250 yds. white, 50 yds. pink and 4 yds. green; size 30 crochet cotton — 100 yds. white; small white feathers; 1¼" x 24" piece of white or beige tulle; 1 yd. of ⅝"-wide double-edged white lace; 14" piece of cord elastic; 10 small snaps; 9" square piece cardboard; polyester fiberfill; dried beans; craft glue or hot glue gun; white and beige sewing thread; sewing and tapestry needles; No. 12, No. 7 and No. 0 steel crochet hooks or sizes needed to obtain gauges.

GAUGES
With **No. 0 hook** and 2 strands size 10 bedspread cotton held tog, 5 sts = 1"; 4 dc rows = 1½". With **No. 7 hook** and one strand size 10 bedspread cotton, 8 sts = 1"; 11 sc rows = 1". With **No. 12 hook** and one strand size 30 crochet cotton, 15 sts = 1".

SKILL LEVEL
★★ Average

PILLOW FORM
Inner Circle
NOTES: Do not join rnds unless otherwise stated. Mark first st of each rnd.

When changing colors (see page 159), work over dropped color and carry across to next section of same color.

Rnd 1: With No. 0 hook and 2 strands white bedspread cotton held tog, ch 2, 6 sc in 2nd ch from hook (6 sc).

Rnd 2: 2 sc in each st around (12).

Rnd 3: (Sc in next st, 2 sc in next st) around (18).

Rnd 4: (Sc in each of next 2 sts, 2 sc in next st) around (24).

Rnd 5: Sc in each st around.

Rnd 6: (Sc in each of next 3 sts, 2 sc in next st) around, join with sl st in first sc, fasten off.

Using crocheted piece as pattern, cut 2 circles from cardboard ⅛" smaller around outer edge.

Inner Tube Base
Rnds 1-6: Work same rnds as Inner Circle. At end of last rnd, **do not** fasten off.

Rnd 7: Working this rnd in **back lps** only, ch 2, hdc in each st around, join with sl st in top of ch-2 (30 hdc).

Rnds 8-9: Ch 2, hdc in each st around, join.

Rnd 10: Place one cardboard circle in bottom of Inner Tube Base; matching sts, sl st last rnds of Inner Circle and Inner Tube Base tog, filling with dried beans and inserting other cardboard circle on top of beans before closing, **do not** fasten off.

Inner Tube
Rnd 1: Working in **back lps** only of sl sts, ch 3, dc in each st around, join with sl st in top of ch-3 (30 dc).

Rnds 2-11: Ch 3, dc in each st around, join.

Rnd 12: Working this rnd in **back lps** only, ch 3, dc in each st around, join.

Rnd 13: Ch 3, dc in each st around, join.

Rnd 14: With No. 7 hook and one strand white bedspread cotton, (ch 3, skip next st, dc in next st) 14 times, ch 3, dc in last st, fasten off.

For **Drawstring,** with No. 7 hook and one strand white bedspread cotton, ch 120, fasten off. Weave Drawstring through sts of row 14 on Inner Tube.

Skirt
Rnd 1: With open end of Tube facing you, working in remaining **front lps** of rnd 11, with No. 0 hook and 2 strands white bedspread cotton held tog, join with sl st in center back st, ch 3, dc in each st around, join (30 dc).

Rnds 2-8: Ch 3, dc in each st around, join.

Rnd 9: Ch 3, dc in next 4 sts, 2 dc in next st, (dc in next 5 sts, 2 dc in next st) around, join (35).

Rnd 10: Ch 3, dc in each st around, join.

Rnd 11: Ch 3, dc in next 5 sts, 2 dc in next st, (dc in next 6 sts, 2 dc in next st) around, join (40).

Rnd 12: Ch 3, dc in each st around, join.

Rnd 13: Ch 3, dc in next 6 sts, 2 dc in next st, (dc in next 7 sts, 2 dc in next st) around, join (45).

Rnd 14: Ch 3, dc in each st around, join.

Rnd 15: Ch 3, dc in next 7 sts, 2 dc in next st, (dc in next 8 sts, 2 dc in next st) around, join (50).

Continued on page 40

Rnd 16: Working this rnd in **back lps** only, ch 4, skip next st, (dc in next st, ch 1, skip next st) around, join with sl st in 3rd ch of ch-4, fasten off.

Weave 11" piece of cord elastic through top of sts on last rnd, overlap ends about ½" and securely sew ends together.

Cut 3¾" circle from cardboard. Place doll in Tube, stretching top edge up to just below doll's waist and tie ends of drawstring at back into a bow. Stuff lower back half of Skirt behind Tube being careful not to over stuff; front half of Inner Tube Base should be touching the front of Skirt; then place cardboard circle in bottom of Pillow Form, covering fiberfill.

GOWN
Skirt

Row 1: With No. 7 hook and beige, ch 27, sc in 2nd ch from hook, sc in each ch across, turn (26 sc).

Row 2: Ch 1, sc in each of first 2 sts, 2 sc in next st, sc in next st, 2 sc in next st, (sc in each of next 2 sts, 2 sc in next st, sc in next st, 2 sc in next st) 4 times, sc in last st, turn (36).

Rows 3-4: Ch 1, sc in each st across, turn.

Row 5: Ch 1, sc in first 5 sts, 2 sc in next st, (sc in next 5 sts, 2 sc in next st) across, turn (42).

Row 6: Ch 1, sc in each st across, turn.

Row 7: Ch 1, 2 sc in first st, sc in next 6 sts, (2 sc in next st, sc in next 6 sts) across, turn (48).

Row 8: Ch 1, 2 sc in first st, sc in next 7 sts, (2 sc in next st, sc in next 7 sts) across, turn (54).

Row 9: Ch 1, 2 sc in first st, sc in next 8 sts, (2 sc in next st, sc in next 8 sts) across, turn (60).

Rows 10-46: Ch 1, sc in each st across, turn.

Row 47: Ch 1, sc in first 9 sts, 2 sc in next st, (sc in next 14 sts, 2 sc in next st) 3 times, sc in last 5 sts, turn (64).

Row 48: Ch 1, sc in each st across, turn.

Row 49: Ch 1, sc in first 4 sts, (2 sc in next st, sc in next 9 sts) across, turn (70).

Rnd 50: Working in rnds, overlap 2 sts at beginning of row over last 2 sts; working through both thicknesses through overlapped sts, sc in each of first 2 sts, sc in each st around, join with sl st in first sc, **turn** (68).

Rnd 51: Ch 1, sc in first 8 sts, (2 sc in next st, sc in next 16 sts) 3 times, 2 sc in next st, sc in last 8 sts, join, **turn** (72).

Rnds 52-54: Ch 1, sc in each st around, join, **turn.**

Rnd 55: Ch 1, sc in first 17 sts, 2 sc in next st, (sc in next 17 sts, 2 sc in next st) around, join, **turn** (76).

Rnds 56-58: Ch 1, sc in each st around, join, **turn.**

Rnd 59: Ch 1, sc in first 10 sts, 2 sc in next st, (sc in next 10 sts, 2 sc in next st) 5 times, sc in last 10 sts, join, **turn** (82).

Rnds 60-61: Ch 1, sc in each st around, join, **turn.**

Rnd 62: Ch 1, sc in first 4 sts, (2 sc in next st, sc in next 12 sts) around, join, **turn** (88).

Rnds 63-66: Ch 1, sc in each st around, join, **turn.**

Rnd 67: Ch 1, sc in first 21 sts, 2 sc in next st, (sc in next 21 sts, 2 sc in next st) around, join, **turn** (92).

Rnd 68: Ch 1, sc in each each st around, join, **turn.**

Rnd 69: Ch 1, sc in first 6 sts, (2 sc in next st, sc in next 19 sts) 4 times, sc in next 6 sts, join, **turn** (96).

Rnds 70-71: Ch 1, sc in each st around, join, **turn.**

Rnd 72: Ch 1, sc in first 23 sts, 2 sc in next st, (sc in next 23 sts, 2 sc in next st) around, join, **turn** (100).

Rnds 73-74: Ch 1, sc in each st around, join, **turn.**

Rnd 75: Ch 1, sc in first 12 sts, 2 sc in next st, (sc in next 24 sts, 2 sc in next st) 3 times, sc in last 12 sts, join, **turn** (104).

Rnds 76-79: Ch 1, sc in each st around join, **turn.**

Rnd 80: Ch 1, sc in each st around, join, fasten off.

Skirt Placket

Row 1: Working in ends of rows across left edge of back opening on Skirt, with No. 7 hook and beige, join with sc in end of first row at bottom of opening, sc in each row across to waistline, turn.

Row 2: Ch 1, sc in each st across, fasten off.

Bodice

Row 1: With No. 7 hook and beige, ch 11, sc in 2nd ch from hook, sc in each ch across, turn (10 sc).

NOTE: Work remaining rows in **back lps** only unless otherwise stated.

Row 2: Ch 1, sc in each st across with 2 sc in last st, turn (11).

Row 3: Ch 1, 2 sc in first st, sc in each st across, turn (12).

Row 4: Ch 1, sc in first 11 sts, 2 sc in next st, ch 9, turn (13 sts, 9 chs).

Row 5: Sc in 2nd ch from hook, sc in next 7 chs, sc in next 13 sts, turn (21).

Rows 6-8: Repeat rows 2 and 3 alternately, ending with row 2 and 24 sts in last row.

Rows 9-10: Ch 1, sc in each st across, turn.

Row 11: Ch 1, sc first 2 sts tog, sc in each st across, turn (23).

Row 12: Ch 1, sc in each st across, turn.

Rows 13-16: Repeat rows 11 and 12 alternately, ending with 21 sts in last row.

Row 17: Ch 1, sc in each st across, turn.

Row 18: Repeat row 2 (22).

Row 19: Ch 1, sc in each st across, turn.

Rows 20-23: Repeat rows 2 and 19 alternately, ending with 24 sts in last row.

Row 24: Ch 1, sc in each st across, turn.

Row 25: Repeat row 11 (23).

Row 26: Ch 1, sc in each st across to last 2 sts, sc last 2 sts tog, turn (22).

Row 27: Repeat row 11 (21).

Row 28: Ch 1, sc in first 13 sts leaving remaining 8 sts unworked, turn (13).

Row 29: Repeat row 11 (12).

Row 30: Repeat row 26 (11).

Row 31: Repeat row 11 (10).

Row 32: Ch 1, sc in each st across, turn.

Row 33: Repeat row 3 (11).

Row 34: Ch 1, sc in each st across with 2 sc in last st, ch 10, turn (12 sc, 10 chs).

Row 35: Sc in 2nd ch from hook, sc in next 8 chs, sc in next 12 sts, turn (21).

Row 36: Repeat row 2 (22).

Rows 37-43: Ch 1, sc in each st across, turn. At end of last row, fasten off.

Row 44: Working in starting ch on oppostie side of row 1, join beige with sc in first ch at waistline edge, sc in each ch across, turn (10).

Row 45: Repeat row 3 (11).

Row 46: Ch 1, sc in each st across with 2 sc in last st, ch 11, turn (12 sc, 11 chs).

Row 47: Sc in 2nd ch from hook, sc in next 9 chs, sc in next 12 sts, turn (22).

Rows 48-55: Ch 1, sc in each st across, turn. At end of last row, fasten off.

Sew ends of matching 5 rows on one back and front together for shoulder seam. Repeat on other side of Bodice.

Run a long piece of beige through end of every other row at waistline edge and gather to fit around doll's waist with enough overlap for a snap. Secure ends.

Collar

Row 1: With No. 7 hook and beige, with right side of Bodice facing out, join with sl st in top corner of back opening, ch 1, work 17 sc evenly spaced across to opposite corner, turn (17 sc).

Row 2: Ch 1, sc in first 7 sts, sc next 2 sts tog, sc in last 8 sts, turn (16).

Rows 3-5: Ch 1, sc in each st across, turn. At end of last row, **do not** turn, fasten off.

Row 6: For **lace trim**, with No. 12 hook and white size 30 crochet cotton, join with sc in first st, ch 2, sl st in 2nd ch from hook, sc in next st, (ch 2, sl st in 2nd ch from hook, skip next st, sc in next st) across, fasten off.

Matching corners and easing Bodice to fit, sew bottom edge of Bodice to remaining lps of row 1 on Skirt.

Sew 9 snaps evenly spaced down back opening of Bodice and Skirt.

Sleeve (make 2)

Foundation: With No. 7 hook and beige, ch 20, sl st in first ch to form ring.

Row 1: Working in foundation to form the cap of Sleeve, sc in next 4 chs, sl st in next ch, turn (5 sts).

Row 2: Ch 1, sc in first sl st, sc in next 4 sc, sl st in next ch on foundation, turn (6).

Row 3: Ch 1, sc in first sl st, sc in next 5 sc, sl st in next ch on foundation, turn (7).

Row 4: Ch 1, sc in first sl st, sc in next 6 sc, sl st in next ch on foundation, turn (8).

Row 5: Ch 1, sc in first sl st, sc in next 7 sc, sl st in next ch on foundation, turn (9).

Row 6: Ch 1, sc in first sl st, sc in next 8 sc, sl st in next ch on foundation, turn (10).

Rnd 7: Working in rnds, ch 1, sc in next sl st, sc in next 9 sc, sc in next ch on foundation, sc in next 9 chs, **do not** join or turn.

Rnd 8: Sc in first 10 sts, skip next st, sc in last 9 sts (19).

Continued on next page

Rnd 9: Skip first sc, sc in last 18 sts.

Rnd 10: Sc in each st around.

Rnd 11: Sc in each st around skipping one st at center of underarm (17).

Rnd 12: Sc in each st around.

Rnd 13: Sc in each st around skipping one st at center of underarm (16).

Rnds 14-19: Sc in each st around.

Rnd 20: Skip first st, sc in each st around (15).

Rnds 21-26: Sc in each st around.

Rnd 27: Skip first st, sc in each st around (14).

Rnds 28-31: Sc in each st around.

Rnd 32: Fold Sleeve in half (see Sleeve Diagram), sc in each st to top of wrist, (hdc, dc, ch 2, sl st in 2nd ch from hook, dc, hdc) in st at top of wrist, sc in each st to bottom of wrist, sl st in next st, fasten off.

Rnd 33: For **lace trim,** with No. 12 hook and white size 30 crochet cotton, join with sc in st at center bottom of wrist, ch 2, sl st in 2nd ch from hook, skip next st, (sc in next st, ch 2, sl st in 2nd ch from hook, skip next st) around, join with sl st in first sc, fasten off.

Sew foundation of Sleeve into armhole on Bodice, easing edges to fit.

Place dress on doll, stuffing Sleeve caps lightly.

SLEEVE DIAGRAM

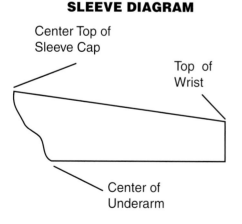

Center Top of Sleeve Cap

Top of Wrist

Center of Underarm

Skirt Ruffle

Row 1: With No. 7 hook and beige, ch 25, sc in 2nd ch form hook, sc in each ch across, turn (24 sc).

NOTE: Work remaining rows in **back lps** only unless otherwise stated.

Rows 2-128: Ch 1, sc in each st across, turn. At end of last row, **do not** turn.

Row 129: Working across top edge of Ruffle,

skip first row, sc in next row and in every other row across, fasten off.

Row 130: Workig across bottom edge of Ruffle, with No. 12 hook and white size 30 crochet cotton, join with sc in first row, (ch 2, sl st in 2nd ch from hook, ch 2, sc in next row) across, fasten off.

Sew first row and **back lps** of last row together. Glue top edge of Ruffle around Skirt with seam at center back and bottom edge touching the floor.

Skirt Lace

Row 1: With No. 12 hook and white size 30 crochet cotton, (ch 137, sc in 2nd ch from hook, sc in each ch across, turn (136 sc).

Row 2: Ch 1, sc in first st, (ch 3, skip next 2 sts, sc in next st) across, turn.

Row 3: Ch 1, sc in first ch sp, (ch 2, sl st in 2nd ch from hook, ch 2, sc in next ch sp) across, fasten off.

Row 4: Working in starting ch on opposite side of row 1, join with sc in first ch, (ch 3, skip next 2 chs, sc in next ch) across, turn.

Row 5: Repeat row 3.

Tack Skirt Lace around top of Skirt Ruffle with ends touching at back. With pink, using French Knot (see page 159), embroider st over every third sc on row 1 of Lace.

Bodice Lace Piece (make 2)

Row 1: With No. 12 hook and white size 30 crochet cotton, ch 95, sc in 2nd ch from hook, sc in each ch across, turn (94 sc).

Rows 2-5: Repeat same rows of Skirt Lace.

Tack Bodice Lace over Bodice as shown in photo, overlapping ends at front. Embroider in same manner as Skirt Lace.

Sleeve Lace

Row 1: With No. 12 hook and white size 30 crochet cotton, ch 62, sc in 2nd ch from hook, sc in each ch across, turn (61 sc).

Rows 2-5: Repeat rows 2-5 of Skirt Lace.

Tack one Sleeve Lace piece on front of each Sleeve as shown in photo, embroider Sleeve Lace in same manner as Skirt Lace.

Belt

With No. 7 hook and beige, ch 39; working in back bar of ch (see illustration), dc in 4th ch from hook, dc in each ch across, fasten off.

Sew one snap to ends of Belt. Place around doll's waist with snap in back.

BACK BAR OF CHAIN

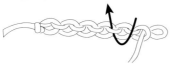

HAT
Rnd 1: With No. 7 hook and beige, ch 2, 6 sc in 2nd ch from hook, **do not** join.

Rnd 2: 2 sc in each st around (12).

Rnd 3: (2 sc in next st, sc in next st) around (18).

Rnd 4: (2 sc in next st, sc in each of next 2 sts) around (24).

Rnd 5: (2 sc in next st, sc in each of next 3 sts) around (30).

Rnds 6-7: Sc in each st around. At end of last rnd, sl st in next st.

Rnd 8: For **brim**, working this rnd in **front lps** only, 2 sc in same st as sl st, sc in next 4 sts, (2 sc in next st, sc in next 4 sts) around (36).

Rnd 9: (2 sc in next st, sc in next 5 sts) around, (42).

Rnd 10: (2 sc in next st, sc in next 6 sts) around (48).

Rnd 11: (2 sc in next st, sc in next 7 sts) around (54).

Rnd 12: (2 sc in next st, sc in next 8 sts) around (60).

Rnd 13: (2 sc in next st, sc in next 9 sts) around (66).

Rnd 14: (2 sc in next st, sc in next 10 sts) around (72).

Rnd 15: (2 sc in next st, sc in next 11 sts) around, join with sl st in first sc, fasten off.

Rnd 16: For **lace trim**, with No. 12 hook and white size 30 crochet cotton, join with sc in first st, ch 2, sl st in 2nd ch from hook, skip next st, (sc in next st, ch 2, sl st in 2nd ch from hook, skip next st) around, join as before, fasten off.

For **sl st trim**, working between sts of rnds 6 and 7, with No. 7 hook and pink, holding crochet cotton to back of Hat, insert hook between 2 sts, yo, pull lp through to front, (insert hook between next 2 sts, yo, pull lp through to front and through lp on hook) around, fasten off.

Cut 1¼" x 24" piece tulle into two 1¼" x 12" pieces; fold one end of each piece in half. For Hat ties, sew folded end of one tulle piece inside crown of Hat on each side.

FAN
Row 1: With No. 7 hook and beige, ch 8, sc in 2nd ch from hook, sc in each ch across, turn (7 sc).

NOTE: Work remaining rows in **back lps** only.

Rows 2-30: Ch 1, sc in each st across, turn. At end of last row, **do not** turn.

Row 31: Working across bottom edge of Fan, skip first row, sc in end of every other row across, turn (15).

Row 32: Ch 1, sc in first st, (skip next st, sc in next st) across, turn (8 sc).

Row 33: Ch 1, sc in first st, (skip next st, dc in next st) 3 times, sc in last st; for **handle**, ch 9; turn, sl st in first st of row 33, fasten off.

Row 34: For **lace edging**, working across ends of rows on top edge of Fan, with No. 12 hook and white size 30 crochet cotton, join with sc in first row, (ch 2, sl st in 2nd ch from hook, ch 2, sc in next row) across, fasten off.

LARGE ROSE
With No. 12 hook and pink, ch 18, sc in sixth ch from hook, (ch 3, skip next ch, sc in next ch) across, fasten off.

Roll Rose into a coil, tack together at bottom.

SMALL ROSE (make 11)
Row 1: With No. 12 hook and pink, ch 12, sc in 4th ch from hook, (ch 3, skip next ch, sc in next ch) across, fasten off.

Roll Rose into a coil, tack together at bottom.

LEAF (make 13)
With No. 12 hook and green, ch 4, sc in 2nd ch from hook, sc in each of last 2 chs, fasten off.

FINISHING
1: Glue 3 Small Flowers and 3 Leaves to Fan as Shown in photo.

2: Glue 6 Small Flowers and 7 Leaves to front of Skirt and Bodice as shown.

3: Glue remaining Flowers and Leaves to Hat as shown. Glue feathers to Hat next to Flowers and Leaves.

4: Style doll's hair as desired. Place Hat on head and tie around chin with bow at side of head.❖

Tea Party Doily

DESIGNED BY JUDY TEAGUE TREECE

SIZE
9" across.

MATERIALS
Size 10 bedspread cotton — 150 yds. white, small amount each mint and pink; No. 6 steel crochet hook or size needed to obtain gauge.

GAUGE
Rnds 1-3 = 1¾" across.

SKILL LEVEL
★★ Average

DOILY
Rnd 1: With white, ch 4, sl st in first ch to form ring, ch 3, 15 dc in ring, join with sl st in top of ch-3 (16 dc).

Rnd 2: Ch 3, dc in same st, ch 2, skip next st, (2 dc in next st, ch 2, skip next st) around, join (8 ch sps).

Rnd 3: Sl st in next st, sl st in next ch sp, ch 3, 2 dc in same sp, ch 3, (3 dc in next ch sp, ch 3) around, join.

Rnd 4: Sl st in each of next 2 sts, sl st in next ch sp, ch 3, 3 dc in same sp, ch 4, (4 dc in next ch sp, ch 4) around, join.

Rnd 5: Sl st in each of next 3 sts, sl st in next ch sp, ch 3, 4 dc in same sp, ch 6, (5 dc in next ch sp, ch 6) around, join.

Rnd 6: Ch 3, dc in next st, ch 2, skip next st, dc in each of next 2 sts, ch 3, sc in next ch sp, ch 3, *dc in each of next 2 sts, ch 2, skip next st, dc in each of next 2 sts, ch 3, sc in next ch sp, ch 3; repeat from * around, join (16 ch-3 sps, 8 ch-2 sps).

NOTES: For **beginning shell (beg shell),** ch 3, (dc, ch 2, 2 dc) in same sp.

For **shell,** (2 dc, ch 2, 2 dc) in next ch sp.

For **cluster (cl),** *yo, insert hook in next ch sp, yo, draw lp through, yo, draw through 2 lps on hook; repeat from * 2 more times in same ch sp, yo, draw through all 4 lps on hook.

Rnd 7: Sl st in next st, sl st in next ch-2 sp, beg shell, ch 4, (sc in next ch-3 sp, ch 4) 2 times, *shell in next ch-2 sp, ch 4, (sc in next ch-3 sp, ch 4) 2 times; repeat from * around, join (24 ch-4 sps, 8 shells).

Rnd 8: Sl st in next st, sl st in next ch sp, beg shell, *[ch 4, sc in next ch-4 sp, ch 3, cl in next ch-4 sp, ch 3, sc in next ch-4 sp, ch 4], shell in ch sp of next shell; repeat from * 6 more times; repeat between [ ], join.

Rnd 9: Sl st in next st, sl st in next ch sp, beg shell, *[ch 4, sc in next ch-4 sp, ch 3, (cl in next ch-3 sp, ch 3) 2 times, sc in next ch-4 sp, ch 4], shell in next shell; repeat from * 6 more times; repeat between [ ], join.

Rnd 10: Sl st in next st, sl st in next ch sp, beg shell, *[ch 4, sc in next ch-4 sp, ch 3, (cl in next ch-3 sp, ch 3) 3 times, sc in next ch-4 sp, ch 4], shell in next shell; repeat from * 6 more times; repeat between [ ], join.

Rnd 11: Sl st in next st, sl st in next ch sp, ch 3, (dc, ch 2, 2 dc, ch 2, 2 dc) in same sp, *[(ch 4, sc in next ch sp) 2 times, ch 3, cl in next ch-3 sp, ch 2, cl in next ch-3 sp, ch 3, (sc in next ch sp, ch 4) 2 times], (2 dc, ch 2, 2 dc, ch 2, 2 dc) in next shell; repeat from * 6 more times; repeat between [ ], join, fasten off.

NOTE: For **beginning cluster (beg cl),** ch 2, (yo, insert hook in same sp, yo, draw lp through, yo, draw through 2 lps on hook) 2 times, yo, draw through all 3 lps on hook.

Rnd 12: Join mint with sl st in first ch-2 sp, beg cl, (ch 2, cl) 2 times in same sp, (cl, ch 2, cl, ch 2, cl) in next ch-2 sp, *[ch 3, (sc in next ch sp, ch 3) 3 times, (cl, ch 2, cl) in next ch-2 sp, ch 3, (sc in next ch sp, ch 3) 3 times], (cl, ch 2, cl, ch 2, cl) in each of next 2 ch-2 sps; repeat from * 6 more times; repeat between [ ], join with sl st in top of beg cl, fasten off.

Rnd 13: Join pink with sc in first ch-2 sp, ch 2, sc in same sp, (sc, ch 2, sc) in next ch-2 sp, *[skip next cl, sc in next cl, (sc, ch 2, sc) in each of next 2 ch-2 sps, ch 3, (sc in next ch-3 sp, ch 3) 4 times, (sc, ch 2, sc) in next ch-2 sp, ch 3, (sc in next ch-3 sp, ch 3) 4 times], (sc, ch 2, sc) in each of next 2 ch-2 sps; repeat from * 6 more times; repeat between [ ], join with sl st in first sc, fasten off.

Rnd 14: Join white with sl st in first ch-2 sp, beg shell, shell in each of next 3 ch-2 sps, *[ch 2, (sc in next ch-3 sp, ch 2) 5 times, (dc, ch 1, dc) in next ch-2 sp, ch 2, (sc in next ch-3 sp, ch 2) 5

Continued on page 56

Butterfly Afghan

DESIGNED BY SANDRA MILLER MAXFIELD

SIZE

46½" x 66" not including Fringe.

MATERIALS

Worsted-weight yarn — 24 oz. lt. yellow, 24 oz. variegated and 21 oz. black; I crochet hook or size needed to obtain gauge.

GAUGE

3 dc sts = 1"; 7 dc rows = 4".

SKILL LEVEL

★★ Average

BLOCK (make 6)

Row 1: With black, ch 70, dc in 4th ch from hook, dc in each ch across, turn (68 dc).

NOTES: When changing colors (see page 159), always drop all colors to same side of work. Do not carry dropped colors across to next section of same color. Use a separate ball of yarn for each color section. Fasten off colors when no longer needed.

Each square on graph equals 2 dc.

Ch-3 counts as first dc.

Row 2: For row 2 of graph, ch 3, dc in next st changing to variegated, dc in next 64 sts changing to black in last st made, dc in each of last 2 sts, turn.

Rows 3-38: Ch 3, dc in each st across changing colors according to graph, turn. At end of last row, fasten off.

Holding blocks wrong sides together, matching sts, sew together through **back lps** in two rows of three Blocks each.

For **border,** working around entire outer edge, join black with sl st in any corner, ch 3, (dc, ch 2, 2 dc) in same sp, dc in each st and 2 dc in end of each row around with (2 dc, ch 2, 2 dc) in each corner, join with sl st in top of ch-3, fasten off.

FRINGE

For **each Fringe,** cut 4 strands yarn each 18" long. Holding all strands together, fold in half, insert hook in st or ch sp, draw fold through, draw all loose ends through fold, tighten. Trim ends.

Fringe in each st and in each corner ch sp across each short end of Afghan.❖

GRAPH

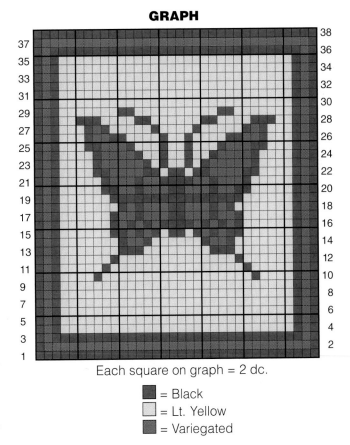

Each square on graph = 2 dc.

■ = Black
□ = Lt. Yellow
■ = Variegated

Dangling Ornaments

DESIGNED BY JO ANN MAXWELL

SNOWFLAKES

SIZE

Ornament is 9" long when assembled, not including hanger.

MATERIALS

Size 10 bedspread cotton — 150 yds. cream; 8 round 7-mm acrylic gemstones; 2 heart-shaped 13-mm x 15-mm acrylic gemstones; invisible thread; liquid fabric stiffener; rustproof pins; plastic wrap; Styrofoam® or blocking board; craft glue or hot glue gun; No. 5 steel crochet hook or size needed to obtain gauge.

GAUGE

Rnd 1 of Large Snowflake = ½" across.

SKILL LEVEL

★★ Average

LARGE SNOWFLAKE (make 3)

Rnd 1: Ch 3, sl st in first ch to form ring, ch 1, 8 sc in ring, join with sl st in first sc (8 sc).

Rnd 2: Ch 14, (sl st in next st, ch 14) around, join with sl st in joining sl st of last rnd, fasten off.

MEDIUM SNOWFLAKE (make 3)

Rnd 1: Ch 3, sl st in first ch to form ring, ch 1, 8 sc in ring, join with sl st in first sc (8 sc).

Rnd 2: Ch 12, (sl st in next st, ch 12) around, join with sl st in joining sl st of last rnd, fasten off.

SMALL SNOWFLAKE (make 3)

Rnd 1: Ch 3, sl st in first ch to form ring, ch 1, 8 sc in ring, join with sl st in first sc (8 sc).

Rnd 2: Ch 10, (sl st in next st, ch 10) around, join with sl st in joining sl st of last rnd, fasten off.

TINY SNOWFLAKE (make 3)

Rnd 1: Ch 3, sl st in first ch to form ring, ch 1, 8 sc in ring, join with sl st in first sc (8 sc).

Rnd 2: Ch 8, (sl st in next st, ch 8) around, join with sl st in joining sl st of last rnd, fasten off.

FINISHING

1: Apply fabric stiffener to all pieces according to manufacturer's instructions.

2: Pin all Snowflakes flat to plastic-covered blocking board, stretching out ch lps. When almost dry, unpin two of each size and bend into a curved shape. Let dry completely.

3: Matching sizes, glue one curved Snowflake to each side of flat Snowflake as shown in photo. Glue one gemstone to center of each curved Snowflake.

4: Using invisible thread, tie ch lps on flat Snowflakes together so that they hang about ¼" apart with the largest Snowflake on top and smallest Snowflake on bottom.

5: Glue backs of heart gemstones together, tie to Tiny Snowflake on bottom of ornament.

6: For **hanger,** tie a piece of invisible thread to ch lp at center top of Large Snowflake.

HEARTS

SIZE

Ornament is 8½" long when assembled, not including hanger.

MATERIALS

Size 10 bedspread cotton — 75 yds. cream; 6 red ⅝" silk flowers with leaves; metallic gold dried baby's breath flowers; one red 8-mm faceted bead; one clear 17-mm x 17-mm heart-shaped acrylic gemstone with hanger; invisible thread; gold metallic thread; liquid fabric stiffener; rustproof pins; plastic wrap; Styrofoam® or blocking board; craft glue or hot glue gun; sewing needle; No. 5 steel crochet hook or size needed to obtain gauge.

GAUGE

Rnds 1-2 of Large Heart = ½" wide.

SKILL LEVEL

★★ Average

LARGE HEART

Rnd 1: Ch 42, sl st in first ch to form ring, ch 1, sc in same ch, sc in next ch, 2 sc in each of next 13 chs, sc in next 6 chs, (2 sc, ch 2, 2 sc) in next ch, sc in next 6 chs, 2 sc in each of next 13 chs, sc in last ch, join with sl st in first sc (71 sc, 1 ch-2 sp).

Continued on page 50

Rnd 2: Working this rnd in **back lps,** ch 1, sc in same st, ch 2, skip next st, (hdc in next st, ch 2, skip next st) 17 times, (hdc, ch 3, hdc) in next ch-2 sp, ch 2, skip next st, (hdc in next st, ch 2, skip next st) around, join with sl st in first sc, fasten off.

MEDIUM HEART

Rnd 1: Ch 36, sl st in first ch to form ring, ch 1, sc in same ch, sc in next ch, 2 sc in each of next 9 chs, sc in next 7 chs, (2 sc, ch 2, 2 sc) in next ch, sc in next 7 chs, 2 sc in each of next 9 chs, sc in last ch, join with sl st in first sc (57 sc, 1 ch-2 sp).

Rnd 2: Working this rnd in **back lps,** ch 1, sc in same st, (ch 2, skip next st, hdc in next st) 14 times, ch 2, (hdc, ch 3, hdc) in next ch-2 sp, ch 2, (hdc in next st, ch 2, skip next st) around, join, fasten off.

SMALL HEART

Rnd 1: Ch 30, sl st in first ch to form ring, ch 1, sc in same ch, sc in next ch, 2 sc in each of next 7 chs, sc in next 6 chs, (2 sc, ch 2, 2 sc) in next ch, sc in next 6 chs, 2 sc in each of next 7 chs, sc in last ch, join with sl st in first sc (47 sc, 1 ch-2 sp).

Rnd 2: Working this rnd in **back lps,** ch 1, sc in same st, ch 2, skip next st, (hdc in next st, ch 2, skip next st) 11 times, (hdc, ch 3, hdc) in next ch-2 sp, ch 2, skip next st, (hdc in next st, ch 2, skip next st) around, join, fasten off.

FINISHING

1: Apply fabric stiffener to each Heart according to manufacturer's instructions.

2: Pin Hearts to plastic-covered blocking board, forming dip at center top and point at center bottom. Let dry completely.

3: For **hanger,** fold 7" piece of gold thread in half. Twist together until it winds around itself. Glue ends to dip at center top on back of Large heart.

4: Glue one flower and small amount of dried baby's breath to dip on each side of each Heart.

5: Using invisible thread, tie Hearts together so they hang about ¼" apart with the Large Heart on top, Medium Heart in the center and Small Heart on the bottom.

6: Using sewing needle, thread clear heart and red bead onto invisible thread. Tie to point of Small Heart on bottom of ornament.

BELLS

SIZE

Ornament is 8½" long when assembled, not including hanger.

MATERIALS

Size 10 bedspread cotton — 200 yds. cream; 6 maroon ¾" silk flowers with leaves; metallic gold dried baby's breath flowers; 2 yds. pink ⅛" satin ribbon; invisible thread; gold metallic cord; 3 gold 10-mm jingle bells; three 1" Styrofoam® balls; 3 small Styrofoam® cones or plastic funnels; liquid fabric stiffener; rustproof pins; plastic wrap; craft glue or glue gun; sewing and tapestry needles; No. 5 steel crochet hook or size needed to obtain gauge.

GAUGE

Rnd 1 of Large Bell = 1" across.

SKILL LEVEL

★★ Average

LARGE BELL

Rnd 1: Ch 4, 15 dc in 4th ch from hook, join with sl st in top of ch-4 (16 dc).

NOTE: For **quadruple treble crochet (quad tr),** yo 5 times, insert hook in next st, yo, draw lp through, (yo, draw through 2 lps on hook) 6 times.

Rnd 2: Ch 8, (quad tr in next st, ch 1) around, join with sl st in 7th ch of ch-8 (16 quad tr, 16 ch sps).

Rnd 3: Ch 4, (dc in next st, ch 1) around, join with sl st in 3rd ch of ch-4.

Rnd 4: Ch 5, (dc in next st, ch 2) around, join with sl st in 3rd ch of ch-5.

NOTE: For **picot,** ch 3, sl st in top of last st made.

Rnd 5: Ch 3, dc in same st, dc in next ch sp, (dc, picot) in next st, dc in next ch sp, *2 dc in next st, dc in next ch sp, (dc, picot) in next st, dc in next ch sp; repeat from * around, join with sl st in top of ch-3.

Rnd 6: Sl st in next st, ch 1, sc in same st, ch 5, skip next 4 sts and one picot, (sc in next st, ch 5, skip next 4 sts and one picot) around, join with sl st in first sc.

Rnd 7: Sc in next ch, (2 sc in next ch, sc in next ch) 2 times, *sl st in next st, sc in next ch, (2 sc in next ch, sc in next ch) 2 times; repeat from * around, join with sl st in joining sl st of last rnd, fasten off.

MEDIUM BELL

Rnd 1: Ch 4, 13 dc in 4th ch from hook, join with sl st in top of ch-4 (14 dc).

NOTE: For **triple treble crochet (tr tr),** yo 4 times, insert hook in next st, yo, draw lp through, (yo, draw through 2 lps on hook) 5 times.

Rnd 2: Ch 7, (tr tr in next st, ch 1) around, join with sl st in 6th ch of ch-7 (14 tr tr, 14 ch sps).

Rnd 3: Ch 4, (dc in next st, ch 1) around, join with sl st in 3rd ch of ch-4.

Rnds 4-6: Repeat rnds 5-7 of Large Bell.

SMALL BELL

Rnd 1: Ch 4, 13 dc in 4th ch from hook, join with sl st in top of ch-4 (14 dc).

NOTE: For **double treble crochet (dtr),** yo 3 times, insert hook in next st, yo, draw lp through, (yo, draw through 2 lps on hook) 4 times.

Rnd 2: Ch 6, (dtr in next st, ch 1) around, join with sl st in 5th ch of ch-6 (14 dtr, 14 ch sps).

Rnds 3-5: Repeat rnds 5-7 of Large Bell.

FINISHING

1: Apply fabric stiffener to Bells according to manufacturer's instructions.

2: For **form,** push one foam ball onto top of each cone. Cover with plastic wrap. Shape Bells over forms, let dry completely,

3: With tapestry needle, thread 18" piece of gold cord inside Small Bell through center of rnd 1 (knot end so it won't slide off bell). Tie a second knot 3" above first knot, thread cord inside Medium Bell through center of rnd 1. Tie third knot 3½" above second knot, thread cord inside Large Bell through center of rnd 1. Remove tapestry needle. For **hanger,** fold end of cord down through rnd 1 (trim to desired length); glue to secure.

4: With sewing needle and invisible thread, attach one jingle bell inside each crocheted Bell.

5: For **bow** (make 3), cut two 9" pieces of ribbon. Holding both pieces together, tie into a bow. Glue one bow to top of each Bell, trim ends of each bow to desired length. Weave 4" piece of ribbon through rnd 3 on Large Bell. Trim ends; glue to secure. Repeat in rnd 4 of Large Bell, rnd 3 of Medium Bell and through top of rnd 2 of Small Bell.

6: Glue 3 flowers and small amount baby's breath to top of Large Bell in front of bow. Glue 2 flowers and small amount baby's breath to top of Medium Bell in front of bow. Glue one flower and small amount baby's breath to top of Small Bell in front of bow.✤

Easter Egg Pillow

DESIGNED BY MICHELLE WILCOX

SIZE

11½" x 15½" without Ruffle.

MATERIALS

Worsted-weight yarn — 3½ oz. white, 2 oz. blue, small amount each dk. peach, gold, green and purple; polyester fiberfill; tapestry needle; G crochet hook or size needed to obtain gauge.

GAUGE

4 sc sts = 1"; 4 sc rows = 1".

SKILL LEVEL

★★ Average

FRONT

Row 1: Starting at **bottom,** with white, ch 25, sc in 2nd ch from hook, sc in each ch across, turn (24 sc).

Rows 2-7: Ch 1, 2 sc in first st, sc in each st across with 2 sc in last st, turn, ending with 36 sts in last row.

Row 8: Ch 1, sc in each st across, turn.

Row 9: Repeat row 2 (38).

Rows 10-11: Ch 1, sc in each st across, turn. At end of last row, fasten off.

Row 12: Join blue with sc in first st, sc in each st across, turn.

Rows 13-17: Ch 1, sc in each st across, turn. At end of last row, fasten off.

Row 18: With white, repeat row 12.

Row 19: Ch 1, sc in each st across, turn, fasten off.

Rows 20-25: With purple, repeat rows 12-17.

Row 26: With white, repeat row 12.

Rows 26-31: Ch 1, sc in each st across, turn.

Row 32: Ch 1, sc first 2 sts tog, sc in each st across to last 2 sts, sc last 2 sts tog, turn (36).

Rows 33-34: Ch 1, sc in each st across, turn.

Row 35: Repeat row 32 (34).

Row 36: Ch 1, sc in each st across, turn, fasten off.

Row 37: With gold, repeat row 12.

Row 38: Repeat row 32 (32).

Rows 39-40: Ch 1, sc in each st across, turn.

Row 41: Repeat row 32 (30).

Row 42: Ch 1, sc in each st across, turn, fasten off.

Row 43: With white, repeat row 12.

Row 44: Repeat row 32 (28).

Rows 45-46: Ch 1, sc in each st across, turn.

Row 47: Repeat row 32 (26).

Row 48: Ch 1, sc in each st across, turn.

Row 49: Repeat row 32 (24).

Row 50: Ch 1, sc in each st across, turn.

Rows 51-55: Repeat row 32, ending with 14 sts in last row.

Rnd 56: Working in rnds, ch 1, sc in each st and in end of each row around, join with sl st in first sc, fasten off.

Embroider Front using sts and colors according to Embroidery Diagram.

EMBROIDERY DIAGRAM

☐ = Gold
☐ = Dk. Peach
☐ = Purple
☐ = Green
☐ = Blue

● = French Knot
∅ = Lazy Daisy Stitch
| = Straight Stitch

BACK

Row 1: Starting at **bottom,** with white, ch 25, sc in 2nd ch from hook, sc in each ch across, turn (24 sc).

Rows 2-7: Ch 1, 2 sc in first st, sc in each st across with 2 sc in last st, turn, ending with 36 sts in last row.

Row 8: Ch 1, sc in each st across, turn.

Continued on page 57

Oval Pineapples

DESIGNED BY SANDRA SMITH

SIZE
18" x 19".

MATERIALS
Size 10 bedspread cotton — 350 yds. ecru; No. 8 steel crochet hook or size needed to obtain gauge.

GAUGE
Rnds 1-2 = 1½" x 2½".

SKILL LEVEL
★★ Average

DOILY

Rnd 1: Ch 12, sl st in first ch to form ring, ch 3, 35 dc in ring, join with sl st in top of ch-3 (36 dc).

Rnd 2: Working this rnd in **back lps** only, *ch 6, sl st in each of next 2 sts, ch 8, sl st in each of next 2 sts, ch 10, sl st in each of next 2 sts, ch 12, sl st in each of next 2 sts, ch 10, sl st in each of next 2 sts, ch 8, sl st in each of next 2 sts, ch 6, (sl st in each of next 2 sts, ch 4) 2 times*, sl st in each of next 2 sts; repeat between **, sl st in last st, join with sl st in joining sl st of last rnd, fasten off (18 ch lps).

Rnd 3: Join with sl st in first ch-6 lp, *ch 8, sl st in next ch lp, ch 10, sl st in next ch lp, ch 12, (sl st, ch 12, sl st) in next ch lp, ch 12, sl st in next ch lp, ch 10, sl st in next ch lp, ch 8, (sl st in next ch lp, ch 6) 3 times*, sl st in next ch lp; repeat between **, join with sl st in first sl st (20 ch lps).

NOTES: For **beginning shell (beg shell)**, ch 3, (2 dc, ch 2, 3 dc) in same sp.

For **shell,** (3 dc, ch 2, 3 dc) in next ch sp.

Rnd 4: Sl st in each of next 3 chs, beg shell, shell in each ch lp around, join with sl st in top of ch-3.

Rnds 5-7: Sl st in each of next 2 sts, sl st in next ch sp, beg shell, shell in ch sp of each shell around, join.

Rnd 8: Ch 3, (3 dc, ch 12, 3 dc) in next shell, ch 3, *sl st in next sp between shells, ch 3, (3 dc, ch 12, 3 dc) in next shell, ch 3; repeat from * around, join with sl st in joining sl st of last rnd, fasten off.

Rnd 9: Join with sl st in first ch-12 lp, beg shell, ch 3, 9 dc in next ch-12 lp, ch 3, (shell in next ch-12 lp, ch 3, 9 dc in next ch-12 lp, ch 3) around, join with sl st in top of ch-3.

Rnd 10: Sl st in each of next 2 sts, sl st in next ch sp, beg shell, *[ch 2, skip next ch-3 sp, dc in next dc, (ch 1, dc in next dc) 8 times, ch 2, skip next ch-3 sp], shell in next shell; repeat from * 8 more times; repeat between [ ], join.

Rnd 11: Sl st in each of next 2 sts, sl st in next ch sp, beg shell, *[ch 2, skip next ch-2 sp, sc in next dc, (sc in next ch-1 sp, sc in next dc) 8 times, ch 2, skip next ch-2 sp], shell in next shell; repeat from * 8 more times; repeat between [ ], join.

NOTES: For **beginning double shell (beg dbl shell),** ch 3, (2 dc, ch 2, 3 dc, ch 2, 3 dc) in same sp.

For **double shell (dbl shell),** (3 dc, ch 2, 3 dc, ch 2, 3 dc) in next ch sp.

Rnd 12: Sl st in each of next 2 sts, sl st in next ch sp, beg dbl shell, *[ch 2, skip next ch-2 sp, sl st in next sc, (ch 3, skip next sc, sl st in next sc) 8 times, ch 2, skip next ch-2 sp], dbl shell in next shell; repeat from * 8 more times; repeat between [ ], join.

Rnd 13: Sl st in each of next 2 sts, sl st in next ch sp, beg shell, *[ch 12, shell in next ch-2 sp, ch 2, skip next ch-2 sp, sl st in next ch-3 sp, (ch 3, sl st in next ch-3 sp) 7 times, ch 2, skip next ch-2 sp], shell in next ch-2 sp; repeat from * 8 more times; repeat between [ ], join.

Rnd 14: Sl st in each of next 2 sts, sl st in next ch sp, beg shell, *[ch 3, (sl st, ch 8, sl st, ch 12, sl st, ch 8, sl st) in next ch-12 lp, ch 3, shell in next shell, ch 2, skip next ch-2 sp, sl st in next ch-3 sp, (ch 3, sl st in next ch-3 sp) 6 times, ch 2, skip next ch-2 sp], shell in next shell; repeat from * 8 more times; repeat between [ ], join.

Rnd 15: Sl st in each of next 2 sts, sl st in next ch sp, beg shell, *[skip next ch-3 sp, shell in next ch-8 lp, ch 2, 9 dc in next ch-12 lp, ch 2, shell in next ch-8 lp, skip next ch-3 sp, shell in next shell, ch 2, skip next ch-2 sp, sl st in next ch-3 sp, (ch 3, sl st in next ch-3 sp) 5 times, ch 2, skip next ch-2 sp], shell in next shell; repeat from * 8 more times; repeat between [ ], join.

Rnd 16: Sl st in each of next 2 sts, sl st in next ch sp, beg shell, shell in next shell, *[ch 2, skip next ch-2 sp, dc in next dc, (ch 1, dc in next dc) 8 times, ch 2, skip next ch-2 sp, shell in each of next 2 shells, ch 2, skip next ch-2 sp, sl st in next ch-3 sp, (ch 3, sl st in next ch-3 sp) 4 times, ch 2, skip next ch-2 sp], shell in each of next 2 shells; repeat from * 8 more times; repeat between [ ], join.

Rnd 17: Sl st in each of next 2 sts, sl st in next ch

Continued on page 56

Oval Pineapples

Continued from page 54

sp, beg shell, shell in next shell, *[ch 2, skip next ch-2 sp, sc in next dc, (sc in next ch-1 sp, sc in next dc) 8 times, ch 2, skip next ch-2 sp, shell in each of next 2 shells, ch 2, skip next ch-2 sp, sl st in next ch-3 sp, (ch 3, sl st in next ch-3 sp) 3 times, ch 2, skip next ch-2 sp], shell in each of next 2 shells; repeat from * 8 more times; repeat between [ ], join.

Rnd 18: Sl st in each of next 2 sts, sl st in next ch sp, beg shell, shell in next shell, *[ch 2, skip next ch-2 sp, sl st in next sc, (ch 3, skip next sc, sl st in next sc) 8 times, ch 2, skip next ch-2 sp, shell in each of next 2 shells, ch 2, skip next ch-2 sp, sl st in next ch-3 sp, (ch 3, sl st in next ch-3 sp) 2 times, ch 2, skip next ch-2 sp], shell in each of next 2 shells; repeat from * 8 more times; repeat between [ ], join.

Rnd 19: Sl st in each of next 2 sts, sl st in next ch sp, beg shell, *[◊ch 2, sl st in next sp between shells, ch 2, shell in next shell, ch 2, skip next ch-2 sp, sl st in next ch-3 sp◊, (ch 3, sl st in next ch-3 sp) 7 times, ch 2, skip next ch-2 sp, shell in next shell; repeat between ◊◊, ch 3, sl st in next ch-3 sp, ch 2, skip next ch-2 sp], shell in next shell; repeat from * 8 more times; repeat between [ ], join (80 ch-3 sps, 70 ch-2 sps, 40 shells).

Rnd 20: Sl st in each of next 2 sts, sl st in next ch sp, beg shell, *[◊ch 3, (sl st in next ch-2 sp, ch 3) 2 times, shell in next shell, ch 2, skip next ch-2 sp, sl st in next ch-3 sp◊, (ch 3, sl st in next ch-3 sp) 6 times, ch 2, skip next ch-2 sp, shell in next shell; repeat between ◊◊, ch 2, skip next ch-2 sp], shell in next shell; repeat from * 8 more times; repeat between [ ], join, fasten off.

Rnd 21: Join with sl st in 2nd shell, beg shell, *[ch 2, skip next ch-2 sp, sl st in next ch-3 sp, (ch 3, sl st in next ch-3 sp) 5 times, ch 2, skip next ch-2 sp, shell in next shell, ch 5, skip next ch-3 sp, sl st in next ch-3 sp, ch 5, skip next ch-3 sp, 3 dc in next shell, ch 8, skip next 2 ch-2 sps, 3 dc in next shell, ch 5, skip next ch-3 sp, sl st in next ch-3 sp, ch 5, skip next ch-3 sp], shell in next shell; repeat from * 8 more times; repeat between [ ], join.

Row 22: For **first pineapple,** working in rows, sl st in each of next 2 sts, sl st in next ch sp, beg shell, ch 2, skip next ch-2 sp, sl st in next ch-3 sp, (ch 3, sl st in next ch-3 sp) 4 times, ch 2, skip next ch-2 sp, shell in next shell leaving remaining sts unworked, **turn.**

Rows 23-25: Ch 1, sl st in each of first 3 sts, sl st in next ch sp, beg shell, ch 2, skip next ch-2 sp, sl st in next ch-3 sp, (ch 3, sl st in next ch-3 sp) across to next ch-2 sp, ch 2, skip next ch-2 sp, shell in last shell, **turn,** ending with 2 shells, 2 ch-2 sps and one ch-3 sp in last row.

Row 26: Ch 1, sl st in each of first 3 sts, sl st in next ch sp, beg shell, ch 2, skip next ch-2 sp, sl st in next ch-3 sp, ch 2, skip next ch-2 sp, shell in last shell, **turn.**

Row 27: Ch 1, sl st in each of first 3 sts, ch 3, 2 dc in same sp, ch 8, skip next 2 ch-2 sps, 3 dc in last shell, **turn,** fasten off.

Row 22: For **next pineapple,** join with sl st in next shell on rnd 21, beg shell, ch 2, skip next ch-2 sp, sl st in next ch-3 sp, (ch 3, sl st in next ch-3 sp) 4 times, ch 2, skip next ch-2 sp, shell in next shell leaving remaining sts unworked, **turn.**

Rows 23-27: Repeat same rows of first pineapple.

Repeat next pineapple around entire Doily, ending with 10 pineapples.❖

Tea Party Doily

Continued from page 45

times], shell in next 4 ch-2 sps; repeat from * 6 more times; repeat between [ ], join with sl st in top of ch-3.

Rnd 15: Sl st in next st, sl st in next ch sp, ch 1, (sc, ch 3, sc) in same sp, *[◊ch 3, (sc, ch 3, sc) in next shell; repeat from ◊ 2 more times, (ch 3, sc in next ch-2 sp) 5 times, ch 3, skip next ch-2 sp, (sc, ch 3, sc) in next ch-1 sp, ch 3, skip next ch-2 sp, (sc in next ch-2 sp, ch 3) 5 times], (sc, ch 3, sc) in next shell; repeat from * 6 more times; repeat between [ ], join with sl st in first sc, fasten off.❖

Easter Egg Pillow

Continued from page 53

Row 9: Repeat row 2 (38).

Rows 10-31: Ch 1, sc in each st across, turn.

Row 32: Ch 1, sc first 2 sts tog, sc in each st across to last 2 sts, sc last 2 sts tog, turn (36).

Rows 33-34: Ch 1, sc in each st across, turn.

Rows 35-47: Repeat rows 32-34 consecutively, ending with row 32 and 26 sts in last row.

Row 48: Ch 1, sc in each st across, turn.

Row 49: Repeat row 32 (24).

Row 50: Ch 1, sc in each st across, turn.

Rows 51-55: Repeat row 32, ending with 14 sts in last row.

Rnd 56: Working in rnds, ch 1, sc in each st and in end of each row around, join with sl st in first sc, fasten off.

RUFFLE

Rnd 1: To **join Front and Back,** with wrong sides held tog, having Front facing you and working through both thicknesses, join blue with sc in any st, sc in each st around stuffing before closing, join with sl st in first sc (158 sc).

Rnd 2: Ch 1, sc in first st, ch 3, skip next st, (sc in next st, ch 3, skip next st) around, join.

Rnd 3: Ch 1, sc in each sc and 5 sc in each ch-3 sp around, join, fasten off.❖

Sewing Angel

Continued from page 29

Rows 9-12: Repeat rows 7 and 8 alternately, ending with 5 sts in last row.

Rnd 13: Working around outer edge, ch 1, sc first 2 sts tog, sc in next st, sc next 2 sts tog, sc in end of each row across; working in starting ch on opposite side of row 1, sc in next ch, 3 sc in next ch, sc in next ch; sc in end of each row across, join with sl st in first sc, fasten off.

Sew first 3 sts of rnd 13 on both Wings together. Sew center of Wings to back of doll.

For **hanger,** tie desired length glitter white to back of Head above Wings.

FINISHING

1: For **hair** (make 9), wrap gray yarn around 2 fingers 10 times. Remove from fingers and tie separate strand gray yarn tightly around middle of all loops. Sew around sides, back and top of Head as desired. For **bangs,** fray ends of yarn on hair at top of Head.

2: With black, using French Knot, embroider **eyes** over rnd 5 of Head ½" apart. With black embroidery floss, using Fly Stitch (see illustration) and Straight Stitch, embroider **mouth** and **eyebrows** as shown in photo. Push 2 straight pins into Head on one side of mouth. Insert glasses stems in Head on each side of eyes.

FLY STITCH

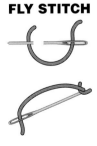

3: For **halo,** insert one end of wired gold braid through a few strands of hair. Twist ends of braid together forming a circle.❖

Fashions & Comforts

When Autumn's chilly breezes chase
away Summer's languid heat,
pamper yourself and those you love
with stylish sweaters and lavishly
thick throws, perfect for relaxing indoors
or out. Regardless of the weather, you're
sure to find the perfect pattern among
these inviting indulgences.

Kitty Angel

DESIGNED BY ESTELLA WHITFORD

SIZE
9" tall.

MATERIALS
Worsted-weight yarn — 3½ oz. warm brown, 2 oz. each burgundy and off-white, small amount each green, blue and black; small amount gold size 10 bedspread cotton; 2½" x 16" piece off-white lace; 2 off-white ⅜" buttons; 6 buttons in assorted colors and sizes; 3 mini wooden spring-type clothespins; 6" piece wired metallic gold braid; polyester fiberfill; off-white sewing thread; burgundy sewing thread; sewing and tapestry needles; G crochet hook or size needed to obtain gauge.

GAUGE
4 sc sts = 1"; 4 sc rows = 1".

SKILL LEVEL
★★ Average

SPECIAL NOTE
Do not join rnds unless otherwise stated. Mark first st of each rnd.

HEAD & BODY
Rnd 1: Starting at **Head,** with warm brown, ch 2, 6 sc in 2nd ch from hook (6 sc).

Rnd 2: 2 sc in each st around (12).

Rnd 3: (Sc in next st, 2 sc in next st) around (18).

Rnd 4: (Sc in each of next 2 sts, 2 sc in next st) around (24).

Rnds 5-7: Sc in each st around.

Rnd 8: (Sc in each of next 2 sts, sc next 2 sts tog) around (18).

Rnd 9: (Sc next 2 sts tog) around (9).

Rnd 10: 2 sc in each st around (18).

Rnd 11: (Sc in each of next 2 sts, 2 sc in next st) around (24).

Rnds 12-17: Sc in each st around.

Rnd 18: (Sc in each of next 2 sts, sc next 2 sts tog) around (18). Stuff.

Rnd 19: (Sc next 2 sts tog) around (9).

Rnd 20: Sc in next st, (sc next 2 sts tog) around, join with sl st in first sc, fasten off leaving 8" for sewing (5).

ARM (make 2)
Rnd 1: Starting at **paw,** with warm brown, ch 2, 6 sc in 2nd ch from hook (6 sc).

Rnd 2: (Sc in next st, 2 sc in next st) around (9).

Rnds 3-10: Sc in each st around. At end of last rnd, join with sl st in first sc, fasten off leaving 10" for sewing. Stuff.

Sew Arms over rnds 11-13 on each side of Body.

LEG (make 2)
Rnd 1: Starting at **foot,** with warm brown, ch 2, 6 sc in 2nd ch from hook (6 sc).

Rnd 2: (Sc in next st, 2 sc in next st) around (9).

Rnds 3-16: Sc in each st around. At end of last rnd, join with sl st in first sc, fasten off leaving 10" for sewing. Stuff.

Sew Legs to bottom of Body.

EAR (make 2)
Row 1: Starting at **bottom,** with warm brown, ch 6, sc in 2nd ch from hook, sc in each ch across, turn (5 sc).

Row 2: Ch 1, sc first 2 sts tog, sc in next st, sc last 2 sts tog, turn (3).

Row 3: Ch 1, sc in first st, skip next st, sc in last st, turn (2).

Row 4: Ch 1, skip first st, sl st in last st, fasten off.

Row 5: Join warm brown with sc in end of row 1, sc in end of each row across to opposite side of row 1 with 3 sc in st at top of Ear, fasten off.

Sew Ears ¼" apart to top of Head.

For **eyes,** embroider 2 black French Knots (see page 159) ¼" apart over rnds 3 and 4. Using Satin and Straight Stitches (see page 159), embroider **nose** and **mouthline** below eyes as shown in photo.

For **whiskers,** thread 2¼" piece off-white yarn through st below nose. Fray ends. For **halo,** twist ends of wired gold braid together. Place over one Ear and tack to back of Head.

DRESS
Row 1: Starting at **top,** with burgundy, ch 7, sc in 2nd ch from hook, sc in each ch across, turn (6 sc).

Row 2: Ch 1, 2 sc in first st, sc in each st across

with 2 sc in last st, turn (8).

Row 3: Ch 1, sc in each st across, turn.

Row 4: Repeat row 2 (10).

Rnd 5: Working in rnds, ch 1, 2 sc in first st, sc in next 8 sts, 2 sc in last st, ch 17, join with sl st in first st (12 sc, 17 chs).

Rnd 6: Ch 1, sc in each st and in each ch around, join with sl st in first sc (29).

Rnd 7: Ch 1, sc in each st around, join.

Rnd 8: Ch 3, dc in same st, 2 dc in each st around, join with sl st in top of ch-3 (58 dc).

Rnd 9: Ch 3, dc in each st around, join, fasten off. With sewing needle and off-white thread, sew lace around bottom of Dress.

For **straps,** with burgundy, ch 23, sc in 2nd ch from hook, sc in each ch across, fasten off. Sew ends to top corners of Dress, sew middle to center back of Dress. Sew one off-white button over each end of straps. Place Dress on Kitty.

WING (make 2)

Row 1: With off-white yarn, ch 4, sc in 2nd ch from hook, sc in each ch across, turn (3 sc).

Rows 2-5: Ch 1, 2 sc in first st, sc in each st across with 2 sc in last st, turn, ending with 11 sts in last row.

Row 6: Ch 1, sc in each st across, turn.

Row 7: Ch 1, sc first 2 sts tog, sc in each st across to last 2 sts, sc last 2 sts tog, turn (9).

Row 8: Ch 1, sc in each st across, turn.

Rows 9-12: Repeat rows 7 and 8 alternately, ending with 5 sts in last row.

Rnd 13: Working around outer edge, ch 1, sc first 2 sts tog, sc in next st, sc next 2 sts tog, sc in end of each row around to row 1; working in starting ch on opposite side of row 1, sc in next ch, 3 sc in next ch, sc in next ch; sc in end of each row around, join with sl st in first sc, fasten off.

With tapestry needle and gold bedspread cotton, Straight Stitch (see page 159) around base of rnd 13. Sew first 3 sts of rnd 13 on both Wings together. Sew center of Wings to back of Kitty, gathering slightly. Sew 3 buttons to front of one Wing.

For **hanger,** tie desired length yarn to back of Head above Wings.

MITTEN (make 2 green and one blue)
Hand

Rnd 1: Ch 2, 6 sc in 2nd ch from hook (6 sc).

Rnd 2: (Sc in next st, 2 sc in next st) around (9).

Rnds 3-4: Sc in each st around.

Rnd 5: Ch 3, dc in each st around, join with sl st in top of ch-3, fasten off.

Thumb

Rnd 1: Ch 2, 6 sc in 2nd ch from hook (6 sc).

Rnd 2: Sc in each st around, join with sl st in first sc, fasten off leaving 6" for sewing.

Sew Thumb to one side of Hand.

Sew one button to front of each Mitten.

For **clothesline,** cut 10" piece off-white yarn, tie to each paw 2" from end. Fray ends. Clip Mittens onto clothesline using clothespins.❖

Garden Blouse

DESIGNED BY NAZANIN S. FARD

SIZE
Fits lady's 32"-38" bust.

MATERIALS
Size 10 bedspread cotton — 2700 yds. ecru;
No. 5 steel crochet hook or size
needed to obtain gauge.

GAUGE
Rnds 1-2 of Large Motif = 1¼". Large Motif
is 3" across. Small Motif is 1½" across.

SKILL LEVEL
★★★ Advanced

LARGE MOTIF
Rnd 1: Ch 8, sl st in first ch to form ring, ch 6, (dc in ring, ch 3) 7 times, join with sl st in 3rd ch of ch-6 (8 dc, 8 ch-3 sps).

Rnd 2: Ch 3, 5 dc in next ch sp, (dc in next st, 5 dc in next ch sp) around, join with sl st in top of ch-3 (48 dc).

Rnd 3: Sl st in next st, ch 3, dc in next 4 sts, ch 3, skip next st, (dc in next 5 sts, ch 3, skip next st) around, join (40 dc, 8 ch-3 sps).

NOTES: For **beginning cluster variation (beg cl),** ch 4, *yo 2 times, insert hook in next st, yo, draw lp through, (yo, draw through 2 lps on hook) 2 times; repeat from * 3 more times, yo, draw through all 5 lps on hook.

For **cluster variation (cl),** *yo 2 times, insert hook in next st, yo, draw lp through, (yo, draw through 2 lps on hook) 2 times; repeat from * 4 more times, yo, draw through all 6 lps on hook.

Rnd 4: Beg cl, ch 9, sl st in 2nd ch of next ch-3, ch 9, (cl, ch 9, sl st in 2nd ch of next ch-3, ch 9) around, join with sl st in top of beg cl (16 ch-9 sps).

NOTES: For **joining ch-7 sp,** ch 3, sl st in center ch of corresponding ch sp on designated Motif, ch 3.

Rnd 5: Sl st in next 5 chs, *[ch 9, sl st in 5th ch of next ch-9, ch 7, (sl st in 5th ch of next ch-9, ch 7) 2 times], sl st in 5th ch of next ch-9; repeat from * 2 more times; repeat between [ ], join with sl st in first sl st, fasten off (12 ch-7 sps, 4 ch-9 sps).

For **joining ch-9 sp,** ch 4, sl st in center ch of corresponding ch sp on designated Motif, ch 4.

Use joining ch-7 sps or joining ch-9 sps on last rnd when joining on to other Motifs (see Joining Diagram).

SMALL MOTIF
NOTES: For **joining ch-7 sp,** ch 3, sl st in center ch of corresponding ch sp on designated Motif, ch 3.

For **joining ch-3 sp,** ch 1, sl st in center ch of corresponding ch sp on designated Motif, ch 1.

Use joining ch-3 sps or joining ch-7 sps on last rnd when joining on to other Motifs (see Joining Diagram).

Rnd 1: Ch 6, sl st in first ch to form ring, ch 6, (dc in ring, ch 3) 7 times, join with sl st in 3rd ch of ch-6 (8 dc, 8 ch-3 sps).

Rnd 2: Sl st in next ch sp, ch 3, 3 dc in same sp, ch 9, 4 dc in next ch sp, ch 3, (4 dc in next ch sp, ch 9, 4 dc in next ch sp, ch 3) around, join with sl st in top of ch-3, fasten off (32 dc, 4 ch-9 sps, 4 ch-3 sps).

JOINING DIAGRAM

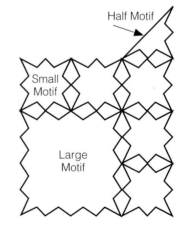

HALF MOTIF
Row 1: Ch 6, sl st in first ch to form ring, ch 6, (dc in ring, ch 3) 3 times, dc in ring, turn (5 dc, 4 ch-3 sps).

NOTES: For **joining ch-9 sp,** ch 4, sl st in center ch of corresponding ch sp on designated Motif, ch 4.

For **joining ch-3 sp,** ch 1, sl st in center ch of corresponding ch sp on designated Motif, ch 1.

Continued on page 81

Polka-Dot Set

DESIGNED BY CHRISTINA MCNEESE

SIZE
Instructions are for 6 mos.; changes for 12 mos. and 18 mos. are in [ ].

MATERIALS
Worsted-weight yarn — 11 [13, 15] oz. hunter green sprinkles; 5 yellow $\frac{9}{16}$" shank buttons; four 40-count packages each blue, red and yellow 5-mm pom-poms (optional—see Note below); one red $1\frac{1}{2}$" pom-pom; fabric glue or sewing thread to match pom-poms (optional); tapestry needle; I (5.5 mm) afghan hook and G crochet hook or sizes needed to obtain gauge.

GAUGES
Afghan hook, 7 afghan knit sts = 2"; 15 knit st rows = 4". **G hook,** 15 sc = 4", 9 sc rows = 2"; 5 ribbing sts = 1", 5 ribbing rows = 1".

SKILL LEVEL
★★ Average

SPECIAL NOTE
Use discretion when making items for small children that have pieces that could be swallowed. If desired, decorative pom-poms shown on photographed items can be replaced with French Knots (see page 159) of the same color.

SWEATER
Back
Row 1: With afghan hook, ch 36 [40, 42]; leaving all lps on hook, insert hook in 2nd ch from hook, yo, draw lp through, (insert hook in next ch, yo, draw lp through) across, **do not** turn; to **work lps off hook,** yo, draw through one lp on hook (see page 159), (yo, draw through 2 lps on hook) across leaving one lp on hook at end of row (see ill. B), **do not** turn (36 sts) [40 sts, 42 sts]. Lp (or vertical bar) left on hook at end of row is first st of next row.

Row 2: For **afghan knit stitch (K),** skip first vertical bar, insert hook from front to back through center of next vertical st (see ill. C), yo, draw lp through; repeat from * across; work lps off hook (36 K sts) [40 K sts, 42 K sts].

Rows 3-34 [3-38, 3-40]: K across; work lps off hook.

Row 35 [39, 41]: For **right shoulder,** K 12 [13, 14] leaving remaining sts unworked, turn (12) [13, 14].

Row 36 [40, 42]: K across; work lps off hook, fasten off.

Row 35 [39, 41]: For **neck,** skip next 12 [14, 14] sts on row 34 [38, 40]; for **left shoulder,** join with sl st in next st, K across; work lps off hook (12) [13, 14].

Row 36 [40, 42]: K across; work lps off hook, fasten off.

Left Front
Row 1: Using ch 16 [18, 19], repeat same row of Back (16) [18, 19].

Rows 2-28 [2-32, 2-34]: K across; work lps off hook.

Row 29 [33, 35]: For **neck shaping,** st st 12 [13, 14] leaving remaining sts unworked (12) [13, 14].

Rows 30-36 [34-40, 36-42]: K across; work lps off hook. At end of last row, fasten off.

Right Front
Row 1: Using ch 16 [18, 19], repeat same row of Back (16) [18, 19].

Rows 2-28 [2-32, 2-34]: K across; work lps off hook. At end of last row, fasten off.

Row 29 [33, 35]: For **neck shaping,** skip first 4 [5, 5] sts, join with sl st in next st, K across; work lps off hook (12) [13, 14].

Rows 30-36 [34-40, 36-42]: K across; work lps off hook. At end of last row, fasten off.

Matching sts, sew shoulder seams.

Sleeve (make 2)
Row 1: Using ch 20, repeat row 1 of Back (20).

NOTE: For **increase (inc),** insert hook under next horizontal bar between sts, yo, draw lp through.

Row 2: Inc, K across to last st, inc, K 1 (22).

Rows 3-4: K across; work lps off hook.

Rows 5-20 [5-23, 5-26]: Repeat rows 2-4 consecutively, ending with row 2 and 34 [36, 38] sts in last row.

Row 21 [24-25, 27-29]: K across; work lps off hook. At end of last row, fasten off.

Matching center of last row to shoulder seam,

Continued on next page

sew Sleeve to body. Sew Sleeve and side seams.

Waist Ribbing

Row 1: Working in starting ch on opposite side of row 1 on each Front and Back, with G crochet hook, join with sl st in first ch on Left Front, ch 6, sc in 2nd ch from hook, sc in next 4 chs, sl st in same ch on body as joining sl st, sl st in next ch, turn (5 sc).

Row 2: Working the following rows in **back lps** only, ch 1, skip first 2 sl sts, sc in each st across, turn.

Row 3: Ch 1, sc in each st across, sl st in each of next 2 chs on body, turn.

Rows 4-68 [4-76, 4-80]: Repeat rows 2 and 3 alternately, ending with row 2. At end of last row, fasten off.

Sleeve Ribbing

Row 1: Working in starting ch on opposite side of row 1 on Sleeve, with G crochet hook, join with sl st in first ch, ch 6, sc in 2nd ch from hook, sc in next 4 chs, sl st in same ch on Sleeve as joining sl st, sl st in next ch, turn (5 sc).

Row 2: Working the following rows in **back lps** only, ch 1, skip first 2 sl sts, sc in each st across, turn.

Row 3: Ch 1, sc in each st across, turn, sl st in each of next 2 chs on Sleeve, turn.

Rows 4-20: Repeat rows 2 and 3 alternately, ending with row 2. At end of last row, fasten off. Repeat on other Sleeve.

Neck Ribbing

Row 1: Working in sts and ends of rows across neck edge, with G crochet hook, join with sl st in first st on row 28 [32, 34] of Right Front, ch 6, sc in 2nd ch from hook, sc in next 4 chs, sl st in same st on body as joining sl st, sl st in next st, turn (5 sc).

Row 2: Working the following rows in **back lps** only, ch 1, skip first 2 sl sts, sc in each st across, turn.

Row 3: Ch 1, sc in each st across, sl st in each of next 2 sts or ends of row on Body, turn.

Next Rows: Repeat rows 2 and 3 alternately across neck edge, ending with row 2. At end of last row, fasten off.

Button Band

Row 1: Working across Left Front opening, with G crochet hook, join with sc in first st on

Neck Ribbing, sc in each st and in end of each row across, turn (38 sc) [42 sc, 44 sc].

Rows 2-5: Ch 1, sc in each st across, turn. At end of last row, fasten off.

Buttonhole Band

Row 1: Working across Right Front opening, with G crochet hook, join with sc in first st on Waist Ribbing, sc in each st and in end of each row across, turn (38 sc) [42 sc, 44 sc].

Row 2: Ch 1, sc in each st across, turn.

Row 3: Ch 1, sc in each of first 2 [2, 3] sts; for **buttonhole,** ch 2, skip next 2 sts; *sc in next 6 [7, 7] sts; for **buttonhole,** ch 2, skip next 2 sts; repeat from * 3 more times, sc in each of last 2 [2, 3] sts, turn (5 buttonholes).

Row 4: Ch 1, sc in each st and 2 sc in each ch-2 sp across, turn.

Row 5: Ch 1, sc in each st across, fasten off.

Finishing

1: Sew buttons to Button Band opposite buttonholes.

2: Alternating red, blue and yellow 5-mm pom-poms, sew or glue one pom-pom to (optional — embroider one French Knot on) each st and end of row around outer edge of entire body as shown in photo. Repeat around row 1 of each Sleeve.

CAP

Row 1: Using ch 52 [56, 62], repeat row 1 of Sweater's Back (52) [56, 62].

Rows 2-6 [2-10, 2-14]: K across; work lps off hook.

Row 7 [11, 15]: *K 9 [10, 11], skip next st; repeat from * 4 more times, K 2 [1, 2]; work lps off hook (47) [51, 57].

Rows 8-9 [12-13, 16-17]: K across; work lps off hook.

Row 10 [14, 18]: *K 8 [9, 10], skip next st; repeat from * 4 more times, K 2 [1, 2]; work lps off hook (42) [46, 52].

Rows 11-12 [15-16, 19-20]: K across; work lps off hook.

Row 13 [17, 21]: *K 7 [8, 9], skip next st; repeat from * 4 more times, K 2 [1, 2]; work lps off hook (37) [41, 47].

Rows 14-15 [18-19, 22-23]: K across; work lps off hook.

Row 16 [20, 24]: *K 6 [7, 8], skip next st; repeat from * 4 more times, K 2 [1, 2]; work lps off hook (32) [36, 42].

Rows 17-18 [21-22, 25-26]: K across; work lps off hook.

Row 19 [23, 27]: *K 5 [6, 7], skip next st; repeat from * 4 more times, K 2 [1, 2]; work lps off hook (27) [31, 37].

Row 20 [24, 28]: K across; work lps off hook, fasten off leaving long end for sewing.

With long end, sew ends of rows together. Weave same end through sts on last row, pull tight to gather, secure.

Ribbing

Row 1: Working in starting ch on opposite side of row 1, with G crochet hook, join with sl st in first ch, ch 6, sc in 2nd ch from hook, sc in next 4 chs, sl st in same ch on Cap as joining sl st, sl st in next ch, turn (5 sc).

Row 2: Working the following rows in **back lps** only, ch 1, skip first 2 sl sts, sc in each st across, turn.

Row 3: Ch 1, sc in each st across, sl st in each of next 2 chs on Cap, turn.

Rows 4-52 [4-56, 4-62]: Repeat rows 2 and 3 alternately, ending with row 2. At end of last row, fasten off.

Finishing

1: Glue 1½" pom-pom to top of Cap.

2: Alternating red, blue and yellow 5-mm pom-poms, sew or glue one pom-pom to (optional—embroider one French Knot on) each st on rows 1 and 5.

MITTEN (make 2)

Row 1: Using ch 20 [22, 24], repeat same row of Sweater's Back (20) [22, 24].

Rows 2-6 [2-6, 2-7]: K across; work lps off hook.

Row 7 [7, 8]: For **first side of thumb**, K 3 [3, 4] leaving remaining sts unworked; work lps off hook (3) [3, 4].

Row 8 [8, 9-10]: K across; work lps off hook.

Row 9 [9, 11]: K across, yo, draw through all 3 [3, 4] lps on hook, fasten off.

Row 7 [7, 8]: For **palm**, join with sl st in next unworked st on row 6 [6, 7], K 13 [15, 15] leaving remaining sts unworked; work lps off hook (14) [16, 16].

Rows 8-10 [8-11, 8-12]: K across; work lps off hook.

Rows 11-12 [12-13, 13-14]: K 1, skip next st, K across to last 2 sts, skip next st, K 1; work lps off hook, ending with 12 [14, 16] sts in last row. At end of last row, fasten off.

Row 7 [7, 8]: For **second side of thumb**, join with sl st in next unworked st on row 6 [6, 7], K across; work lps off hook (3) [3, 4].

Rows 8-9 [8-9, 9-11]: Repeat same rows of first side of thumb.

Fold Mitten in half vertically; matching sts and ends of rows, sew together.

Ribbing

Row 1: Working in starting ch on opposite side of row 1, with G crochet hook, join with sl st in first ch, ch 6, sc in 2nd ch from hook, sc in next 4 chs, sl st in same ch on Mitten as joining sl st, sl st in next ch, turn (5 sc).

Row 2: Working the following rows in **back lps** only, ch 1, skip first 2 sl sts, sc in each st across, turn.

Row 3: Ch 1, sc in each st across, sl st in each of next 2 chs on Mitten, turn.

Rows 4-20 [4-22, 4-24]: Repeat rows 2 and 3 alternately, ending with row 2. At end of last row, fasten off.

Finishing

Alternating red, blue and yellow 5-mm pom-poms, sew or glue one pom-pom to (optional—embroider one French Knot on) each st on row 1 of Mitten.❖

Tweed Cables

DESIGNED BY CHRISTINA MCNEESE

SIZES

Instructions are for lady's size 30"-32" bust; changes for 34"-36", 38"-40" and 42"-44" are in [ ].

MATERIALS

Worsted-weight yarn — 16 [18, 20, 22] oz. beige heather, 6 [7, 8, 9] oz. green sprinkles; tapestry needle; H and I crochet hooks or sizes needed to obtain gauges.

GAUGES

H hook, 7 ribbing sts = 2"; 9 ribbing rows = 2".
I hook, 3 dc = 1"; 3 dc rows = 2".

SKILL LEVEL

★★★ Advanced

BODY
Back

Row 1: With I hook and beige, ch 56 [62, 68, 74], dc in 4th ch from hook, dc in each ch across, turn (54 dc) [60 dc, 66 dc, 72 dc].

Rows 2-32 [2-32, 2-34, 2-34]: Ch 3, dc in each st across, turn.

Row 33 [33, 35, 35]: For **right shoulder,** ch 3, dc in next 17 [19, 21, 23] sts, fasten off; for **neck,** skip next 18 [20, 22, 24] sts; for **left shoulder,** join with sl st in next st, ch 3, dc in each st across, fasten off (18) [20, 22, 24] sts on each shoulder.

Front

NOTES: For **double crochet front post (dc fp, see page 159),** yo, insert hook from front to back around post of next st, yo, draw lp through, (yo, draw through 2 lps on hook) 2 times. Skip one st on last row behind each post st.

For **double crochet back post (dc bp),** yo, insert hook from back to front around post of next st, yo, draw lp through, (yo, draw through 2 lps on hook) 2 times.

For **treble crochet front post (tr fp),** yo 2 times, insert hook around post of designated st, yo, draw lp through, (yo, draw through 2 lps on hook) 3 times.

For **popcorn (pc),** 5 dc in next st, drop lp from hook, insert hook in first st of 5-dc group, draw dropped lp through st, ch 1.

When changing colors (see page 159), always drop color to wrong side of work. Carry dropped color to next section of same color.

Row 1: With I hook and beige, ch 56 [62, 68, 74], dc in 4th ch from hook, dc in each of next 2 [3, 4, 5] chs changing to green in last st made, *◊dc in each of next 2 chs changing to beige in last st made, dc in next 4 chs changing to green in last st made, dc in each of next 2 chs changing to beige in last st made◊, dc in next 5 [6, 7, 8] chs changing to green in last st made, pc in next ch changing to beige, dc in next 5 [6, 7, 8] chs changing to green in last st made; repeat from *; repeat between ◊◊, dc in last 4 [5, 6, 7] chs, turn (52 dc, 2 pc) [58 dc, 2 pc; 64 dc, 2 pc; 70 dc, 2 pc].

Row 2: Ch 3, dc in each of next 3 [4, 5, 6] sts changing to green in last st made, *◊dc bp around each of next 2 sts changing to beige in last st made, dc bp around next 4 sts changing to green in last st made, dc bp around each of next 2 sts changing to beige in last st made◊, dc in next 4 [5, 6, 7] sts changing to green in last st made, pc in next st changing to beige, dc in next st changing to green, pc in next st changing to beige, dc in next 4 [5, 6, 7] sts changing to green in last st made; repeat from *; repeat between ◊◊, dc in last 4 [5, 6, 7] sts, turn (26 dc, 24 dc bp, 4 pc) [32 dc, 24 dc bp, 4 pc; 38 dc, 24 dc bp, 4 pc; 44 dc, 24 dc bp, 4 pc].

Row 3: Ch 3, dc in each of next 3 [4, 5, 6] sts, *◊skip next 2 sts, tr fp around each of next 2 sts changing to green in last st made; working behind last 2 sts made, tr fp around each of last 2 skipped sts, skip next 2 sts, tr fp around each of next 2 sts changing to beige in last st made; working in front of last 2 sts made, tr fp around each of last 2 skipped sts◊, dc in next 5 [6, 7, 8] sts changing to green in last st made, pc in next st changing to beige, dc in next 5 [6, 7, 8] sts; repeat from *; repeat between ◊◊, dc in last 4 [5, 6, 7] sts, turn (28 dc, 24 tr fp, 2 pc) [34 dc, 24 tr fp, 2 pc; 40 dc, 24 tr fp, 2 pc; 46 dc, 24 tr fp, 2 pc].

Row 4: Ch 3, dc in each of next 3 [4, 5, 6] sts, *◊dc bp around each of next 2 sts changing to

Continued on page 82

Autumn Wheat

DESIGNED BY ROSETTA HARSHMAN

SIZE
49" x 68".

MATERIALS
Worsted-weight yarn — 32½ oz. tan, 12 oz. brown, 6 oz. orange; tapestry needle; G crochet hook or size needed to obtain gauge.

GAUGE
2 cl = 1"; 6 cl rows = 5". Each Strip is 4½" across.

SKILL LEVEL
★★★ Advanced

STRIP A (make 6)
Row 1: With tan, ch 9, sc in 2nd ch from hook, sc in each ch across, turn (8 sc).

Row 2: Ch 3, dc in each st across, turn (8 dc).

Row 3: Ch 1, sc in each st across, turn (8 sc).

NOTE: For **front post cluster (fp cl),** yo, insert hook from right to left around post of next st on last dc row (see page 159), yo, draw lp through, yo, draw through 2 lps on hook, (yo, insert hook aroundsame st, yo, draw lp through, yo, draw through 2 lps on hook) 2 times, yo, draw through all 4 lps on hook.

Row 4: Ch 3, dc in next st, fp cl, dc in each of next 2 sts, fp cl, dc in each of last 2 sts, turn (6 dc, 2 fp cl).

Row 5: Ch 1, sc in each st across, turn (8 sc).

Row 6: Ch 3, dc in next st, skip next st, fp cl, dc in each of next 2 sts, fp cl, skip next st, dc in each of last 2 sts, turn (6 dc, 2 fp cl).

Rows 7-164: Repeat rows 5 and 6 alternately.

Row 165: Ch 1, sc in each st across, **turn,** fasten off.

Edging
NOTE: For **double treble crochet (dtr, see page 158),** yo 3 times, insert hook in next st, yo, draw lp through, (yo, draw through 2 lps on hook) 4 times.

Rnd 1: Working in rnds, join orange with sl st in first sc on row 165, ch 2, dc in next st, 2 tr in next st, 2 dtr in next st, 2 tr in next st, dc in next st, hdc in next st; *working in end rows on long edge, skip first sc row, (2 dc around posts of 2 dc at end of next dc row, hdc in end of next sc row) across to last 2 rows, 2 dc around posts of 2 dc at end of last dc row, skip last sc row*; working in starting ch on opposite side of row 1, hdc in first ch, dc in next ch, 2 tr in next ch, 2 dtr in next st, 2 tr in next st, dc in next st, hdc

in next st; repeat between **, join with sl st in top of ch-2, fasten off.

NOTE: For **treble crochet front post (tr fp),** yo 2 times, insert hook from right to left around post of next st, complete as tr.

Rnd 2: Join brown with sl st in first st, ch 3, dc in same st, dc in next st, (2 dc in next st, dc in next st) 5 times; *working on long edge, (tr fp around each of next 2 dc, hdc in next hdc) across to last 2 dc, tr fp around each of last 2 dc*, (2 dc in next st, dc in next st) 6 times; repeat between **, join with sl st in top of ch-3.

Rnd 3: Ch 1, (2 sc in first dc, sc in next dc) 9 times; working on long edge, sc in each st across to first dc on next short end; repeat between ( ) 9 times; working on long edge, sc in each st across, join with sl st in first sc, fasten off.

STRIP B (make 5)
Rows 1-165: Repeat same rows of Strip A. At end of last row, **turn, do not** fasten off.

Edging
Rnd 1: Working in rnds, ch 2, dc in next st, 2 tr in next st, 2 dtr in next st, 2 tr in next st, dc in next st, hdc in next st; *working in end rows on long edge, skip first sc row, (2 dc around posts of 2 dc at end of next dc row, hdc in end of next sc row) across to last 2 rows, 2 dc around posts of 2 dc at end of last dc row, skip last sc row*; working in starting ch on opposite side of row 1, hdc in first ch, dc in next ch, 2 tr in next ch, 2 dtr in next st, 2 tr in next st, dc in next st, hdc in next st; repeat between **, join with sl st in top of ch-2.

Rnd 2: Ch 3, dc in same st, dc in next st, (2 dc in next st, dc in next st) 5 times; *working on long edge, (tr fp around each of next 2 dc, hdc in next hdc) across to last 2 dc, tr fp around each of last 2 dc*, (2 dc in next st, dc in next st) 6 times; repeat between **, join with sl st in top of ch-3.

Rnd 3: Ch 1, 2 sc in first st, sc in next dc, (2 sc in next dc, sc in next dc) 8 times; working on long edge, sc in each st across to first dc on next short end; repeat between ( ) 9 times; working on long edge, sc in each st across, join with sl st in first sc, fasten off.

To **join Strips,** working in **back lps,** matching sts and alternating Strips, sew Strips together with tan leaving 27 sts at each end of Strips unsewn.❧

Snowballs Sweater

DESIGNED BY CHRISTINA MCNEESE

SIZES
Instructions are for children's size 8; changes for size 12 are in [ ].

MATERIALS
Worsted-weight yarn — 21 [25] oz. white; tapestry needle; G and I crochet hooks or sizes needed to obtain gauge.

GAUGES
G hook, 4 ribbing sts = 1"; 5 ribbing rows = 1".
I hook, 3 sts = 1"; 13 sc rows = 4".

SKILL LEVEL
★★ Average

BODY
Back
Row 1: With I hook, ch 48 [52], sc in 2nd ch from hook, sc in each ch across, turn (47 sc) [51 sc].

Row 2: Ch 1, sc in each st across, turn.

NOTES: For **front post stitch (fp, see page 159),** yo, insert hook from front to back around post of corresponding st on row before last, yo, draw lp through, (yo, draw through 2 lps on hook) 2 times. Skip next st on last row behind fp.

For **puff stitch (puff st),** yo, insert hook in next st, yo, draw up long lp, (yo, insert hook in same st, yo, draw up long lp) 4 times, yo, draw through 10 lps on hook, yo, draw through remaining 2 lps on hook.

Row 3: Ch 1, sc in each of first 2 [4] sts, *fp, sc in next st, fp, sc in next 4 sts, puff st, sc in next 4 sts, fp, sc in next st, fp*, sc in next 6 sts, puff st, sc in next 6 sts; repeat between **, sc in each of last 2 [4] sts, turn (36 sc, 8 fp, 3 puff sts) [40 sc, 8 fp, 3 puff sts].

Row 4: Repeat row 2.

Row 5: Ch 1, sc in each of first 2 [4] sts, *fp, sc in next st, fp, sc in each of next 2 sts, puff st, sc in each of next 3 sts, puff st, sc in each of next 2 sts, fp, sc in next st, fp*, sc in next 4 sts, puff st, sc in each of next 3 sts, puff st, sc in next 4 sts; repeat between **, sc in each of last 2 [4] sts, turn (33 sc, 8 fp, 6 puff sts) [37 sc, 8 fp, 6 puff sts].

Row 6: Repeat row 2.

Row 7: Ch 1, sc in each of first 2 [4] sts, *fp, sc in next st, fp, sc in next 4 sts, puff st, sc in next 4 sts, fp, sc in next st, fp*, sc in each of next 2 sts, puff st, sc in next 7 sts, puff st, sc in each of next 2 sts; repeat between **, sc in each of last 2 [4] sts, turn (35 sc, 8 fp, 4 puff sts) [39 sc, 8 fp, 4 puff sts].

Row 8: Repeat row 2.

Row 9: Repeat row 5.

NOTE: Pattern is established in rows 2-9.

Rows 10-50 [10-58]: Work in pattern.

Row 51 [59]: For **right shoulder,** work in pattern across first 16 [18] sts leaving remaining sts unworked, turn (16 sts) [18 sts].

Row 52 [60]: Work in pattern across, turn, fasten off.

Row 51 [59]: For **neck,** skip next 15 sts on row 50 [58]; for **left shoulder,** join with sc in next st, work in pattern across, turn (16 sts) [18 sts].

Row 52 [60]: Work in pattern across, fasten off.

Front
Rows 1-44 [1-52]: Repeat same rows of Back.

Row 45 [53]: For **left shoulder,** work in pattern across first 16 [18] sts leaving remaining sts unworked, turn (16 sts) [18 sts].

Rows 46-52 [54-60]: Work in pattern. At end of last row, fasten off.

Row 45 [53]: For **neck,** skip next 15 sts on row 44 [52]; for **right shoulder,** join with sc in next st, work in pattern across, turn (16 sts) [18 sts].

Rows 46-52 [54-60]: Work in pattern. At end of last row, fasten off.

With right sides together, matching sts and working through both thicknesses, sc or sew shoulder seams.

SLEEVE (make 2)
Row 1: With I hook, ch 26, sc in 2nd ch from hook, sc in each ch across, turn (25 sc).

Row 2: Ch 1, sc in each st across, turn.

Row 3: Ch 1, sc in each of first 3 sts, fp, sc in next st, fp, sc in next 6 sts, puff st, sc in next 6 sts, fp, sc in next st, fp, sc in each of last 3 sts, turn (20 sc, 4 fp, 1 puff st).

Row 4: Repeat row 2.

Row 5: Ch 1, (sc, puff st) in first st, sc in each of next 2 sts, fp, sc in next st, fp, sc in next 4 sts,

Continued on page 74

Continued from page 72

puff st, sc in each of next 3 sts, puff st, sc in next 4 sts, fp, sc in next st, fp, sc in each of next 2 sts, (puff st, sc) in last st, turn (19 sc, 4 fp, 4 puff sts).

Row 6: Repeat row 2.

Row 7: Ch 1, sc in first 4 sts, fp, sc in next st, fp, sc in each of next 2 sts, puff st, sc in next 7 sts, puff st, sc in each of next 2 sts, fp, sc in next st, fp, sc in last 4 sts, turn (21 sc, 4 fp, 2 puff sts).

Row 8: Repeat row 2.

Row 9: Ch 1, 2 sc in first st, puff st, sc in each of next 2 sts, fp, sc in next st, fp, sc in next 4 sts, puff st, sc in each of next 3 sts, puff st, sc in next 4 sts, fp, sc in next st, fp, sc in each of next 2 sts, puff st, 2 sc in last st, turn (21 sc, 4 fp, 4 puff sts).

Row 10: Repeat row 2.

NOTE: For **beginning puff stitch (beg puff st),** ch 2, (yo, insert hook in same st, yo, draw up long lp) 4 times, yo, draw through 8 lps on hook, yo, draw through remaining 2 lps on hook.

Row 11: Beg puff st, sc in next 4 sts, fp, sc in next st, fp, sc in next 6 sts, puff st, sc in next 6 sts, fp, sc in next st, fp, sc in next 4 sts, puff st, turn (22 sc, 4 fp, 3 puff sts).

Row 12: Repeat row 2.

Row 13: Ch 1, 2 sc in first st, sc in next st, puff st, sc in each of next 2 sts, fp, sc in next st, fp, sc in next 4 sts, puff st, sc in each of next 3 sts, puff st, sc in next 4 sts, fp, sc in next st, fp, sc in each of next 2 sts, puff st, sc in next st, 2 sc in last st, turn (23 sc, 4 fp, 4 puff sts).

Row 14: Repeat row 2.

Row 15: Ch 1, sc in first st, puff st, sc in next 4 sts, fp, sc in next st, fp, sc in each of next 2 sts, puff st, sc in next 7 sts, puff st, sc in each of next 2 sts, fp, sc in next st, fp, sc in next 4 sts, puff st, sc in last st, turn.

Row 16: Repeat row 2.

Row 17: Ch 1, 2 sc in first st, sc in each of next 2 sts, puff st, sc in each of next 2 sts, fp, sc in next st, fp, sc in next 4 sts, puff st, sc in each of next 3 sts, puff st, sc in next 4 sts, fp, sc in next st, fp, sc in each of next 2 sts, puff st, sc in each of next 2 sts, 2 sc in last st, turn (33 sts).

Row 18: Repeat row 2.

Row 19: Ch 1, sc in each of first 2 sts, puff st, sc in next 4 sts, fp, sc in next st, fp, sc in next 6 sts, puff st, sc in next 6 sts, fp, sc in next st, fp, sc in next 4 sts, puff st, sc in each of last 2 sts, turn.

Row 20: Repeat row 2.

Row 21: Ch 1, (sc, puff st) in first st, sc in each of next 3 sts, puff st, sc in each of next 2 sts, fp, sc in next st, fp, sc in next 4 sts, puff st, sc in each of next 3 sts, puff st, sc in next 4 sts, fp, sc in next st, fp, sc in each of next 2 sts, puff st, sc in each of next 3 sts, (puff st, sc) in last st, turn (35 sts).

Row 22: Repeat row 2.

Row 23: Ch 1, sc in each of first 3 sts, puff st, sc in next 4 sts, fp, sc in next st, fp, sc in each of next 2 sts, puff st, sc in next 7 sts, puff st, sc in each of next 2 sts, fp, sc in next st, fp, sc in next 4 sts, puff st, sc in each of last 3 sts, turn.

Row 24: Repeat row 2.

Row 25: Ch 1, 2 sc in first st, puff st, sc in each of next 3 sts, puff st, sc in each of next 2 sts, fp, sc in next st, fp, sc in next 4 sts, puff st, sc in each of next 3 sts, puff st, sc in next 4 sts, fp, sc in next st, fp, sc in each of next 2 sts, puff st, sc in each of next 3 sts, puff st, 2 sc in last st, turn (37 sts).

Row 26: Repeat row 2.

Row 27: Ch 1, sc in first 4 sts, puff st, sc in next 4 sts, fp, sc in next st, fp, sc in next 6 sts, puff st, sc in next 6 sts, fp, sc in next st, fp, sc in next 4 sts, puff st, sc in last 4 sts, turn.

Row 28: Repeat row 2.

Row 29: Ch 1, 2 sc in first st, sc in next st, puff st, sc in each of next 3 sts, puff st, sc in each of next 2 sts, fp, sc in next st, fp, sc in next 4 sts, puff st, sc in each of next 3 sts, puff st, sc in next 4 sts, fp, sc in next st, fp, sc in each of next 2 sts, puff st, sc in each of next 3 sts, puff st, sc in next st, 2 sc in last st, turn (39 sts).

Row 30: Repeat row 2.

Row 31: Ch 1, fp around first st on row before last, sc in next 4 sts, puff st, sc in next 4 sts, fp, sc in next st, fp, sc in each of next 2 sts, puff st, sc in next 7 sts, puff st, sc in each of next 2 sts, fp, sc in next st, fp, sc in next 4 sts, puff st, sc in next 4 sts, fp, turn.

Row 32: Repeat row 2.

Row 33: Ch 1, sc in first st, fp around first st on row before last **(do not** skip st on last row behind fp), *sc in each of next 2 sts, puff st, sc in each of next 3 sts, puff st, sc in each of next 2 sts*, fp, sc in next st, fp, sc in next 4 sts, puff st, sc in each of next 3 sts, puff st, sc in next 4 sts, fp, sc in next st, fp; repeat between **, fp around last st on row before last, sc in last st on last row, turn (41 sts).

Row 34: Repeat row 2.

Row 35: Ch 1, sc in first st, fp, sc in next 4 sts, puff st, sc in next 4 sts, fp, sc in next st, fp, sc in next 6 sts, puff st, sc in next 6 sts, fp, sc in next st, fp, sc in next 4 sts, puff st, sc in next 4 sts, fp, sc in last st, turn.

Row 36: Repeat row 2.

Row 37: Ch 1, 2 sc in first st, fp, *sc in each of next 2 sts, puff st, sc in each of next 3 sts, puff st, sc in each of next 2 sts*, fp, sc in next st, fp, sc in next 4 sts, puff st, sc in each of next 3 sts, puff st, sc in next 4 sts, fp, sc in next st, fp; repeat between **, fp, 2 sc in last st, turn (43 sts).

Row 38: Repeat row 2.

Row 39: Ch 1, sc in each of first 2 sts, fp, sc in next 4 sts, puff st, sc in next 4 sts, fp, sc in next st, fp, sc in each of next 2 sts, puff st, sc in next 7 sts, puff st, sc in each of next 2 sts, fp, sc in next st, fp, sc in next 4 sts, puff st, sc in next 4 sts, fp, sc in each of last 2 sts, turn; for **size 8 only,** fasten off.

Row [40]: For **size 12 only,** repeat row 2.

Row [41]: Ch 1, 2 sc in first st, sc in next st, fp, *sc in each of next 2 sts, puff st, sc in each of next 3 sts, puff st, sc in each of next 2 sts*, fp, sc in next st, fp, sc in next 4 sts, puff st, sc in each of next 3 sts, puff st, sc in next 4 sts, fp, sc in next st, fp; repeat between **, fp, sc in next st, 2 sc in last st, turn [45 sts].

Row [42]: Repeat row 2.

Row [43]: Ch 1, sc in first st, fp, sc in next st, fp, sc in next 4 sts, puff st, sc in next 4 sts, fp, sc in next st, fp, sc in next 6 sts, puff st, sc in next 6 sts, fp, sc in next st, fp, sc in next 4 sts, puff st, sc in next 4 sts, (fp, sc in next st) 2 times, turn.

Row [44]: Repeat row 2.

Row [45]: Ch 1, 2 sc in first st, fp, sc in next st, fp, *sc in each of next 2 sts, puff st, sc in each of next 3 sts, puff st, sc in each of next 2 sts*, fp, sc in next st, fp, sc in next 4 sts, puff st, sc in each of next 3 sts, puff st, sc in next 4 sts, fp, sc in next st, fp; repeat between **, fp, sc in next st, fp, 2 sc in last st, turn (47 sts).

Row [46]: Repeat row 2.

Row [47]: Ch 1, sc in each of first 2 sts, fp, sc in next st, fp, sc in next 4 sts, puff st, sc in next 4 sts, fp, sc in next st, fp, sc in each of next 2 sts, puff st, sc in next 7 sts, puff st, sc in each of next 2 sts, fp, sc in next st, fp, sc in next 4 sts, puff st, sc in next 4 sts, fp, sc in next st, fp, sc in each of

last 2 sts, turn, fasten off.

With wrong sides together, matching center of last row on Sleeve to shoulder seam and working through both thicknesses, sc or sew Sleeve to Body; sc or sew Sleeve and side seams.

SLEEVE RIBBING

Row 1: Working in starting ch on opposite side of row 1 on Sleeve, with G hook, join with sl st in first ch, ch 6, sc in 2nd ch from hook, sc in next 4 chs, skip first ch on Sleeve, sl st in each of next 2 chs, turn (5 sc).

Row 2: Working the following rows in **back lps** only, ch 1, skip first 2 sl sts, sc in each st across, turn.

Row 3: Ch 1, sc in each st across, sl st in each of next 2 chs on Sleeve, turn.

Rows 4-24: Repeat rows 2 and 3 alternately, ending with row 2.

Row 25: Matching sts of first and last rows, working through both thicknesses in starting ch on opposite side of row 1 and in **back lps** only of last row, ch 1, sc in each st across, fasten off.

Repeat on other Sleeve.

WAIST RIBBING

Row 1: Working in starting ch on opposite side of row 1 on Front and Back, with G hook, join with sl st in first ch on Back, ch 6, sc in 2nd ch from hook, sc in next 4 chs, sl st in same ch on Body as joining sl st, sl st in next ch, turn (5 sc).

Next Rows: Working around Body, repeat rows 2 and 3 of Sleeve Ribbing, ending with row 2.

Last Row: Repeat row 25 of Sleeve Ribbing.

NECK RIBBING

Row 1: Working in sts and ends of rows around neck opening, with G hook, join with sl st in first row on Front, ch 6, sc in 2nd ch from hook, sc in next 4 chs, sl st in same ch on Body as joining sl st, sl st in next ch, turn (5 sc).

Row 2: Working the following rows in **back lps** only, ch 1, skip first 2 sl sts, sc in each st across, turn.

Row 3: Ch 1, sc in each st across, sl st in each of next 2 rows or sts on Body, turn.

Next Rows: Repeat rows 2 and 3 alternately around neck opening, ending with row 2.

Last Row: Repeat row 25 of Sleeve Ribbing.❖

Victorian Eyelet

DESIGNED BY ROBERTA MAIER

SIZE
44½" x 71" without Fringe.

MATERIALS
Worsted-weight yarn — 29 oz. off-white, 20 oz. blue; H crochet hook or size needed to obtain gauge.

GAUGE
2 dc, ch 1 = 1½"; 2 dc rows = 1½".

SKILL LEVEL
★★ Average

AFGHAN

Row 1: With off-white, ch 251, dc in 4th ch from hook, skip next 2 chs, *(dc, ch 1, dc) in next ch, skip next 2 chs; repeat from * across to last 2 chs, dc in each of last 2 chs, turn (166 dc, 81 ch sps).

Row 2: Ch 3, dc in next st, skip next st, (dc, ch 1, dc) in next ch sp, *skip next 2 sts, (dc, ch 1, dc) in next ch sp; repeat from * across to last 3 sts, skip next st, dc in each of last 2 sts, turn, fasten off.

Row 3: Join blue with sl st in first dc, ch 4, tr in next st, skip next st, (tr, ch 1, tr) in next ch sp, *skip next 2 sts, (tr, ch 1, tr) in next ch sp; repeat from * across to last 3 sts, skip next st, tr in each of last 2 sts, turn, fasten off.

Row 4: Join off-white with sl st in first st, ch 3, dc in next st, skip next st, (dc, ch 1, dc) in next ch sp, *skip next 2 sts, (dc, ch 1, dc) in next ch sp; repeat from * across to last 3 sts, skip next st, dc in each of last 2 sts, turn.

Row 5: Ch 3, dc in next st, skip next st, (dc, ch 1, dc) in next ch sp, *skip next 2 sts, (dc, ch 1, dc) in next ch sp; repeat from * across to last 3 sts, skip next st, dc in each of last 2 sts, turn, fasten off.

Rows 6-59: Repeat rows 3-5 consecutively. At end of last row, **do not** turn, fasten off.

EDGING

Join off-white with sc in first st of long edge on row 59, 2 sc in same st, sc in each ch and in each st across to last st, 3 sc in last st; *working in end rows on short end, 2 sc in each of first 2 dc rows, (3 sc in next tr row, 2 sc in each of next 2 dc rows) across*; working in starting ch on opposite side of row 1, 3 sc in first ch, sc in each ch across to last ch, 3 sc in last ch; repeat between **, join with sl st in first sc, fasten off.

FRINGE

For **each Fringe**, with off-white, cut 2 strands each 14" long. With both strands held together, fold in half, insert hook in st, draw fold through st, draw all loose ends through fold, tighten. Trim ends. Fringe in each st on short ends of Afghan.❖

Fancy Cardigan

DESIGNED BY CHRISTINA MCNEESE

SIZES

Child's size 5, G hook, 4 sc = 1"; 5 sc rows = 1". **H hook,** 4 dc worked in pattern = 1"; 4 pattern rows 3". **Child's size 8, H hook,** 7 sc = 2"; 9 sc rows = 2". **I hook,** 7 dc worked in pattern = 2"; 12 pattern rows = 11".

MATERIALS

Worsted-weight yarn — 16 [19] oz. beige heather; 6 pearl ⅝" shank novelty buttons; tapestry needle; crochet hooks needed to obtain size and gauge given above.

SKILL LEVEL

★★ Average

BODY
Back

Row 1: With larger hook, ch 55, 4 dc in 5th ch from hook, (skip next 3 chs, 4 dc in next ch) 12 times, skip next ch, dc in last ch, turn (13 4-dc groups, 2 dc).

NOTE: For **cross stitch (cr st),** skip next 3 sts, dc in next st, ch 2; working behind last st made, dc in first skipped st leaving 2 center sts unworked.

Row 2: Ch 3, cr st across to last st, dc in last st, turn (13 cr sts, 2 dc).

Row 3: Ch 3, 4 dc in each ch-2 sp across, dc in last st, turn (13 4-dc groups, 2 dc).

Rows 4-18: Repeat rows 2 and 3 alternately, ending with row 2.

Row 19: For **right shoulder,** *ch 3, 4 dc in each of next 4 ch-2 sps, skip next st, dc in next st, fasten off*; for **neck,** skip next 5 ch-2 sps; for **left shoulder,** join with sl st in next st; repeat between ** (4 4-dc groups and 2 dc on each shoulder).

Left Front

Row 1: With larger hook, ch 27, 4 dc in 5th ch from hook, (skip next 3 chs, 4 dc in next ch) 5 times, skip next ch, dc in last ch, turn (6 4-dc groups, 2 dc).

Rows 2-14: Repeat rows 2 and 3 of Back alternately, ending with row 2.

Row 15: For **neck shaping,** ch 3, 4 dc in each of next 4 ch-2 sps, skip next st, dc in next st leaving remaining sts unworked, turn (4 4-dc groups, 2 dc).

Rows 16-19: Repeat rows 2 and 3 of Back alternately. At end of last row, fasten off.

Right Front

Rows 1-14: Repeat same rows of Left Front.

Row 15: For **neck shaping,** skip next 2 ch-2 sps, join with sl st in next st, ch 3, 4 dc in each ch-2 sp across, dc in last st, turn (4 4-dc groups, 2 dc).

Rows 16-19: Repeat rows 2 and 3 of Back alternately. At end of last row, fasten off.

With wrong sides together, matching sts and working through both thicknesses, sc or sew shoulder seams.

SLEEVE (make 2)
Arm

Row 1: With larger hook, ch 27, 4 dc in 5th ch from hook, (skip next 3 chs, 4 dc in next ch) 5 times, skip next ch, dc in last ch, turn (6 4-dc groups, 2 dc).

Row 2: Ch 3, cr st across to last st, dc in last st, turn (6 cr sts, 2 dc).

Row 3: Ch 3, dc in same st, 4 dc in each ch-2 sp across, 2 dc in last st, turn (6 4-dc groups, 4 dc).

Row 4: Ch 3, dc in next st, cr st across to last 2 sts, dc in each of last 2 sts, turn (6 cr sts, 4 dc).

Row 5: Ch 3, dc in same st, dc in next st, 4 dc in each ch-2 sp across to last 2 sts, dc in next st, 2 dc in last st, turn (6 4-dc groups, 6 dc).

Row 6: Ch 3, dc in each of next 2 sts, cr st across to last 3 sts, dc in each of last 3 sts, turn (6 cr sts, 6 dc).

Row 7: Ch 3, dc in same st, dc in each of next 2 sts, 4 dc in each ch-2 sp across to last 3 sts, dc in each of next 2 sts, 2 dc in last st, turn (6 4-dc groups, 8 dc).

Row 8: Ch 3, dc in each of next 3 sts, cr st across to last 4 sts, dc in last 4 sts, turn (6 cr sts, 8 dc).

Row 9: Ch 3, dc in same st, dc in each of next 3 sts, 4 dc in each ch-2 sp across to last 4 sts, dc in each of next 3 sts, 2 dc in last st, turn (6 4-dc groups, 10 dc).

Row 10: Ch 3, cr st across to last st, dc in last st, turn (8 cr sts, 2 dc).

Continued on page 80

Fancy Cardigan

Continued from page 78

Rows 11-13: Repeat rows 3-5, ending with 8 4-dc groups and 6 dc in last row. At end of last row, fasten off.

Cuff

Row 1: Working in starting ch on opposite side of row 1 on Arm, with smaller hook, join with sc in first ch, sc in each ch across, turn.

Rows 2-5: Ch 1, sc in each st across, turn. At end of last row, fasten off.

Matching center of last row on Arm to shoulder seam, sc or sew Sleeve to Body. Sc or sew Sleeve and side seams.

Waistband

Row 1: Working in starting ch on opposite side of row 1 on each Front and Back, with smaller hook, join with sc in first ch on Left front, sc in each ch across, turn.

Rows 2-5: Ch 1, sc in each st across, turn. At end of last row, fasten off.

Neck Band

Row 1: Working across neck edge, with smaller hook, join with sc in first st on row 14 of Right Front, sc in each ch, in each st and 2 sc in end of each dc row across neck edge, turn.

Rows 2-5: Ch 1, sc in each st across, turn. At end of last row, fasten off.

Button Band

Row 1: Working in ends of rows across Left Front opening, with smaller hook, join with sc in first row on Neck Band, sc in next 4 rows, sc in next row on Body, 2 sc in each of next 12 rows, sc in next row, sc in last 5 rows on Waistband, turn (36 sc).

Rows 2-5: Ch 1, sc in each st across, turn. At end of last row, fasten off.

Buttonhole Band

Row 1: Working in ends of rows across Right Front opening, with smaller hook, join with sc on first row of Waist Band, sc in next 4 rows, sc in next row on Body, 2 sc in each of next 12 rows, sc in next row, sc in last 5 rows on Neck Band, turn (36 sc).

Row 2: Ch 1, sc in each st across, turn.

Row 3: Ch 1, sc in each of first 2 sts; for **buttonhole,** ch 2, skip next 2 sts; *sc in next 4 sts; for **buttonhole,** ch 2, skip next 2 sts; repeat from * across to last 2 sts, sc in each of last 2 sts, turn (6 buttonholes).

Row 4: Ch 1, sc in each st and 2 sc in each ch-2 sp across, turn.

Row 5: Ch 1, sc in each st across, turn, fasten off.

Sew buttons to Button Band opposite buttonholes. ❖

Garden Blouse

Continued from page 62

Rnd 2: Work joining ch-9 sp, (4 dc in next ch sp on this Motif, work joining ch-3 sp, 4 dc in next ch sp on this Motif, work joining ch-9 sp) 2 times, sl st in last st on this Motif, fasten off (16 dc, 3 ch-9 sps, 2 ch-3 sps).

BODY

Using instructions that follow, work Motifs as shown in Body Assembly Diagram, using joining ch sps when needed to join adjacent Motifs.

SLEEVE (make 2)

Work Motifs as shown in Sleeve Assembly Diagram, using joining ch sps to join on to adjoining Motifs and to designated Motifs on Body.

BODY EDGING

Rnd 1: Working around bottom opening of Body, join with sc in any dc; skipping each sl st, sc in each dc, 4 sc in each ch-9 sp, 4 sc in each ch-7 sp and 2 sc in each ch-3 sp around, join with sl st in first sc.

Rnd 2: Ch 1, sc in each st around, join.

Rnd 3: For **reverse sc** (see page 159), working from left to right, insert hook in next st to the right, yo, draw through st, complete as a sc; reverse sc in each st around, join, fasten off.

NECK EDGING

Working around neck opening, work same as Body Edging.

SLEEVE EDGING

Working around Sleeve opening, work same as Body Edging.

Repeat on other Sleeve.❖

**BODY
ASSEMBLY DIAGRAM**

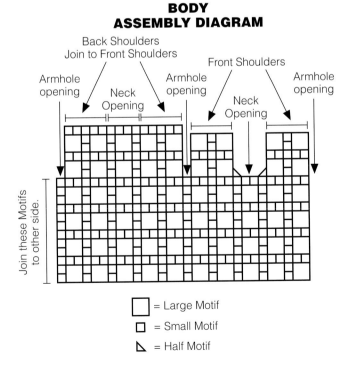

**SLEEVE
ASSEMBLY DIAGRAM**

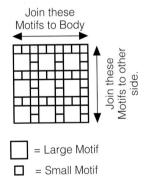

Tweed Cables

Continued from page 68

green in last st made, dc bp around next 4 sts changing to beige in last st made, dc bp around each of next 2 sts◊, dc in next 4 [5, 6, 7] sts changing to green in last st made, pc changing to beige, dc in next st changing to green, pc in next st changing to beige, dc in next 4 [5, 6, 7] sts; repeat from *; repeat between ◊◊, dc in last 4 [5, 6, 7] sts, turn (26 dc, 24 dc bp, 4 pc) [32 dc, 24 dc bp, 4 pc; 38 dc, 24 dc bp, 4 pc; 44 dc, 24 dc bp, 4 pc].

Row 5: Ch 3, dc in each of next 3 [4, 5, 6] sts changing to green in last st made, *◊skip next 2 sts, tr fp around each of next 2 sts changing to beige in last st made; working behind last 2 sts made, tr fp around each of last 2 skipped sts, skip next 2 sts, tr fp around each of next 2 sts changing to green in last st made; working in front of last 2 sts made, tr fp around each of last 2 skipped sts changing to beige in last st made◊, dc in next 5 [6, 7, 8] sts changing to green in last st made, pc in next st changing to beige, dc in next 5 [6, 7, 8] sts; repeat from *; repeat between ◊◊, dc in last 4 [5, 6, 7] sts, turn (28 dc, 24 tr fp, 2 pc) [34 dc, 24 tr fp, 2 pc; 40 dc, 24 tr fp, 2 pc; 46 dc, 24 tr fp, 2 pc].

NOTE: Pattern is established in rows 2-5.

Rows 6-27 [6-27, 6-29, 6-29]: Work in pattern.

Row 28 [28, 30, 30]: For **right shoulder,** work in pattern across first 18 [20, 22, 24] sts leaving remaining sts unworked, turn (18 sts) [20 sts, 22 sts, 24 sts].

Rows 29-33 [29-33, 31-35, 31-35]: Work in pattern. At end of last row, fasten off.

Row 28 [28, 30, 30]: For **neck,** skip next 18 [20, 22, 24] sts on row 27 [27, 29, 29]; for **left shoulder,** join with sl st in next st, work in pattern across, turn (18 sts) [20 sts, 22 sts, 24 sts].

Rows 29-33 [29-33, 31-35, 31-35]: Work in pattern. At end of last row, fasten off.

With right sides together, matching sts, sew or sc shoulder seams using beige.

SLEEVE (make 2)

Row 1: With I hook and beige, ch 32 [34, 36, 38], dc in 4th ch from hook, dc in next 9 [10, 11, 12] chs changing to green in last st made, dc in each of next 2 chs changing to beige in last st made, dc in next 4 chs changing to green in last st made, dc in each of next 2 chs changing to

beige in last st made, dc in last 11 [12, 13, 14] chs, turn (30 dc) [32 dc, 34 dc, 36 dc].

Row 2: Ch 3, dc in each st across to next green st changing to green in last st made, dc bp around each of next 2 sts changing to beige in last st made, dc bp around next 4 sts changing to green in last st made, dc bp around each of next 2 sts changing to beige in last st made, dc in each st across, turn (22 dc, 8 dc bp) [24 dc, 8 dc bp; 26 dc, 8 dc bp; 28 dc, 8 dc bp].

Row 3: Ch 3, dc in same st, dc in each st across to next dc bp, skip next 2 sts, tr fp around each of next 2 sts changing to green in last st made; working behind last 2 sts made, tr fp around each of last 2 skipped sts, skip next 2 sts, tr fp around each of next 2 sts changing to beige in last st made; working in front of last 2 sts made, tr fp around each of last 2 skipped sts, dc in each st across to last st, 2 dc in last st, turn (32 sts) [34 sts, 36 sts, 38 sts].

Row 4: Ch 3, dc in each st across to next tr fp, dc bp around each of next 2 sts changing to green in last st made, dc bp around next 4 sts changing to beige in last st made, dc bp around each of next 2 sts, dc in each st across, turn.

Row 5: Ch 3, dc in same st, dc in each st across to next dc bp changing to green in last st made, skip next 2 sts, tr fp around each of next 2 sts changing to beige in last st made; working behind last 2 sts made, tr fp around each of last 2 skipped sts, skip next 2 sts, tr fp around each of next 2 sts changing to green in last st made; working in front of last 2 sts made, tr fp around each of last 2 skipped sts changing to beige in last st made, dc in each st across to last st, 2 dc in last st, turn (34 sts) [36 sts, 38 sts, 40 sts].

Rows 6-25 [6-26, 6-28, 6-31]: Repeat rows 2-5 consecutively, ending with row 5 [2, 4, 3] and 54 sts [56 sts, 58 sts, 60 sts] in last row. At end of last row, fasten off.

With right sides together, matching center of last row on Sleeve to shoulder seam, sew or sc Sleeve to Body. Sew or sc Sleeve and side seams.

SLEEVE RIBBING

Row 1: Working in starting ch on opposite side of row 1 on Sleeve, with H hook and green, join with sl st in first ch, ch 11, sc in 2nd ch from hook, sc in next 9 chs, sl st in same ch on Sleeve as joining sl st, sl st in next ch, turn (10 sc).

Row 2: Working the following rows in **back lps** only, ch 1, skip first 2 sl sts, sc in each st across, turn.

Row 3: Ch 1, sc in each st across, sl st in each of next 2 chs on Sleeve, turn.

Rows 4-30 [4-32, 4-34, 4-36]: Repeat rows 2 and 3 alternately, ending with row 2.

Row 31 [33, 35, 37]: Matching sts of first and last rows, working through both thicknesses in starting ch on opposite side of row 1 and in **back lps** only of last row, ch 1, sc in each st across, fasten off.

Repeat on other Sleeve.

WAIST RIBBING

Row 1: Working in starting ch on opposite side of row 1 on Front and Back, with H hook and green, join with sl st in first ch on Back, ch 11, sc in 2nd ch from hook, sc in next 9 chs, sl st in same ch on Body as joining sl st, sl st in next ch, turn (10 sc).

Next Rows: Working around Body, repeat rows 2 and 3 of Sleeve Ribbing, ending with row 2.

Last Row: Work same as last row of Sleeve Ribbing.

NECK RIBBING

Row 1: Working in sts and ends of rows around neck opening, with H hook and green, join with sl st in first row on Front, ch 7, sc in 2nd ch from hook, sc in next 5 chs, sl st 2 times in 2nd row on Body, turn (6 sc).

Row 2: Working the following rows in **back lps** only, ch 1, skip first 2 sl sts, sc in each st across, turn.

Row 3: Ch 1, sc in each st across, sl st in each of next sts **or** sl st 2 times in next row on Body, turn.

Next Rows: Repeat rows 2 and 3 alternately around neck opening, ending with row 2.

Last Row: Work same as last row of Sleeve Ribbing.❖

Grandma's Garden

Harvest a rainbow of color for
your home with this freshly-picked
collection, lavishly arrayed in blossoms
and buds. Dazzling selections
reflecting the glory of Nature's pallette
will keep spring alive all year long.

Garden Angel

DESIGNED BY ESTELLA WHITFORD

SIZE
9" tall.

MATERIALS
Worsted-weight yarn — 3½ oz. gray, 2 oz. blue, 1 oz. each variegated and glitter white, small amount each black and white; 3 white ⅜" buttons; miniature clay flower pot; small amount spanish moss; one artificial flower sprig; 6" piece wired metallic gold braid; polyester fiberfill; white sewing thread; sewing and tapestry needles; F crochet hook or size needed to obtain gauge.

GAUGE
4 sc sts = 1"; 4 sc rows = 1".

SKILL LEVEL
★★ Average

ANGEL
Head & Body
NOTE: Do not join rnds unless otherwise stated. Mark first st of each rnd.

Rnd 1: Starting at **Head,** with gray, ch 2, 6 sc in 2nd ch from hook (6 sc).

Rnd 2: 2 sc in each st around (12).

Rnd 3: (Sc in next st, 2 sc in next st) around (18).

Rnd 4: (Sc in each of next 2 sts, 2 sc in next st) around (24).

Rnds 5-7: Sc in each st around.

Rnd 8: (Sc in each of next 2 sts, sc next 2 sts tog) around (18).

Rnd 9: (Sc next 2 sts tog) around (9).

Rnd 10: 2 sc in each st around (18).

Rnd 11: (Sc in each of next 2 sts, 2 sc in next st) around (24).

Rnds 12-17: Sc in each st around.

Rnd 18: (Sc in each of next 2 sts, sc next 2 sts tog) around (18). Stuff.

Rnd 19: (Sc next 2 sts tog) around (9).

Rnd 20: Sc in next st, (sc next 2 sts tog) around, join with sl st in first sc, leaving 8" for sewing, fasten off (5).

ARM (make 2)
Rnd 1: Starting at **paw,** with gray, ch 2, 6 sc in 2nd ch from hook (6 sc).

Rnd 2: (Sc in next st, 2 sc in next st) around (9).

Rnds 3-10: Sc in each st around. At end of last rnd, join with sl st in first sc, leaving 10" for sewing, fasten off. Stuff.

Sew Arms over rnds 11-13 on each side of Body.

LEG (make 2)
Rnd 1: Starting at **foot,** with gray, ch 2, 6 sc in 2nd ch from hook (6 sc).

Rnd 2: (Sc in next st, 2 sc in next st) around (9).

Rnds 3-16: Sc in each st around. At end of last rnd, join with sl st in first sc, leaving 10" for sewing, fasten off. Stuff.

Sew Legs to bottom of Body.

EAR (make 2)
Row 1: With gray, ch 4, sc in 2nd ch from hook, sc in each ch across, turn (3 sc).

Row 2: Ch 1, sc in each st across with 2 sc in last st, turn (4).

Row 3: Ch 1, 2 sc in first st, sc in each st across, turn (5).

Row 4: Ch 1, sc in each st across, turn.

Row 5: Ch 1, sc first 2 sts tog, sc in each st across, turn (4).

Row 6: Ch 1, sc in each st across to last 2 sts, sc last 2 sts tog, turn (3).

Row 7: Ch 1, sc first 2 sts tog, sc in last st, turn (2).

Rnd 8: Working around outer edge, ch 1, sc in each st and in end of each row around, join with sl st in first sc, leaving 8" for sewing, fasten off.

Sew straight edge of Ears to top of Head spaced 1¼" apart.

NOSE
Rnd 1: With gray, ch 2, 6 sc in 2nd ch from hook (6 sc).

Rnd 2: Sc in each st around.

Rnd 3: (Sc in next st, 2 sc in next st) around (9).

Rnd 4: (Sc in each of next 2 sts, 2 sc in next st) around, join with sl st in first sc, leaving 8" for sewing, fasten off. Stuff and sew over rnds 4-7 of Head.

With black, using French Knot (page 159), embroider eyes, centered above nose ¼" apart, and end of nose as shown in photo.

For **whiskers,** pull 3 pieces white yarn each 3" long through end of nose. For **halo,** twist ends of wired gold braid together. Tack to top of Head between Ears.

DRESS

NOTE: Front of row 1 is wrong side of work.

Row 1: Starting at **neckline,** with blue, ch 23, sc in 2nd ch from hook, sc in each ch across, turn (22 sc).

Row 2: Ch 1, sc in each st across, turn.

Row 3: Ch 1, sc in first 4 sts; for **armhole,** ch 5, skip next 3 sts; sc in next 8 sts; for **armhole,** ch 5, skip next 3 sts; sc in last 4 sts, turn (16 sc, 10 chs).

Row 4: Ch 1, sc in each st and in each ch across, turn (26 sc).

Row 5: Ch 1, sc in each of first 2 sts, (2 sc in next st, sc in each of next 2 sts) across, turn (34).

Row 6: Ch 3, 2 dc in next st, (dc in next st, 2 dc in next st) across, turn (51 dc).

Rows 7-8: Ch 3, dc in each st across, turn.

Row 9: Working this row in **back lps** only, ch 3, dc in each st across, fasten off.

Row 10: With right side facing you, working in **front lps** of row 8, join variegated with sl st in first st, ch 3, dc in each st across, turn.

Row 11: Ch 3, dc in each st across, turn.

Row 12: Ch 1, skip first 2 sts, 6 dc in next st, (skip next 2 sts, 6 dc in next st) across, fasten off.

SLEEVES

Rnd 1: Working around armhole, with wrong side of Dress facing you, join variegated with sc in center st at underarm, sc in same st, 2 sc in each st and in each ch around, join with sl st in first sc (16 sc).

Rnds 2-4: Ch 1, sc in each st around, join.

Rnd 5: Ch 1, sc in first st, ch 2, skip next st, (sc in next st, ch 2, skip next st) around, join, fasten off.

Repeat in other armhole. Turn right side out. Place Dress on Angel, sew ends of rows 1-9 together in front. Sew buttons evenly spaced down center front.

WING (make 2)

Row 1: With glitter white, ch 4, sc in 2nd ch from hook, sc in each ch across, turn (3 sc).

Rows 2-5: Ch 1, 2 sc in first st, sc in each st across with 2 sc in last st, turn, ending with 11 sts in last row.

Row 6: Ch 1, sc in each st across, turn.

Row 7: Ch 1, sc first 2 sts tog, sc in each st across to last 2 sts, sc last 2 sts tog, turn (9).

Row 8: Ch 1, sc in each st across, turn.

Rows 9-12: Repeat rows 7 and 8 alternately, ending with 5 sts in last row.

Rnd 13: Working around outer edge, ch 1, sc first 2 sts tog, sc in next st, sc last 2 sts tog, sc in end of each row across to row 1; working in starting ch on opposite side of row 1, sc in first ch, 3 sc in next ch, sc in last ch, sc in end of each row across, join with sl st in first sc.

Rnd 14: Ch 1, sc in first st, ch 3, skip next st, (sc in next st, ch 3, skip next st) around, join, fasten off.

Sew first 3 sts of rnd 13 on both Wings together. Sew center of Wings to back of Angel, gathering slightly.

For **hanger,** with glitter white, tie desired length yarn to back of Head above Wings.

FINISHING

1: Place moss and flower in flower pot.

2: With blue, sew flower pot to left paw and front left side of Dress by wrapping yarn around pot several times.❖

Pastel Dress

DESIGNED BY BEVERLY MEWHORTER

SIZE
Fits 11½" fashion doll.

MATERIALS
Size 10 bedspread cotton — 600 yds. pastel variegated; 1⅔ yds. pale pink ¼" satin picot ribbon; 8" white 1¼" gathered lace; several bunches of small silk flowers; 6" x 72" lavender tulle; 4" x 36" lavender tulle; 3 small snaps; sewing thread; craft glue or hot glue gun; sewing and tapestry needles; No. 7 crochet hook or size needed to obtain gauge.

GAUGE
8 sts = 1"; 9 sc rows = 1"; 4 dc rows = 1¼".

SKILL LEVEL
★★ Average

BODICE
Row 1: Starting at **waist**, ch 27, sc in 2nd ch from hook, sc in each ch across, turn (26 sc).

Rows 2-4: Ch 1, sc in each st across, turn.

Row 5: Ch 1, sc in each st across with 2 sc in last st, turn (27).

Row 6: Ch 1, sc in first 7 sts, 2 sc in next st, (sc in each of next 3 sts, 2 sc in next st) 3 times, sc in last 7 sts, turn (31).

Row 7: Ch 1, sc in first 8 sts, 2 sc in next st, sc in next 13 sts, 2 sc in next st, sc in last 8 sts, turn (33).

Row 8: Ch 1, sc in each st across, turn.

Row 9: Ch 1, sc in first 8 sts, 2 sc in next st, sc in next 15 sts, 2 sc in next st, sc in last 8 sts, turn (35).

Row 10: Ch 1, sc in each st across, turn.

Row 11: Ch 1, sc in first 8 sts, 2 sc in next st, sc in next 17 sts, 2 sc in next st, sc in last 8 sts, turn (37).

Row 12: Ch 1, sc in each st across, turn.

Row 13: Ch 1, sc in first st, 2 sc in next st, sc in next 13 sts; for **bust shaping,** skip next st, 10 dc in next st, skip next st, sc in next st, skip next st, 10 dc in next st, skip next st; sc in next 13 sts, 2 sc in next st, sc in last st, turn (53 sts).

Row 14: Ch 1, sc in first 15 sts, skip next st, dc in next 9 sts, skip next st, sc in next st, skip next st, dc in next 9 sts, skip next st, sc in last 15 sts, turn (49).

Row 15: Ch 1, sc in first 14 sts, skip next st, sc in next 9 sts, skip next st, sc in next 9 sts, skip next st, sc in last 14 sts, turn (46 sc).

Row 16: Ch 1, sc in first 22 sts, sc next 2 sts tog, sc in last 22 sts, turn (45).

Row 17: Ch 1, sc in first 8 sts; for **armhole,** ch 10, skip next 5 sts; sl st in next 19 sts; for **armhole,** ch 10, skip next 5 sts; sc in last 8 sts, fasten off.

SLEEVES
Rnd 1: Working around armhole, join with sc in center st at underarm, sc in each st and 2 sc in each ch around, join with sl st in first sc (25 sc).

Rnd 2: Ch 3, dc in each of next 2 sts, 4 dc in next 20 sts, dc in each of last 2 sts, join with sl st in top of ch-3 (85 dc).

Rnds 3-8: Ch 3, dc in each st around, join.

Rnds 9-10: Ch 1, sc in first st, (sc next 2 sts tog) around, join with sl st in first sc (43, 22).

Rnd 11: Ch 1, sc first 2 sts tog, (sc next 2 sts tog) around, join (11).

Rnd 12: Ch 1, sc in first st, sc next 2 sts tog, (sc in each of next 2 sts, sc next 2 sts tog) around, join, fasten off.

Repeat in other armhole.

SKIRT
Row 1: Working in starting ch on opposite side of row 1 on Bodice, join with sl st in first ch, ch 3, dc in each ch across, turn (26 dc).

Row 2: Ch 3, 2 dc in next st, (dc in next st, 2 dc in next st) across, turn (39).

Rnd 3: Working in rnds, ch 3, dc in same st, (dc in next st, 2 dc in next st) around, join with sl st in top of ch-3 (59).

Rnd 4: (Ch 3, sc in next st) around; to **join,** ch 1, hdc in in joining sl st of last rnd.

Rnd 5: Ch 1, (sc, ch 5, sc) around joining st, *ch 5, (sc, ch 5, sc) in next ch sp; repeat from * around; to **join,** ch 2, dc in first sc.

Rnd 6: Ch 1, sc around joining st, (ch 5, sc in next ch lp) around, join as before.

Rnds 7-8: Ch 1, sc around joining st, (ch 6, sc in next ch lp) around; to **join,** ch 3, dc in first sc.

Rnds 9-10: Ch 1, sc around joining st, (ch 7, sc in next ch lp) around; to **join,** ch 3, tr in first sc.

Rnds 11-12: Ch 1, sc around joining st, (ch 8, sc in next ch lp) around; to **join,** ch 4, tr in first sc.

Rnds 13-14: Repeat rnds 5 and 6.

Rnds 15-16: Repeat rnd 7.

Rnd 17: Repeat rnd 9.

Continued on page 105

Birdhouse Coasters

DESIGNED BY CHERYL BIGHAM KINSER

SCHOOL HOUSE

SIZE

4" x 6".

MATERIALS

Size 10 bedspread cotton — small amount each red, blue, white, black and gray; red sewing thread; sewing and embroidery needles; No. 7 steel crochet hook or size needed to obtain gauge.

GAUGE

5 sts = ½"; 3 hdc rows = ½".

SKILL LEVEL

★★ Average

HOUSE

Row 1: With red, ch 36, dc in 4th ch from hook, dc in each ch across, turn (34 dc).

Rows 2-3: Ch 3, dc in each st across, turn. At end of last row, **do not** turn, fasten off.

NOTE: When changing colors (page 159), always drop yarn to same side of work. Work over dropped color as you carry it across to next section of same color.

Row 4: Join white with sl st in 3rd st, ch 2, hdc in next 4 sts changing to blue in last st made, (hdc in next 5 sts changing to white in last st made, hdc in next 5 sts changing to blue in last st made) 2 times, hdc in next 5 sts leaving last 2 sts unworked, turn (30 hdc).

NOTE: Always change to next color in last st of last color used.

Row 5: Ch 2, hdc in next 4 sts; (with white, hdc in next 5 sts; with blue, hdc in next 5 sts) 2 times; with white, hdc in last 5 sts, turn.

Row 6: Ch 2, hdc in next 4 sts; (with blue, hdc in next 5 sts; with white, hdc in next 5 sts) 2 times; with blue, hdc in last 5 sts changing to white in last st made, turn.

Row 7: Ch 2, hdc in next 4 sts; (with blue, hdc in next 5 sts; with white, hdc in next 5 sts) 2 times; with blue, hdc in last 5 sts, turn.

Row 8: Repeat row 5.

Row 9: Ch 2, hdc in next 4 sts; (with blue, hdc in next 5 sts; with white, hdc in next 5 sts) 2 times; with blue, hdc in last 5 sts changing to white in last st made, turn.

Row 10: Repeat row 7.

Row 11: Repeat row 5.

Row 12: Ch 2, hdc in next 4 sts; with blue, hdc in next 5 sts; with white, hdc in each of next 2 sts; with black, hdc in next 6 sts; with blue, hdc in each of next 2 sts; with white, hdc in next 5 sts; with blue, hdc in last 5 sts changing to white in last st made, turn.

Row 13: Ch 2, hdc in next 4 sts; with blue, hdc in next 5 sts; with white, hdc in each of next 2 sts; with black, hdc in next 6 sts; with blue, hdc in each of next 2 sts; with white, hdc in next 5 sts; with blue, hdc in last 5 sts, turn.

Row 14: Ch 2, hdc next 2 sts tog, hdc in each of next 2 sts; with white, hdc in next 5 sts; with blue, hdc in each of next 2 sts; with black, hdc in next 6 sts; with white, hdc in each of next 2 sts; with blue, hdc in next 5 sts; with white, hdc in each of next 2 sts, hdc next 2 sts tog, hdc in last st, turn (28).

Row 15: Ch 2, hdc in each of next 3 sts; (with blue, hdc in next 5 sts; with white, hdc in next 5 sts) 2 times; with blue, hdc in last 4 sts changing to white in last st made, turn.

Row 16: Ch 2, hdc next 2 sts tog, hdc in next st; (with blue, hdc in next 5 sts; with white, hdc in next 5 sts) 2 times; with blue, hdc in next st, hdc next 2 sts tog, hdc in last st, turn (26).

Row 17: Ch 2, hdc in each of next 2 sts; (with white, hdc in next 5 sts; with blue, hdc in next 5 sts) 2 times; with white, hdc in each of last 3 sts, turn.

Row 18: Ch 2, hdc next 2 sts tog; (with blue, hdc in next 5 sts; with white, hdc in next 5 sts) 2 times; with blue, hdc next 2 sts tog, hdc in last st, fasten off (24).

CENTER BELL SECTION

Row 1: With red, ch 41, sc in 2nd ch from hook, sc in next 6 chs, 2 sc in next ch, sc in next 24 chs, 2 sc in next ch, sc in last 7 chs, turn (42 sc).

Row 2: Ch 2, hdc in each of next 3 sts, sc in each of next 3 sts, 2 sc in next st, sc in next 26 sts, 2 sc in next st, sc in next 3 sts, hdc in last 4 sts, turn (44 sts).

Row 3: Ch 2, hdc in each of next 3 sts, sc in next 4 sts, 2 sc in next st, sc in next 26 sts, 2 sc in next st, sc in next 4 sts, hdc in last 4 sts, turn (46).

Row 4: Ch 2, hdc in each of next 3 sts, sc in next 4 sts, 2 sc in next st, sc in next 28 sts, 2 sc in next st, sc in next 4 sts, hdc in last 4 sts, turn, fasten off (48).

Continued on next page

NOTE: When changing colors, always drop yarn to wrong side of work. Use a separate skein or ball of yarn for each color section. **Do not** carry yarn across from one section to another. Fasten off colors at end of each color section.

Row 5: Join red with sc in 15th st, sc in next 4 sts; with white, sc in next 10 sts; with red, sc in next 5 sts leaving last 14 sts unworked, turn (20 sc).

Rows 6-7: Ch 1, sc in first 5 sts; with white, sc in next 10 sts; with red, sc in last 5 sts, turn.

Row 8: Ch 1, sc in first 5 sts; with white, sc in each of next 3 sts; with gray; for **bell,** sc in next 4 sts; with white, sc in each of next 3 sts; with red, sc in last 5 sts, turn.

Row 9: Ch 1, sc in first 5 sts; with white, sc in next 4 sts; with gray, sc in each of next 3 sts; with white, sc in each of next 3 sts; with red, sc in last 5 sts, turn.

Row 10: Ch 1, sc in first 5 sts; with white, sc in next 4 sts; with gray, sc in each of next 2 sts; with white, sc in next 4 sts; with red, sc in last 5 sts, fasten off.

ROOF

Row 1: With red, ch 27, hdc in 3rd ch from hook, hdc in each ch across, turn (26 hdc).

Rows 2-5: Ch 1, hdc first 2 sts tog, hdc in each st across to last 2 sts, hdc last 2 sts tog, turn, ending with 18 sts in last row.

Rows 6-7: Ch 1, hdc first 2 sts tog, hdc next 2 sts tog, hdc in each st across to last 4 sts, (hdc next 2 sts tog) 2 times, turn (14, 10).

Row 8-9: Repeat row 2 (8, 6).

Row 10: Ch 1, hdc first 2 sts tog, (hdc next 2 sts tog) 2 times, turn (3).

Row 11: Ch 1, hdc next 3 sts tog, **do not** turn.

Row 12: Working around entire outer edge, ch 1, 3 sc in first st, evenly space 18 sc across ends of rows; working in starting ch on opposite side of row 1, 3 sc in first ch, sc in each ch across with 3 sc in last ch, evenly space 18 sc across ends of rows, join with sl st in first sc, fasten off.

FINISHING

1: Sew row 1 of Center Bell Section centered to last row of Schoolhouse. Sew row 1 of Roof centered to last row of Center Bell Section.

2: With black, using Straight Stitch (page 158), embroider one stitch centered belowbell on row 7.

FLOWERED HOUSE
SIZE
4" x 5".

MATERIALS
Size 10 bedspread cotton — small amount each black, lt. purple, med. purple, dk. purple, white, green variegated, yellow variegated, dk. green, lt. pink, dk. pink; small amount gray embroidery floss; purple and white sewing thread; sewing needle; No. 7 steel crochet hook or size needed to obtain gauge.

GAUGE
5 sts = ½"; 5 sc rows = ½".

SKILL LEVEL
★★ Average

HOUSE SIDE
NOTE: When changing colors (page 159), always drop yarn to wrong side of work. Use a separate skein of yarn for each color section. **Do not** carry yarn across from one section to another. Fasten off colors at end of each color section.

Row 1: With white, ch 24, sc in 2nd ch from hook, sc in next 11 chs changing to green variegated in last st made, sc in last 11 chs, turn (23 sc).

Rows 2-28: Ch 1, sc in each st across changing colors according to Side Graph, turn. At end of last row, fasten off.

Row 29: Working in starting ch on opposite side of row 1, join gray with sc in first st, sc in each st across, fasten off.

HOUSE FRONT
Row 1: With white, ch 24, sc in 2nd ch from hook, sc in next 11 chs changing to dk pink in last st made, sc in next ch changing to white, sc in next ch changing to dk. pink, sc in next ch changing to lt. green, sc in next 4 chs changing to dk. pink in last st made, sc in next ch changing to lt. green, sc in each of last 3 chs, turn (23 sc).

Rows 2-15: Ch 1, sc in each st across changing colors according to Front Graph, turn. At end of last row, fasten off.

With white, sew last row of Front to gray row of Side through **back lps.**

EAVE

Row 1: With white, ch 16, sc in 2nd ch from hook, sc in each ch across, turn (15 sc).

Row 2: Ch 1, sc in each st across, turn.

Row 3: Ch 1, sc next 2 sts tog, sc in each st across to last 2 sts, sc last 2 sts tog, turn (13).

Rows 4-11: Repeat rows 2 and 3 alternately, ending with 5 sts in last row.

Row 12: Ch 1, sc in first st, (sc next 2 sts tog) 2 times, turn (3).

Row 13: Ch 1, sc next 3 sts tog, fasten off.
Sew Eave to top of Front as shown in photo.

LARGE ROOF SECTION

Row 1: With dk. purple, ch 30, dc in 4th ch from hook, dc in each ch across, turn (28).

Row 2: Ch 3, dc in each st across to last st, 2 dc in last st, turn (29).

Row 3: Ch 3, dc in each st across to last 2 sts, dc last 2 sts tog, turn.

Rows 4-9: Repeat rows 2 and 3 alternately. At end of last row, **do not** turn or fasten off.

For **edging;** working in ends of rows, 3 sc in first row, evenly space 17 sc across to last row, 3 sc in last row; working in starting ch on opposite side of row 1, sc in each ch across leaving remaining ends of rows and sts unworked, fasten off.

SMALL ROOF SECTION

Row 1: With dk. purple, ch 7, dc in 4th ch from hook, dc in each of last 3 chs, turn (5 dc).

Row 2: Ch 3, dc in same st, dc in each st across, turn (6 dc).

Row 3: Ch 3, dc in each st across to last 2 sts, dc last 2 sts tog, turn.

Rows 4-8: Repeat rows 2 and 3 alternately, ending with row 2. At end of last row, **do not** turn or fasten off.

For **edging,** evenly space 17 sc across ends of rows; working in startng ch on opposite edge of row 1, 2 sc in first ch, sc in each ch across leaving remaining sts and ends of rows unworked, fasten off.

Sew unworked ends of rows on Large and Small Roof Sections to each side of Eave as shown. Sew bottom edge of row 2 on Large Roof Section to top of House Side.

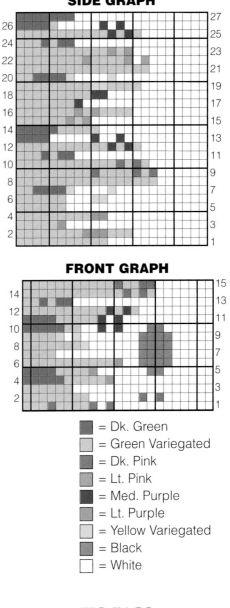

SIDE GRAPH

FRONT GRAPH

■ = Dk. Green
□ = Green Variegated
■ = Dk. Pink
□ = Lt. Pink
■ = Med. Purple
■ = Lt. Purple
□ = Yellow Variegated
■ = Black
□ = White

ZIG-ZAGS
SIZE
4¼" x 4½".

MATERIALS
Size 10 bedspread cotton — small amount each pink, white, black, dk. purple, green and yellow; dk. purple sewing thread; sewing needle; No. 7 steel crochet hook or size needed to obtain gauge.

Continued on next page

Birdhouse Coasters

Continued from page 93

GAUGE
5 sts = ½"; 5 sc rows = ½".

SKILL LEVEL
★★ Average

HOUSE
Row 1: With pink, ch 31, sc in 2nd ch from hook, sc in each ch across, turn (30 sc).

Row 2: Ch 1, sc in each st across, turn.

Row 3: Ch 2, hdc in each st across, turn.

NOTE: When changing colors (page 159), always drop yarn to same side of work. Work over dropped color as you carry it across to next section of same color.

Row 4: Ch 2, hdc in each st across changing to white in last st made, turn.

NOTE: Always change to next st in last st of last color used.

Row 5: Ch 1, hdc in first st; with pink, hdc in next 4 sts; (with white, hdc in each of next 2 sts; with pink, hdc in next 4 sts) 4 times; with white, hdc in last st, turn.

Row 6: Ch 2, hdc in next st; with pink, hdc in next st, (with white, hdc in next 4 sts; with pink, hdc in each of next 2 sts) 4 times; with white, hdc in each of last 3 sts, turn.

Row 7: Ch 2, hdc in next 5 sts; (with pink, hdc in each of next 2 sts; with white, hdc in next 4 sts) 3 times; with pink, hdc in each of next 2 sts; with white, hdc in last 4 sts, turn.

Row 8: Ch 2, hdc in each of next 2 sts; (with pink, hdc in next 4 sts; with white, hdc in each of next 2 sts) 4 times; with pink, hdc in each of last 3 sts, turn.

Rows 9-10: Ch 2, hdc in each st across, turn.

Row 11: Ch 1, sc in each st across changing to white in last st made, turn, fasten off pink.

Rows 12-13: Ch 1, sc in each st across, turn.

Row 14: Ch 1, sc in each st across changing to pink in last st made, turn.

Row 15: Ch 1, sc in first 5 sts; (with green, sc in next st; with pink, sc in next 8 sts) 2 times; with green, sc in next st; with pink, sc in last 6 sts, turn.

Row 16: Ch 2, hdc in next 5 sts; with green, hdc in next st; (with pink, hdc in next 8 sts; with green, hdc in next st) 2 times; with pink, dc in last 5 sts, turn.

Row 17: Ch 1, sc in first 5 sts; with green, sc in each of next 3 sts; with pink, sc in next 6 sts; with green, sc in each of next 2 sts; with pink, sc in next 6 sts; with green, sc in each of next 3 sts; with pink, sc in last 5 sts, turn.

Row 18: Ch 1, sc in first 4 sts; (*with green, sc in each of next 2 sts; with yellow, sc in next st; with green, sc in each of next 2 sts*; with pink, sc in next 4 sts) 2 times; repeat between **; with pink, sc in each of last 3 sts, turn.

Row 19: Ch 1, sc in first 4 sts; (*with yellow, sc in next st; with white, sc in next st; with yellow, sc in each of next 2 sts*; with pink, sc in next 5 sts) 2 times; repeat between **; with pink, sc in last 4 sts, turn.

Row 20: Ch 1, sc in first 5 sts; (*with yellow, sc in each of next 3 sts*; with pink, sc in next 6 sts) 2 times; repeat between **; with pink, sc in last 4 sts, turn.

Row 21: Ch 1, sc in first 5 sts; with yellow, sc in next st; with pink, sc in next 17 sts; with yellow, sc in next st; with pink, sc in last 6 sts, turn.

Row 22: Ch 1, sc first 2 sts tog, sc in each st across to last 2 sts, sc last 2 sts tog, turn (28).

Row 23: Ch 1, sc first 2 sts tog, sc in next 9 sts; with black, sc in next 5 st; with pink, sc in next 10 sts, sc last 2 sts tog, turn (26).

Row 24: Ch 1, sc first 2 sts tog, sc in next 8 sts; with black, sc in next 7 sts; with pink, sc in next 7sts, sc last 2 sts tog, turn (24).

Row 25: Ch 1, sc first 2 sts tog, sc in next 6 sts; with black, sc in next 7 sts; with pink, sc in next 7 sts, sc last 2 sts tog, turn (22).

Row 26: Ch 1, sc first 2 sts tog, sc in next 5 sts; with black , sc in next 9 sts; with pink, sc in next 4 sts, sc last 2 sts tog, turn (20).

Row 27: Ch 1, sc in first 5 sts; with black, sc in next 9 sts; with pink, sc in last 6 sts, turn.

Row 28: Ch 1, sc in first 7 sts; with black, sc in next 7 sts; with pink, sc in last 6 sts, turn.

Row 29: Ch 1, sc in first 8 sts; with black, sc in next 4 sts; with pink, sc in last 8 sts, turn.

Row 30: Ch 1, sc first 2 sts tog, sc in each st across to last 2 sts, sc last 2 sts tog, turn (18).

Row 30: Ch 1, sc in each st across, turn.

Row 31: Repeat row 29 (16).

Row 32: Ch 1, sc in each st across, turn.

Rows 33-35: Ch 1, sc first 2 sts tog, sc next 2 sts tog, sc in each st across to last 4 sts, (sc next 2 sts tog) 2 times, turn (12, 8, 4).

Row 36: Ch 1, sc first 2 sts tog, sc last 2 sts tog, turn (2).

Row 37: Ch 1, sc next 2 sts tog, fasten off.

ROOF SIDE (make 2)

Row 1: With dk. purple, ch 28, sc in 2nd ch from hook, sc in each ch across, turn (27 sc).

Row 2: Ch 1, sc in each st across, turn. At end of last row, fasten off.

Sew Roof Sides to each side of House as shown in photo.

DOWEL

Rnd 1: With dk. purple, ch 3, sl st in first ch to form ring, ch 1, 6 sc in ring, join with sl st in first sc (6 sc).

Rnd 2: Ch 1, 2 sc in each st around, join, fasten off. Sew Dowel to center top of Roof.

"FOR RENT"
SIZE
4¼" x 4½".

MATERIALS

Size 10 bedspread cotton — small amount each blue, pink, white, black, rust, dk. purple and gray; small amount each green, pink, black and yellow embroidery floss; pink and dk. purple sewing thread; tapestry and sewing needles; No. 7 steel crochet hook or size needed to obtain gauge.

GAUGE
5 sts = ½"; 5 sc rows = ½".

SKILL LEVEL
★★ Average

HOUSE

Row 1: With dk. purple, ch 36, sc in 2nd ch from hook, sc in each ch across, turn (35 sc).

NOTE: When changing colors (page 159), always drop yarn to same side of work. Work over dropped color as you carry it across to next section of same color.

Row 2: Ch 2, hdc in next 4 sts changing to pink in last st made, (*hdc in next 5 sts changing to dk. purple in last st made, hdc in next 5 sts* changing to pink in last st made) 2 times; repeat between **, turn.

NOTE: Always change to next color in last st of last color used.

Row 3: Ch 3, dc in next 4 sts; (*with pink, dc in

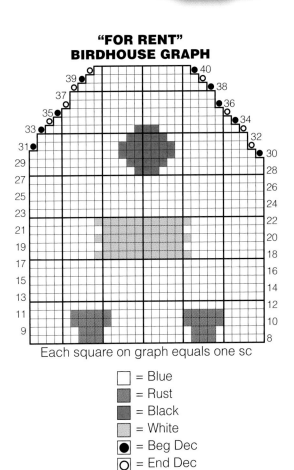

"FOR RENT"
BIRDHOUSE GRAPH

Each square on graph equals one sc

☐ = Blue
▨ = Rust
■ = Black
▤ = White
● = Beg Dec
◉ = End Dec

next 5 sts*; with dk. purple, dc in next 5 sts) 2 times; repeat between **; with dk. purple, dc in last 5 sts changing to pink in last st made, turn.

Row 4: Ch 3, dc in next 4 sts; (*with dk. purple, dc in next 5 sts; with pink, dc in next 5 sts) 3 times, turn.

Row 5: Ch 3, dc in next 4 sts; (*with dk. purple, dc in next 5 sts*; with pink, dc in next 5 sts) 2 times; repeat between **; with pink, dc in last 5 sts changing to dk. purple in last st made, turn.

Rows 6-7: Ch 1, sc in each st across, turn. At end of last row, **do not** turn, fasten off.

Row 8: Join blue with sc in 4th st, sc in next 5 sts; for **flower pot**, with rust, sc in each of next 3 sts; with blue, sc in next 11 sts; for **flower pot**, with rust, sc in each of next 3 sts; with blue, sc in next 6 sts leaving remaining sts unworked, turn (29 sc).

NOTES: For **beginning decrease (beg dec)**, ch 1, sc first 2 sts tog.

For **end decrease (end dec)**, sc last 2 sts tog.

Continued on page 106

Granny's 9-Patch

DESIGNED BY ELLEN ANDERSON

SIZE
51½" x 53".

MATERIALS
Worsted-weight yarn — 32 oz. black, 2 oz. each dk. blue, dk. coral, dk. purple, burgundy, and dk. green, 1½ oz. each lt. blue, med. blue, lt. coral, med. coral, lt. purple, med. purple, lt. pink, med. pink, lt. green, and med. green; tapestry needle; H crochet hook or size needed to obtain gauge.

GAUGE
Each Motif is 5" x 5".

SKILL LEVEL
★★ Average

BLOCK A (make 2)
First Motif (make 5)
Rnd 1: With lt. purple, ch 4, sl st in first ch to form ring, ch 3, 2 dc in ring, ch 2, (3 dc in ring, ch 2) 3 times, join with sl st in top of ch-3, fasten off (12 dc, 4 ch-2 sps).

Rnd 2: Join med. purple with sl st in any ch-2 sp, ch 3, (2 dc, ch 2, 3 dc) in same sp, ch 1, *(3 dc, ch 2, 3 dc) in next ch sp, ch 1; repeat from * 2 more times, join, fasten off (24 dc, 4 ch-2 sps, 4 ch-1 sps).

Rnd 3: Join dk. purple with sl st in any ch-2 sp, ch 3, (2 dc, ch 2, 3 dc) in same sp, ch 1, 3 dc in next ch-1 sp, ch 1, *(3 dc, ch 2, 3 dc) in next ch-2 sp, ch 1, 3 dc in next ch-1 sp, ch 1; repeat from * 2 more times, join, fasten off (36 dc, 8 ch-1 sps, 4 ch-2 sps).

Rnd 4: Join black with sl st in any ch-2 sp, ch 3, (2 dc, ch 2, 3 dc) in same sp, (ch 1, 3 dc in next ch-1 sp) 2 times, ch 1, *(3 dc, ch 2, 3 dc) in next ch-2 sp, (ch 1, 3 dc in next ch-1 sp) 2 times, ch 1; repeat from * 2 more times, join, fasten off.

Second Motif (make 4)
Rnd 1: With dk. purple, repeat same rnd as First Motif.

Rnd 2: Repeat same rnd as First Motif.

Rnd 3: With lt. purple, repeat same rnd as First Motif.

Rnd 4: Repeat same rnd as First Motif.

For **Block,** with black, matching sts and ch sps, sew Motifs together according to Motif Assembly Diagram.

MOTIF ASSEMBLY DIAGRAM

First Motif	Second Motif	First Motif
Second Motif	First Motif	Second Motif
First Motif	Second Motif	First Motif

Edging
Join black with sl st in any corner ch-2 sp, ch 3, (2 dc, ch 2, 3 dc) in same sp, ch 1, [*(3 dc in next ch-1 sp, ch 1) 3 times, dc in next ch-2 sp, dc in next joining seam, dc in next ch-2 sp, ch 1*; repeat between **, (3 dc in next ch-1 sp, ch 1) 3 times, (3 dc, ch 2, 3 dc) in next ch-1 sp, ch 1]; repeat between [ ] 2 more times; repeat between ** 2 times, (3 dc in next ch-1 sp, ch 1) 3 times, join with sl st in top of ch-3, fasten off.

BLOCK B (make 2)
Using shades of pink, work same as Block A.

BLOCK C (make 2)
Using shades of blue, work same as Block A.

BLOCK D (make 2)
Using shades of coral, work same as Block A.

BLOCK E (make 1)
Using shades of green, work same as Block A.

ASSEMBLY
Matching sts and ch sps, sew Blocks together according to Block Diagram on page 107.

BORDER
Rnd 1: Working around entire outer edge, join black with sl st in any corner ch-2 sp, ch 3, (2 dc, ch 2, 3 dc) in same sp, [*ch 1, (3 dc in next ch-1 sp, ch

Continued on page 107

Pin Cushion

DESIGNED BY JUDY TEAGUE TREECE

SIZE
6½" across.

MATERIALS
Size 10 bedspread cotton — 200 yds. pink, 100 yds. each lavender, mint and yellow; 2 pink 5½" fabric circles; pink sewing thread; polyester fiberfill; sewing needle; No. 6 steel crochet hook or size needed to obtain gauge.

GAUGE
Rnds 1-3 of Front = 2" across.

SKILL LEVEL
★★ Average

FRONT
Rnd 1: With lavender, ch 6, sl st in first ch to form ring, ch 3, 23 dc in ring, join with sl st in top of ch-3 (24 dc).

Rnd 2: Ch 3, dc in same st, dc in next st, (2 dc in next st, dc in next st) around, join (36).

Rnd 3: Ch 3, dc in each of next 2 sts, ch 2, (dc in each of next 3 sts, ch 2) around, join, fasten off (12 ch-2 sps).

Rnd 4: Join pink with sl st in any ch sp, ch 3, 5 dc in same sp, ch 1, (6 dc in next ch sp, ch 1) around, join (72 dc, 12 ch-1 sps).

Rnd 5: Ch 3, dc in each of next 2 sts, 2 tr in next st, dc in each of next 2 sts, ch 1, (dc in each of next 3 sts, 2 tr in next st, dc in each of next 2 sts, ch 1) around, join, fasten off (84 sts, 12 ch-1 sps).

NOTE: For **long single crochet (lsc),** sc around next 2 chs of last 2 rnds at same time.

Rnd 6: Join mint with sc in first st, sc in next 6 sts, lsc, (sc in next 7 sts, lsc) around, join with sl st in first sc, fasten off (84 sc, 12 lsc).

Rnd 7: Join yellow with sl st in any lsc, ch 4, (3 tr, ch 2, 4 tr) in same st, ch 1, *(4 tr, ch 2, 4 tr) in next lsc, ch 1; repeat from * around, join with sl st in top of ch-4.

Rnd 8: Ch 3, dc in each of next 3 sts, 4 tr in next ch-2 sp, dc in each of next 4 sts, ch 1, (dc in next 4 sts, 4 tr in next ch-2 sp, dc in next 4 sts, ch 1) around, join with sl st in top of ch-3, fasten off (144 sts, 12 ch-1 sps).

Rnd 9: Join lavender with sc in first st, sc in next 11 sts, lsc, (sc in next 12 sts, lsc) around, join with sl st in first sc, fasten off (144 sc, 12 lsc).

Rnd 10: Working behind sts on last rnd, join mint with sl st in any lsc, ch 4, (3 tr, ch 2, 4 tr) in same st, ch 2, *(4 tr, ch 2, 4 tr) in next lsc, ch 2; repeat from * around, join with sl st in top of ch-4.

Rnd 11: Ch 3, dc in each of next 3 sts, *[(2 tr, ch 1, 2 tr) in next ch-2 sp, dc in next 4 sts, ch 2], dc in next 4 sts; repeat from * 10 more times; repeat between [ ], join with sl st in top of ch-3, fasten off (144 dc, 12 ch-2 sps, 12 ch-1 sps).

Rnd 12: Join yellow with sc in first st, sc in next 5 sts, 3 sc in next ch-2 sp, sc in next 6 sts, lsc, (sc in next 6 sts, 3 sc in next ch-2 sp, sc in next 6 sts, lsc) around, join with sl st in first sc, fasten off (180 sc, 12 lsc).

Rnd 13: Working behind sts on last rnd, join pink with sl st in any lsc, ch 4, (6 tr, ch 2, 7 tr) in same st, ch 1, *(7 tr, ch 2, 7 tr) in next lsc, ch 1; repeat from * around, join with sl st in top of ch-4 (168 tr, 12 ch-2 sps, 12 ch-1 sps).

Rnd 14: Ch 3, dc in next 6 sts, *[(2 dc, ch 1, 2 dc) in next ch-2 sp, dc in next 7 sts, ch 1], dc in next 7 sts; repeat from * 10 more times; repeat between [ ], join with sl st in top of ch-3, fasten off (216 dc, 24 ch-1 sps).

Rnd 15: Join lavender with sc in first st, sc in next 8 sts, 2 sc in next ch sp, sc in next 9 sts, lsc, (sc in next 9 sts, 2 sc in next ch sp, sc in next 9 sts, lsc) around, join with sl st in first sc, fasten off (240 sc, 12 lsc).

BACK
Rnd 1: With pink, ch 6, sl st in first ch to form ring, ch 3, 21 dc in ring, join with sl st in top of ch-3 (22 dc).

Rnd 2: Ch 4, (dc in next st, ch 1) around, join with sl st in 3rd ch of ch-4 (22 dc, 22 ch-1 sps).

Rnd 3: Ch 3, dc in each st and in each ch sp around, join with sl st in top of ch-3 (44 dc).

Rnds 4-5: Repeat rnds 2 and 3 (88).

Rnds 6-7: Ch 3, dc in each st around, join.

Rnds 8-9: Repeat rnds 2 and 3 (176).

Rnd 10: Ch 3, skip next st, (dc in next st, skip next st) around, join (88).

NOTES: For **beginning shell (beg shell),** ch 4, (6 tr, ch 2, 7 tr) in same st.

For **shell,** (7 tr, ch 2, 7 tr) in next st.

Rnd 11: Beg shell, ch 3, skip next 6 sts, shell in next st, ch 3, skip next 6 sts, shell in next st, ch 3,

skip next 7 sts, *(shell in next st, ch 3, skip next 6 sts) 2 times, shell in next st, ch 3, skip next 7 sts; repeat from * around, join with sl st in top of ch-4 (12 shalls, 12 ch-3 sps).

Rnds 12-13: Repeat rnds 14 and 15 of Front.

PILLOW

Holding fabric circles right sides together, allow-ing ¼" for seam allowance, sew together leaving 1" opening. Turn. Stuff. Sew opening closed.

For **joining rnd,** holding Front and Back wrong sides together, with Pillow between, with Front fac-ing you, matching sts and working through both thicknesses, join lavender with sc in any sc, sc in each sc and 2 sc in each lsc around, join with sl st in first sc, fasten off.✣

Posy Patch

DESIGNED BY KATHLEEN GAREN

SIZE
39" x 53".

MATERIALS
Worsted-weight yarn — 20 oz. dk. blue, 4 oz. lt. green, 30 oz. scrap yarn in assorted colors; H rochet hook or size needed to obtain gauge.

GAUGE
Each Flower is 2¾" across.

SKILL LEVEL
★★ Average

FLOWER (make 262)
Rnd 1: With desired color scrap yarn, ch 5, sl st in first ch to form ring, ch 1, 12 sc in ring, join with sl st in first sc, fasten off (12 sc).

Rnd 2: Join desired color scrap yarn with sc in any st, ch 2, skip next st, (sc in next st, ch 2, skip next st) around, join with sl st in first sc (6 sc, 6 ch sps).

Rnd 3: Sl st in next ch sp, ch 1, (sc, hdc, 3 dc, hdc, sc) in same sp, ch 1, *(sc, hdc, 3 dc, hdc, sc) in next ch sp, ch 1; repeat from * around, join, fasten off (6 petals, 6 ch sps).

FIRST ROW OF FLOWERS
First Flower Border
Rnd 1: Join dk. blue with sc in any ch sp on desired color Flower; working behind petals, ch 3, skip next 7 sts, (sc in next ch sp, ch 3, skip next 7 sts) around, join (6 sc, 6 ch sps).

Rnd 2: Sl st in next ch sp, ch 2, 2 hdc in same sp, ch 4, skip next st, (3 hdc in next ch sp, ch 4, skip next st) around, join with sl st in top of ch-2, fasten off.

Second Flower Border
Rnd 1: Repeat same rnd of First Flower Border.
Rnd 2: Sl st in next ch sp, ch 2, 2 hdc in same sp; to **join Flowers,** (ch 2, sl st in corresponding ch-4 sp on last Flower, ch 2, 3 hdc in next ch sp on this Flower) 2 times; ch 4, (3 hdc in next ch sp, ch 4) around, join with sl st in top of ch-2, fasten off.

Repeat 2nd Flower Border until you have a strip of 17 Flowers joined end to end.

SECOND ROW OF FLOWERS
First Flower Border
Rnd 1: Repeat same rnd of First Flower Border on First Row.

Rnd 2: Sl st in next ch sp, ch 2, 2 hdc in same sp; to **join Flowers,** staggering Flower according to diagram on page 104, (ch 2, sl st in corresponding ch-4 sp on last Flower, ch 2, 3 hdc in next ch sp on this Flower) 2 times, ch 4, (3 hdc in next ch sp, ch 4) around, join with sl st in top of ch-2, fasten off.

Second Flower Border
Rnd 1: Repeat same rnd of First Flower Border on First Row.

Rnd 2: Sl st in next ch sp, ch 2, 2 hdc in same sp; to **join Flowers,** place desired color Flower according to diagram, ch 2, sl st in next unworked ch-4 sp of next Flower on last Row, ch 2, (3 hdc in next ch sp on this Flower, ch 2, sl st in next sp formed by joining, ch 2) 2 times, 3 hdc in next ch sp on this Flower, ch 2, sl st in next unworked ch-4 sp of last Flower on this Row, ch 2, (3 hdc in next ch sp on this Flower, ch 4) around, join with sl st in top of ch-2, fasten off.
Repeat 2nd Flower Border until you have a row of 18 Flowers joined.

Last Flower Border
Rnd 1: Repeat same rnd of First Flower Border on First Row.

Rnd 2: Sl st in next ch sp, ch 2, 2 hdc in same sp; to **join Flowers,** place desired color Flower according to diagram, ch 2, sl st in next unworked ch-4 sp of next Flower on last Row, ch 2, (3 hdc in next ch sp on this Flower, ch 2, sl st in next sp formed by joining, ch 2, 3 hdc in next ch sp on this Flower, ch 2, sl st in next unworked ch-4 sp of last Flower on this Row, ch 2, (3 hdc in next ch sp on this Flower, ch 4) around, join with sl st in top of ch-2, fasten off.

THIRD ROW OF FLOWERS
First Flower Border
Rnd 1: Repeat same rnd of First Flower Border on First Row.

Rnd 2: Sl st in next ch sp, ch 2, 2 hdc in same sp; to **join Flowers,** staggering desired color Flower according to diagram, ch 2, sl st in next unworked ch-

Continued on page 104

Sunny Garden

DESIGNED BY MAGGIE WELDON FOR MONSANTO'S DESIGNS FOR AMERICA PROGRAM

SIZE
45" x 64" not including Tassels.

MATERIALS
Worsted-weight yarn — 35 oz. lt. gold, 7 oz. each blue and green, 3½ oz. dk. gold; H crochet hook or size needed to obtain gauge.

GAUGE
3 sts = ¾"; rows 1-4 = 4½" square.

SKILL LEVEL
★ Average

AFGHAN
First Motif
Rnd 1: With yellow, ch 4, sl st in first ch to form ring, ch 3, 2 dc in ring, ch 2, (3 dc in ring, ch 2) 3 times, join with sl st in top of ch-3 (12 dc, 4 ch sps).

Rnd 2: Sl st in each of next 2 sts, sl st in next ch sp, ch 3, (2 dc, ch 2, 3 dc) in same sp, ch 1, *(3 dc, ch 2, 3 dc) in next ch sp, ch 1; repeat from * 2 more times, join with sl st in top of ch-3 (24 dc, 8 ch sps).

Rnd 3: Sl st in each of next 2 sts, sl st in next ch sp, ch 3, (2 dc, ch 2, 3 dc) in same sp, ch 1, 3 dc in next ch sp, ch 1, *(3 dc, ch 2, 3 dc) in next ch sp, ch 1, 3 dc in next ch sp, ch 1; repeat from * 2 more times, join with sl st in top of ch-3 (36 dc, 12 ch sps).

Rnd 4: Sl st in each of next 2 sts, sl st in next ch sp, ch 1, (sc, ch 7, sc) in same sp, ch 5, (sc in next ch sp, ch 5) 2 times, *(sc, ch 7, sc) in next ch sp, ch 5, (sc in next ch sp, ch 5) 2 times; repeat from * 2 more times, join with sl st in first sc, fasten off (16 ch sps).

One-Side Joined Motif
Rnds 1-3: Repeat same rnds of First Motif.

Rnd 4: Sl st in each of next 2 sts, sl st in next ch sp, ch 1, (sc, ch 7, sc) in same sp, *ch 5, (sc in next ch sp, ch 5) 2 times*, (sc, ch 7, sc) in next ch sp; repeat between **; to **join Motifs,** sc in next ch sp on this Motif, ch 3, sl st in 4th ch of corresponding ch-7 on last Motif, ch 3, sc in same ch sp on this Motif, (ch 2, sl st in 3rd ch of corresponding ch-5 on last Motif, ch 2, sc in next ch sp on this Motif) 2 times, ch 2, sl st in 3rd ch of corresponding ch-5 on last Motif, ch 2, sc in next ch sp on this Motif, ch 3,

sl st in 4th ch of corresponding ch-7 on last Motif, ch 3, sc in same ch sp on this Motif; repeat between **, join with sl st in first sc, fasten off.

ASSEMBLY DIAGRAM

Two-Side Joined Motif
Rnds 1-3: Repeat same rnds of First Motif.

Rnd 4: Sl st in each of next 2 sts, sl st in next ch sp, ch 1, (sc, ch 7, sc) in same sp, ch 5, (sc in next ch sp, ch 5) 2 times; [to **join Motifs** (see Assembly Diagram), sc in next ch sp on this Motif, ch 3, sl st in 4th ch of corresponding ch-7 on other Motif, ch 3, sc in same ch sp on this Motif, (ch 2, sl st in 3rd ch of corresponding ch-5 on other Motif, ch 2, sc in next ch sp on this Motif) 2 times, ch 2, sl st in 3rd ch of corresponding ch-5 on other Motif, ch 2]; repeat between [ ], (sc, ch 7, sc) in next ch sp, ch 5, (sc in next ch sp, ch 5) 2 times, join with sl st in first sc, fasten off.

Continued on next page

Sunny Garden

Continued from page 103

Using One- and Two-Side Joined Motifs as needed, work remainder of Afghan according to Assembly Diagram on page 103, ending with a total of 111 Motifs.

FLOWER (make 63)

Rnd 1: With gold, ch 2, 6 sc in 2nd ch from hook, join with sl st in first sc, fasten off (6 sc).

Rnd 2: Join blue with sl st in any st, ch 3, (tr, ch 3, sl st) in same st, (sl st, ch 3, tr, ch 3, sl st) in each st around, join with sl st in first sl st, fasten off.

LEAVES (make 63)

NOTE: For **treble cluster stitch (tr cl)**, yo 2 times, insert hook in next ch, yo, draw lp through, (yo, draw through 2 lps on hook) 2 times, *yo 2 times, insert hook in same ch, yo, draw lp through, (yo, draw through 2 lps on hook) 2 times; repeat from *, yo, draw through all 4 lps on hook.

With green, ch 5, tr cl in 5th ch from hook, ch 8, tr cl in 5th ch of ch-8, fasten off leaving long end for sewing (2 Leaves).

Sew Leaves and Flower to center of Motifs according to Assembly Diagram.

TASSEL (make 14)

Cut 21 strands blue each 12" long. Tie a separate strand blue tightly around center of all strands, fold all strands in half. Tie 18" strand blue around all strands 1" from fold. Trim ends.

Working across short end, attach one Tassel to corner ch sp of each Motif on end.

Repeat on other short end of Afghan.❖

Posy Patch

Continued from page 100

4 sp of 2nd Flower on last Row, ch 2, 3 hdc in next ch sp of this Flower, ch 2, sl st in sp formed by next joining, ch 2, 3 hdc in next ch sp on this Flower, ch 2, sl st in next unworked ch-4 sp of first Flower on last row, ch 2, (3 hdc in next ch sp on this Flower, ch 4) around, join with sl st in top of ch-2, fasten off.

Second Flower Border

Rnd 1: Repeat same rnd of First Flower Border on First Row.

Rnd 2: Sl st in next ch sp, ch 2, 2 hdc in same sp; to **join Flowers**, place desired color Flower according to diagram, ch 2, sl st in next unworked ch-4 sp of next Flower on last Row, ch 2, 3 hdc in next ch sp of this Flower, (ch 2, sl st in sp formed by next joining, ch 2, 3 hdc in next ch sp on this Flower) 2 times, ch 2, sl st in next unworked ch-4 sp of last Flower on this row,

ch 2, (3 hdc in next ch sp on this Flower, ch 4) around, join with sl st in top of ch-2, fasten off.

Repeat 2nd Flower Border until you have a row with 17 Flowers.

Remaining Rows of Flowers

Repeat Second and Third Rows of Flowers alternately until all Flowers are joined.

OUTER BORDER

Rnd 1: Join dk. blue with a sc in first ch-4 sp at

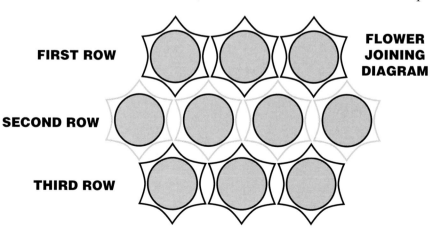

FIRST ROW

SECOND ROW

THIRD ROW

FLOWER JOINING DIAGRAM

any corner Flower, 2 sc in same sp, skip next hdc, hdc in each of next 2 hdc, *(3 sc in next corner ch-4 sp, skip next hdc, hdc in each of next 2 hdc, 2 dc in next ch-2 sp, tr in joining sp, 2 dc in next ch sp, hdc in each of next 2 hdc) across to next corner ch-4 sp, 3 sc in next ch-4 sp, skip next hdc, hdc in each of next 2 hdc; repeat from * 2 more times; repeat between ( ) across to first corner, join with sl st in first sc.

Rnd 2: Ch 4, skip next st, (dc in next st, ch 1, skip next st) around, join with sl st in 3rd ch of ch-4, fasten off.

Rnd 3: Join lt. green with sc in first st, ch 1, skip next ch; *for **corner,** sc in next st, ch 1, sc in next ch-1, ch 1, sc in next st, ch 1, skip next ch, sc in next st, ch 1, sc in next ch-1, ch 1, sc in next st; ch 1, (sc in next st, ch 1, skip next ch) across to next corner; repeat from * 3 more times, join with sl st in first sc, fasten off.

Rnd 4: Join dk. blue with sc in first st, ch 1; skipping chs, (sc, ch 1) in each st around, join with sl st in first sc, fasten off.

Rnd 5: Join lt. green with sc in any st of last rnd, (ch 4, skip next ch, next st and next ch, sc in next st) around, ch 4, join with sl st in first sc.

Rnd 6: (Sl st in each of next 2 chs, ch 4, sl st in each of next 2 chs, sl st in next st) around to last ch-4, sl st in each of next 2 chs, ch 4, sl st in each of next 2 chs, join with sl st in first sl st, fasten off.❖

Pastel Dress

Continued from page 88

Rnd 18: Ch 1, sc around joining st, ch 1, 8 dc in next ch lp, ch 1, (sc in next ch lp, ch 1, 8 dc in next ch lp, ch 1) around, join with sl st in first sc.

Rnd 19: Ch 1, sc in first sc, ch 2, sc in next 8 dc, ch 2, (sc in next sc, ch 2, sc in next 8 dc, ch 2) around, join, fasten off.

HAT

Rnd 1: Ch 4, sl st in first ch to form ring, ch 3, 15 dc in ring, join with sl st in top of ch-3 (16 dc).

Rnd 2: Ch 3, dc in same st, 2 dc in each st around, join (32).

Rnd 3: Ch 1, sc in each st around, join with sl st in first sc.

Rnds 4-5: Ch 3, dc in each st around, join.

Rnd 6: Repeat rnd 2 (64).

Rnd 7: Ch 3, (2 dc in next st, dc in each of next 2 sts) around, join (85).

Rnd 8: Ch 3, dc in each of next 3 sts, 2 dc in next st, (dc in next 4 sts, 2 dc in next st) around, join (102).

Rnd 9: Ch 3, dc in each st around, join.

Rnd 10: Ch 1; working left to right, **reverse sc** (page 159) in each st around, join with sl st in first sc, fasten off.

FINISHING

1: For **petticoat,** baste across one long edge of 6" x 72" piece of tulle. Pull up to fit around doll's waist, place on doll, secure ends in back.

2: Sew snaps evenly spaced to back of Bodice. Place dress on doll.

3: For **ribbon loops,** cut eight pieces of ribbon each 1" long. Fold each piece in half crosswise and tack ends together.

4: Cut 12" piece of ribbon, fold in half crosswise. Tack fold to right shoulder of Bodice Front; tack ends to waist as shown in photo. Tack three ribbon loops to shoulder over fold and three to waist over ends. Glue six flowers over front of Bodice as shown.

5: Cut piece of ribbon to fit around wrist; tack ends together around wrist. Tack or glue remaining ribbon loops to top of wrist over ribbon. Glue flower below loops.

6: Fold 4" x 36" piece tulle in half lengthwise. Run gathering thread through raw edges, pull to gather, secure. Tack or glue inside Hat. Cut two pieces of ribbon each 11" long. Tack one end of one piece to inside of Hat on each side. Place Hat on doll's head; tie ribbon ends into a bow around chin.

7: Sew ends of lace together; tack centered to top of Hat, glue flowers over center covering completely. Tie remaining ribbon into a bow, tack below flowers.❖

Rows 9-40: Ch 1, sc in each st across changing colors accroding to graph, turn. At end of last row, fasten off.

ROOF
First Section
Row 1: With pink, ch 40, hdc in 3rd ch from hook, hdc in next 17 chs, 2 hdc in next ch, hdc in last 19 chs, turn (40 hdc).

Row 2: Ch 2, hdc in next 18 sts, 2 hdc in each of next 2 sts, hdc in last 19 sts, fasten off.

Second Section
Row 1: With dk. purple, ch 43, dc in 3rd ch from hook, tr in next ch, dc in next ch, hdc in next ch, sl st in next ch, (hdc in next ch, dc in next ch, tr in next ch, dc in next ch, hdc in next ch, sl st in next ch) across, turn (42 sts).

Row 2: Ch 1, sc in first 20 sts, 2 sc in next st, sc in last 21 sts, turn (43).

Row 3: Ch 1, sc in first 21 sts, 3 sc in next st, sc in last 21 sts, turn (45).

Row 4: Ch 1, sc in first 22 sts, (sc, ch 3, sc, ch 4, sl st in 3rd ch from hook, sc, ch 3, sc) in next st, sc in last 22 sts, fasten off.

Finishing
1: Sew Roof Second Section to last row of Roof First Section. Sew Roof to top of House as shown in photo.

2: Cut piece white 1¼" long, tack one end to each side of white section on House; tack center of strand centered 4 rows above white section. With gray, using French Knot (page 159), embroider nail over center of strand. With black floss, using Straight Stitch, embroider words "FOR RENT" over center of white section on House.

3: With green, pink and yellow floss, using Straight Stitch and French Knot, embroider flowers and leaves above each flower pot on House.

PICKET FENCE
SIZE
4" x 5½".

MATERIALS
Size 10 bedspread cotton — small amount each green, yellow, white, blue and black; small amount each yellow and blue variegated embroidery floss; blue sewing thread; sewing and tapestry needles; No. 7 steel crochet hook or size needed to obtain gauge.

GAUGE
5 sts = ½"; 7 hdc rows = 1".

SKILL LEVEL
★★ Average

HOUSE
Row 1: With green, for **grass,** ch 35, sc in 2nd ch from hook, sc in each ch across, turn (34 sc).

Row 2: Ch 1, sc in each of first 3 sts, hdc in next st, dc in next st, hdc in next st, sc in each of next 3 sts, hdc in next st, dc in next st, hdc in each of next 2 sts, sc in each of next 3 sts, hdc in each of next 2 sts, dc in next st, tr in next st, dc in each of next 2 sts, hdc in each of next 2 sts, sc in each of next 3 sts, hdc in each of next 2 sts, dc in next st, hdc in next st, sc in each of last 3 sts, turn, fasten off (34 sts).

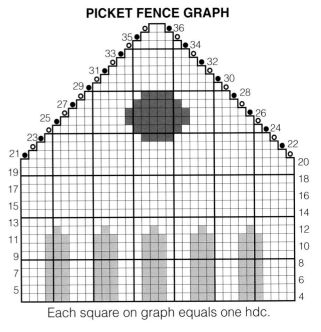

PICKET FENCE GRAPH

Each square on graph equals one hdc.

☐ = Yellow
▨ = Black
▨ = White
● = Beg Dec
○ = End Dec

NOTE: When changing colors (page 159), always drop yarn to same side of work. Work over dropped color as you carry it across to next section of same color.

Row 3: Join yellow with sl st in first st, ch 3, dc in each of next 2 sts changing to white in last st made; for **picket fence,** sc in each of next 3 sts changing to yellow in last st made, hdc in each of next 2 sts, dc in next st changing to white; for **picket fence,** sc in each of next 2 sts, sl st in next st changing to yellow, sl st in each of next 3 sts changing to white in last st made; for **picket fence,** sc in each of next 3 sts changing to yellow in last st made, sc in each of next 3 sts changing to white in last st made; for **picket fence,** sc in each of next 3 sts changing to yellow in last st made, sc in next st, hdc in each of next 2 sts changing to white in last st made; for **picket fence,** sl st in each of next 3 sts changing to yellow in last st made, sc in last 4 sts, turn.

NOTES: First ch-2 counts as first hdc.

For **beginning decrease (beg dec),** ch 1, hdc first 2 sts tog.

For **end decrease (end dec),** hdc last 2 sts tog.

Rows 4-36: Ch 2, hdc in each st across changing colors according to graph, turn. At end of last row, fasten off.

ROOF SIDE (make 2)

Row 1: With med. blue, ch 30, sc in 2nd ch from hook, sc in each ch across, turn (29 sc).

Row 2: Ch 3, dc in each st across, turn.

Row 3: Ch 1, sc in each st across, fasten off.

Sew Roof Sides to each side of House as shown.

DOWEL

Rnd 1: With med. blue, ch 3, sl st in first ch to form ring, ch 1, 6 sc in ring, join with sl st in first sc (6 sc).

Rnd 2: Ch 1, 2 sc in each st around, join, fasten off.

Sew Dowel to center top of Roof.

Finishing

1: With white, using Straight Stitch (see page 158), embroider between fence pickets across rows 7 and 9.

2: With blue variegated and yellow, using Lazy Daisy Stitch (see illustration) and French Knot (see page 159), embroider flowers at random across green rows.❖

LAZY DAISY STITCH

Granny's 9-Patch

Continued from page 96

Continued from page 96

1) across to next corner ch-2 sp], (3 dc, ch 2, 3 dc) in next corner ch-2 sp; repeat from * 2 more times; repeat between [ ], join with sl st in top of ch-3.

Rnds 2-3: Sl st in each of next 2 dc, sl st in next ch-2 sp, ch 3, (2 dc, ch 2, 3 dc) in same sp, [*ch 1, (3 dc in next ch-1 sp, ch 1) across to next corner ch-2 sp], (3 dc, ch 2, 3 dc) in next corner ch-2 sp; repeat from * 2 more times; repeat between [ ], join.

Rnd 4: Sl st in each of next 2 sts, sl st in next corner ch-2 sp, ch 5, (tr, ch 1) 9 times in same sp, [sc in next ch sp, *tr in next ch sp, (ch 1, tr) 5 times in same sp*; repeat between ** across to next corner ch-2 sp, tr in next ch-2 sp, (ch 1, tr) 9 times in same

sp]; repeat between [ ] 2 more times, sc in next ch sp; repeat between ** across to first corner, join with sl st in top of ch-5.

Rnd 5: Sl st in next ch sp, ch 1, sc in same sp, ch 3; working in ch sps only, (sc in next ch sp, ch 3) around, join with sl st in first sc, fasten off.❖

BLOCK DIAGRAM

A	B	C
D	E	D
C	B	A

A = Block A
B = Block B
C = Block C
D = Block D
E = Block E

Heartfelt Hospitality

Fill your home with all the creature
comforts of an old-fashioned inn
and when company comes calling, you'll
be the most gracious hostess they've ever
experienced. When your creations
are seen through their eyes, you'll have
a newfound appreciation for
your crochet skills.

Kitchen Angel

DESIGNED BY ESTELLA WHITFORD

SIZE
11½" tall.

MATERIALS
Worsted-weight yarn — 4½ oz. white, 2 oz. red, 1 oz. each glitter red and royal blue, small amount each black, glitter white and tan; 2½" miniature fork and spoon; 3" square cotton fabric; 6" piece wired metallic gold braid; polyester fiberfill; tapestry needle; G crochet hook or size needed to obtain gauge.

GAUGE
4 sc sts = 1"; 4 sc rows = 1".

SKILL LEVEL
★★ Average

SPECIAL NOTE
Do not join rnds unless otherwise stated.
Mark first st of each rnd.

COW
Head & Body
Rnd 1: Starting at **Head,** with white, ch 2, 6 sc in 2nd ch from hook (6 sc).

Rnd 2: 2 sc in each st around (12).

Rnd 3: (Sc in next st, 2 sc in next st) around (18).

Rnd 4: (Sc in each of next 2 sts, 2 sc in next st) around (24).

Rnds 5-7: Sc in each st around.

Rnd 8: (Sc in each of next 2 sts, sc next 2 sts tog) around (18).

Rnd 9: (Sc next 2 sts tog) around (9).

Rnd 10: 2 sc in each st around (18).

Rnd 11: (Sc in each of next 2 sts, 2 sc in next st) around (24).

Rnds 12-17: Sc in each st around.

Rnd 18: (Sc in each of next 2 sts, sc next 2 sts tog) around (18). Stuff.

Rnd 19: (Sc next 2 sts tog) around (9).

Rnd 20: Sc in next st, (sc next 2 sts tog) around, join with sl st in first sc, fasten off leaving 8" for sewing (5).

Arm (make 2)
Rnd 1: Starting at **hoof,** with black, ch 2, 6 sc in 2nd ch from hook (6 sc).

Rnd 2: (Sc in next st, 2 sc in next st) around (9).

Rnd 3: Working this rnd in **back lps** only (see page 159), sc in each st around, join with sl st in first sc, fasten off.

Rnd 4: Join white with sc in first st, sc in each st around, **do not** join.

Rnds 5-10: Sc in each st around. At end of last rnd, join with sl st in first sc, fasten off leaving 10" for sewing. Stuff.

Sew Arms over rnds 11-13 on each side of Body.

Leg (make 2)
Rnd 1: Starting at **hoof,** with black, ch 2, 6 sc in 2nd ch from hook (6 sc).

Rnd 2: (Sc in next st, 2 sc in next st) around (9).

Rnd 3: Working this rnd in **back lps** only, sc in each st around, join with sl st in first sc, fasten off.

Rnd 4: Join white with sc in first st, sc in each st around, **do not** join.

Rnds 5-16: Sc in each st around. At end of last rnd, join with sl st in first sc, fasten off leaving 10" for sewing. Stuff.

Sew Legs to bottom of Body.

HAT
Rnd 1: Starting at **top,** with white, ch 2, 6 sc in 2nd ch from hook (6 sc).

Rnds 2-3: 2 sc in each st around (12, 24).

Rnd 4: (Sc in each of next 3 sts, 2 sc in next st) around (30).

Rnds 5-6: Sc in each st around.

Rnd 7: (Sc in each of next 3 sts, sc next 2 sts tog) around (24).

Rnd 8: (Sc next 2 sts tog) around (12).

Rnd 9: Working this rnd in **back lps** only, sc in each st around.

Rnds 10-11: Sc in each st around. At end of last rnd, join with sl st in first sc, fasten off.

Stuff lightly and sew to center top of Head. With tapestry needle, using black and Running Stitch (see page 159) embroider around bottom edge of Hat as shown in photo.

Ear (make 2)
With white, ch 4, sc in 2nd ch from hook, sc in next ch, 3 sc in end ch; working on opposite side of starting ch, sc in each of last 2 chs, join with sl st in first sc, fasten off leaving 8" for sewing.

Sew Ears to Head on each side of Hat.

MUZZLE

Rnd 1: With tan, ch 6, 3 sc in 2nd ch from hook, sc in each of next 3 chs, 3 sc in end ch; working on opposite side of starting ch, sc in each of next 3 chs, join with sl st in first sc (12 sc).

Rnds 2-3: Ch 1, sc in each st around, join. At end of last rnd, fasten off.

Stuff lightly and sew over rnds 6-8 of Head.

For **nostrils,** with black, embroider 2 French Knots (see page 159) ¼" apart over Muzzle. For **eyes,** embroider 2 black French Knots ⅜" apart above Muzzle.

For **halo,** wrap wired gold braid around base of Hat and one Ear forming a circle; twist ends together.

DRESS

Row 1: Starting at **neckline,** with red, ch 23, sc in 2nd ch from hook, sc in each ch across, turn (22 sc).

Row 2: Ch 1, sc in each st across, turn.

Row 3: Ch 1, sc in first 4 sts; for **armhole,** ch 5, skip next 3 sts; sc in next 8 sts; for **armhole,** ch 5, skip next 3 sts; sc in last 4 sts, turn (16 sc, 10 chs).

Row 4: Ch 1, sc in each st and in each ch across, turn (26 sc).

Row 5: Ch 1, 2 sc in first st, sc in next st, (2 sc in next st, sc in next st) across, turn (39).

Row 6: Ch 3, (2 dc in next st, dc in next st) across, turn (58 dc).

Rows 7-9: Ch 3, dc in each st across, turn.

Row 10: Working this row in **back lps** only, ch 3, dc in each st across, turn, fasten off.

Row 11: Working in unworked **front lps** of row 9, join glitter red with sl st in first st, ch 3, dc in each st across, turn.

Row 12: Ch 3, dc in each st across, turn.

Row 13: Ch 3, 5 dc in same st, (skip next 2 sts, 6 dc in next st) across, fasten off.

For **neck edging,** working in starting ch on opposite side of row 1, join red with sc in first ch, (ch 3, sc in next ch) across, fasten off.

Place Dress on Cow, sew ends of rows together in back.

APRON

Row 1: With royal blue, ch 7, sc in 2nd ch from hook, sc in each ch across, turn (6 sc).

Row 2: Ch 1, 2 sc in first st, sc in each st across with 2 sc in last st, turn (8).

Row 3: Ch 1, sc in each st across, turn.

Rows 4-6: Repeat row 2 (10, 12, 14).

Rows 7-11: Ch 1, sc in each st across, turn.

Row 12: Ch 1, sc first 2 sts tog, sc in each st across to last 2 sts, sc last 2 sts tog, turn (12).

Rnd 13: Working around outer edge, ch 1, sc in each st and in end of each row around with 2 sc in each corner, join with sl st in first sc, fasten off.

Pocket

Row 1: With royal blue, ch 6, sc in 2nd ch from hook, sc in each ch across, turn (5 sc).

Rows 2-4: Ch 1, sc in each st across, turn.

Rnd 5: Working around outer edge, ch 1, sc in each st and in end of each row around with 2 sc in each corner, join with sl st in first sc, fasten off.

With tapestry needle, using white and Running Stitch, embroider around outer edge of Pocket. Sew Pocket to left side of Apron as shown.

For **neck strap,** with royal blue, ch 28, fasten off. Sew ends to ends of row 1.

For **tie (make 2),** with royal blue, ch 50, fasten off. Sew one end of each tie to end of row 6 on Apron. Place Apron on Cow and tie in bow at back.

Fold cotton fabric to resemble napkin and place inside Pocket with miniature fork.

WING (make 2)

Row 1: With white, ch 4, sc in 2nd ch from hook, sc in each ch across, turn (3 sc).

Rows 2-5: Ch 1, 2 sc in first st, sc in each st across with 2 sc in last st, turn, ending with 11 sts in last row.

Row 6: Ch 1, sc in each st across, turn.

Row 7: Ch 1, sc first 2 sts tog, sc in each st across to last 2 sts, sc last 2 sts tog, turn (9).

Row 8: Ch 1, sc in each st across, turn.

Rows 9-12: Repeat rows 7 and 8 alternately, ending with 5 sts in last row. At end of last row, fasten off.

Rnd 13: Working around outer edge in sts and in ends of rows, join glitter white with sc in first st, evenly space 35 more sc around, join with sl st in first sc, fasten off (36 sc).

Rnd 14: Join royal blue with sl st in first st, ch 3, 5 dc in same st, skip next 2 sts, (6 dc in next st, skip next 2 sts) around, join with sl st in top of ch-3, fasten off.

With tapestry needle, using royal blue and Running Stitch, embroider around base of rnd 13 as shown.

Sew Wings to back of Dress.

For **hanger,** tie desired length yarn to back of Head above Wings. ✤

Halloween Hot Pads

DESIGNED BY BEVERLY MEWHORTER

SIZES
Each Hot Pad is 8" square.

MATERIALS FOR BOTH
Worsted-weight yarn — 4 oz. each black and white, 1 oz. orange; G crochet hook or size needed to obtain gauge.

GAUGE
4 sts = 1"; 4 sc rows = 1".

SKILL LEVEL
★★ Average

SPECIAL NOTE
When changing colors (see page 159), always drop yarn to wrong side of work. Do not work over dropped color; carry yarn loosely across back of work to next section of same color. Fasten off colors when no longer needed.

GHOST HOT PAD

Front
Row 1: With black, ch 31, sc in 2nd ch from hook, sc in each ch across, turn (30 sc).

Rows 2-3: Ch 1, sc in each st across, turn.

Rows 4-27: Ch 1, sc in each st across changing colors according to Ghost Hot Pad Graph, turn.

Rows 28-30: Ch 1, sc in each st across, turn. At end of last row, fasten off.

Back
Row 1: With black, ch 31, sc in 2nd ch from hook, sc in each ch across, turn (30 sc).

Rows 2-30: Ch 1, sc in each st across, turn. At end of last row, fasten off.

Edging
To **join**, holding Front and Back wrong sides together, working through both thicknesses, join orange with sc in top left corner st; for **hanging loop,** ch 10, sc in same st; sc in each st and in end of each row around with 2 sc in each corner st, join with sl st in first sc, fasten off.

BOO HOT PAD

Front
Row 1: With white, ch 31, sc in 2nd ch from hook,
sc in each ch across, turn (30 sc).

Rows 2-8: Ch 1, sc in each st across, turn.

Rows 9-22: Ch 1, sc in each st across changing colors according to Boo Hot Pad Graph, turn.

Rows 23-30: Ch 1, sc in each st across, turn. At end of last row, fasten off.

Back
With white, work same as Ghost Hot Pad Back.

Edging
Work same as Ghost Hot Pad Edging.❖

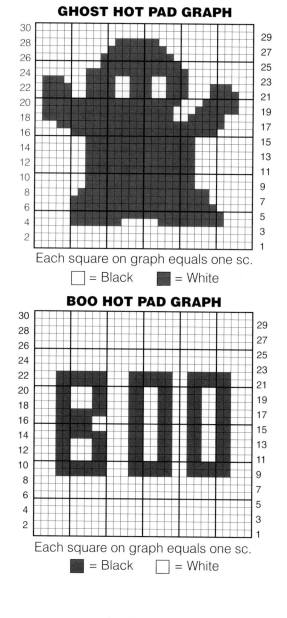

GHOST HOT PAD GRAPH

Each square on graph equals one sc.

□ = Black   ■ = White

BOO HOT PAD GRAPH

Each square on graph equals one sc.

■ = Black   □ = White

Yuletide Hot Pads

DESIGNED BY BEVERLY MEWHORTER

SIZE
Each Hot Pad is 8" square.

MATERIALS FOR BOTH
Worsted-weight yarn — 4 oz. each green and red, 3 oz. white; tapestry needle; G crochet hook or size needed to obtain gauge.

GAUGE
4 sts = 1"; 4 sc rows = 1".

SKILL LEVEL
★★ Average

SPECIAL NOTE
When changing colors (see page 159), always drop yarn to wrong side of work. Do not work over dropped color; carry yarn loosely across back of work to next section of same color. Fasten off colors when no longer needed.

STOCKING HOT PAD
Front
Row 1: With green, ch 31, sc in 2nd ch from hook, sc in each ch across, turn (30 sc).

Rows 2-3: Ch 1, sc in each st across, turn.

Rows 4-27: Ch 1, sc in each st across changing colors according to Stocking Hot Pad Graph, turn.

Rows 28-30: Ch 1, sc in each st across, turn. At end of last row, fasten off.

Using white and Straight Stitch (see page 159), embroider stars at random on stocking as shown in photo.

Back
Row 1: With green, ch 31, sc in 2nd ch from hook, sc in each ch across, turn (30 sc).

Rows 2-30: Ch 1, sc in each st across, turn. At end of last row, fasten off.

Edging
To **join,** holding Front and Back wrong sides together, working through both thicknesses, join white with sc in top left corner st; for **hanging loop,** ch 10, sc in same st; sc in each st and in each end row around with 2 sc in each corner st, join with sl st in first sc, fasten off.

Continued on page 125

PACKAGE HOT PAD
Front
Row 1: With red, ch 31, sc in 2nd ch from hook, sc in each ch across, turn (30 sc).

STOCKING HOT PAD GRAPH

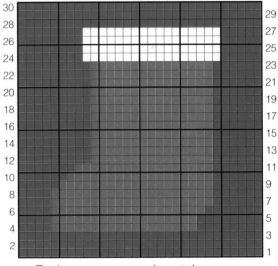

Each square on graph equals one sc.

= Red
= Green
= White

PACKAGE HOT PAD GRAPH

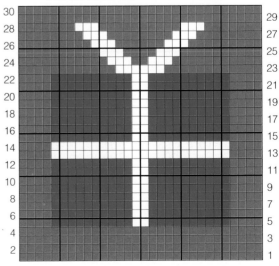

Each square on graph equals one sc.

Blue Kitchen Set

DESIGNED BY CAROL SMITH

SIZES

Place Mat is 12¼" x 14¾" across. Coaster is 5" across. Hot Pad is 8" across. Dish Towel Topper fits standard dish towel.

MATERIALS FOR SET

Cotton worsted-weight yarn — 7 oz. blue; blue 1" button; dish towel; blue thread; sewing needles; J crochet hook or size needed to obtain gauge.

GAUGE

3 hdc = 1"; 4 rows = 2".

SKILL LEVEL

★★ Average

SPECIAL NOTE

For **cluster variation (cl),** yo, insert hook in next st or ch, yo, draw lp through, (insert hook in next st or ch, yo, draw lp through) 2 times, yo, draw through all 5 lps on hook.

PLACE MAT

Row 1: Ch 49, skip first 3 chs from hook, cl, ch 2, (cl, ch 2) across to last ch, hdc in last ch, turn (15 cl, 2 hdc).

Row 2: Ch 2, skip next ch-2 sp, (hdc, ch 1, hdc) in next hdc, *skip next ch-2 sp, (hdc, ch 1, hdc) in next hdc; repeat from * across to last st, hdc in last st, turn (32 hdc).

Row 3: Ch 4, (cl, ch 2) across to last st, hdc in last st, turn.

Rows 4-20: Repeat rows 2 and 3 alternately ending with row 2. At end of last row, turn, **do not** fasten off.

Rnd 21: Working around outer edge, ch 2, 2 hdc in same st, *hdc in each st or ch across to next corner st, 3 hdc in next corner; (hdc in end of next row, 2 hdc in end of next row) across* to next corner, 3 hdc in next corner; repeat between **, join with sl st in top of ch-2.

Rnd 22: Ch 2, hdc in each st around with 3 hdc in each center corner st, join, fasten off.

COASTER

Rnd 1: Ch 4, sl st in first ch to form ring, ch 2, 16 hdc in ring, join with, sl st in top of ch-2 (17 dc).

Rnd 2: Ch 3, yo, insert hook in next st, yo, draw lp through, (insert hook in next st, yo, draw lp through) 2 times, yo, draw through all 5 lps on hook, ch 2, *yo, insert hook in last worked st, yo, draw lp through, (insert hook in next st, yo, draw lp through) 2 times, yo, draw through all 5 lps on hook, ch 2; repeat from * around to last st, yo, insert hook in last worked st, yo, draw lp through, insert hook in last st, yo, draw lp through, insert hook in same st as ch-3, yo, draw lp through, yo, draw through all 5 lps on hook, ch 2, join with sl st in 2nd ch of ch-3.

Rnd 3: Ch 2; skipping ch-2 sps, (hdc, ch 1, hdc) in each st around, (hdc, ch 1, hdc) in same st as first ch-2, join with sl st in top of ch-2.

Rnd 4: Working in sts and in chs, repeat rnd 2.

Rnd 5: Ch 1, sc in each st and in each ch around, join with sl st in first sc, fasten off.

HOT PAD SIDE (make 2)

Row 1: Ch 25, skip first 3 chs from hook, cl, ch 2, (cl, ch 2) across to last ch, hdc in last ch, turn (7 cl, 2 hdc).

Row 2: Ch 2; skipping ch-2 sps, (hdc, ch 1, hdc) in each st across to last st, hdc in last st, turn.

Row 3: Ch 4, (cl, ch 2) across to last st, hdc in last st, turn.

Rows 4-12: Repeat rows 2 and 3 alternately ending with row 2.

Rnd 13: Working around outer edge, ch 2, 2 hdc in same st, *hdc in each st or ch across to next corner st, 3 hdc in next corner st; (hdc in end of next row, 2 hdc in end of next row) across* to next corner st, 3 hdc in next corner st; repeat between **, join with sl st in top of ch-2. For **first side,** fasten off; for **second side,** do not fasten off.

Rnd 14: To **join Sides,** hold first and second Sides wrong sides together; matching sts and working through both thicknesses, ch 2, hdc in each st around, join with sl st in top of ch-2, fasten off.

DISH TOWEL TOPPER

Rnd 1: Ch 43, sl st in first ch to form ring, ch 2, (cl, ch 2) around, join with sl st in top of ch-2, **turn** (14 cl, 1 hdc).

Rnd 2: Sl st in next st, ch 3, hdc in same st; skipping all ch-2 sps, (hdc, ch 1, hdc) in each st around, join with sl st in 2nd ch of ch-3, **turn** (28 hdc).

Rnd 3: Ch 1, (cl, ch 2) around, join with sl st in first cl, **turn.**

Continued on page 125

Green Kitchen Set

DESIGNED BY CAROL SMITH

SIZES

Place Mat is 18" across. Coaster is 5½" across. Hot Pad is 7¾" across. Dish Towel Topper fits standard-size dish towel.

MATERIALS FOR SET

Cotton worsted-weight yarn — 7 oz. green; gold 1" button; double-sided print dish towel; green sewing thread; sewing and tapestry needles; J crochet hook or size needed to obtain gauge.

GAUGE

1 shell and 1 V-st = 2"; 3 rows = 2½".

SKILL LEVEL

★★ Average

SPECIAL NOTES

For **beginning shell (beg shell)**, (ch 3, dc, ch 1, 2 dc) in st or sp.

For **shell**, (2 dc, ch 1, 2 dc) in next st or sp.

For **V-stitch (V-st)**, (dc, ch 1, dc) in next st or sp.

For **picot**, ch 4, sl st in top of last st made.

For **picot shell**, (3 dc, picot, 2 dc) in next ch sp.

PLACE MAT

Rnd 1: Ch 8, dc in 4th ch from hook, (skip next ch, shell in next ch) 2 times; working on opposite side of starting ch, skip next ch, shell in next ch, skip next ch, 2 dc in same ch as first dc; to **join**, sc in top of ch-3 (4 shells).

Rnd 2: Ch 3, dc around joining sc, skip next 2 sts, shell in next sp between shells, skip next 2 sts, (shell in next ch sp of shell, skip next 2 sts, shell in next sp between shells, skip next 2 sts) around, 2 dc in joining sp, join with sc in top of ch-3 (8 shells).

Rnd 3: Ch 3, dc around joining sc, V-st in next sp between shells, (shell in next ch sp of shell, V-st in next sp between shells) around, 2 dc in joining sp, join as before (8 shells, 8 V-sts).

Rnd 4: Ch 3, dc around joining sc, shell in ch sp of each V-st and each shell around, 2 dc in joining sp, join (16 shells).

Rnd 5: Ch 3, dc around joining sc, (*skip next 2 sts, V-st in next sp between shells, shell in each of next 3 shells, skip next 2 sts, V-st in next sp between shells, skip next 2 sts*, shell in next shell) 3 times; repeat between **, 2 dc in joining

sp, join (16 shells, 8 V-sts).

Rnd 6: Repeat rnd 4 (24 shells).

Rnd 7: Ch 3, dc around joining sc, shell in each shell around, 2 dc in joining sp, join (24 shells).

Rnd 8: Ch 3, dc around joining sc, (*skip next 2 sts, V-st in next sp between shells, shell in next 5 shells, skip next 2 sts, V-st in next sp between shells, skip next 2 sts*, shell in next shell) 3 times; repeat between **, 2 dc in joining sp, join (24 shells, 8 V-sts).

Rnd 9: Repeat rnd 4 (32 shells).

Rnd 10: Repeat rnd 7.

Rnd 11: Sl st in next st, (sl st, ch 1, sc) in next st, sc in next st, sc in next ch sp, picot, sc in each of next 2 sts, skip next 2 sts, picot shell, (skip next 2 sts, sc in each of next 2 sts, sc in next ch sp, picot, sc in each of next 2 sts, skip next 2 sts, picot shell) around, join with sl st in first sc, fasten off.

COASTER

Rnd 1: Ch 4, sl st in first ch to form ring, ch 4, dc in ring, 7 V-sts in ring, join with sl st in 3rd ch of ch-4 (8 V-sts).

Rnd 2: Sl st in next ch sp, beg shell in same sp, shell in ch sp of each V-st around, join with sl st in top of ch-3 (8 shells).

Rnd 3: Ch 1, sc in each of first 2 sts, sc in next ch sp, picot, sc in each of next 2 sts, skip next 2 sts, picot shell in next ch sp, skip next 2 sts, (sc in each of next 2 sts, sc in next ch sp, picot, sc in each of next 2 sts, skip next 2 sts, picot shell in next ch sp, skip next 2 sts) around, join with sl st in first sc, fasten off.

HOT PAD SIDE (make 2)

Rnd 1: Ch 4, sl st in first ch to form ring, beg shell in ring, ch 1, (shell in ring, ch 1) 2 times, join with sl st in top of ch-3 (3 shells).

Rnd 2: Sl st in next st, sl st in next ch sp, beg shell in same sp, shell in ch sp of each shell around, join (6 shells).

Rnd 3: Sl st in next st, sl st in next ch sp, beg shell in same sp, skip next 2 sts, V-st in next sp between shells, skip next 2 sts, (shell in next shell, skip next 2 sts, V-st in next sp between shells, skip next 2 sts) around, join (6 shells, 6 V-sts).

Rnd 4: Sl st in next st, sl st in next ch sp, beg shell in same sp, shell in ch sp of each V-st and in each

Continued on page 124

Trinket Box

DESIGNED BY SUSIE SPIER MAXFIELD & SANDRA MILLER MAXFIELD

SIZE
Fits 5½" half-doll.

MATERIALS
Worsted-weight yarn — 2 oz. each pink and white; 25" red ¼" satin ribbon; red ⅜" ribbon rosebud with leaves; craft glue or hot glue gun; 3-pound plastic margarine container with lid (we used Shedd's Spread Country Crock®); polyester fiberfill; F crochet hook or size needed to obtain gauge.

GAUGE
9 sts = 2"; 4 dc rows = 1¾".

SKILL LEVEL
★★ Average

DRESS
Bodice
Row 1: Starting at **waist**, with pink, ch 13, sc in 2nd ch from hook, sc in each ch across, turn (12 sc).

Row 2: Ch 1, sc in each of first 2 sts, 2 sc in next st, sc in each of next 3 sts, (2 sc in next st, sc in each of next 2 sts) 2 times, turn (15).

Row 3: Ch 1, sc in each of first 2 sts, 2 sc in next st, sc in next st, 2 sc in next st, sc in next 5 sts, 2 sc in next st, sc in next st, 2 sc in next st, sc in each of last 2 sts, turn (19).

Rows 4-5: Ch 1, sc in each st across, turn.

Row 6: Ch 1, sc in first 6 sts, hdc in next st, 5 dc in next st, skip next st, sc in next st, skip next st, 5 dc in next st, hdc in next st, sc in last 6 sts, turn (25 sts).

Row 7: Ch 1, sc in first 4 sts; for **armhole**, ch 6, skip next 2 sts; sc next 2 sts tog, sc in each of next 2 sts, sc next 2 sts tog, sc in next st, sc next 2 sts tog, sc in each of next 2 sts, sc next 2 sts tog; for **armhole**, ch 6, skip next 2 sts; sc in last 4 sts, fasten off.

Sleeves
Rnd 1: Working around armhole, join pink with sc in first skipped st at underarm, sc in same st, 2 sc in each st and in each ch around, join with sl st in first sc (16 sc).

Rnds 2-4: Working in **back lps** only, ch 1, sc in each st around, join.

Rnd 5: Working in **back lps** only, ch 1, sc in first st, skip next st, (sc in next st, skip next st) around, join (8).

Rnd 6: Ch 1, 2 sc in each st around, join (16).

Rnd 7: Ch 1, sc in first st, 2 sc in next st, (sc in next st, 2 sc in next st) around, join, fasten off (24).

Rnd 8: Working this rnd in **back lps** only, join white with sc in any st, ch 4, sl st in 3rd ch from hook, ch 1, (sc in next st, ch 4, sl st in 3rd ch from hook, ch 1) around, join with sl st in first sc, fasten off.

Repeat on other armhole.

Skirt
Row 1: Working in starting ch on opposite side of row 1 on Bodice, with right side facing you, join pink with sc in first ch, sc in same ch, 2 sc in each ch across, turn (24 sc).

Row 2: Working in **front lps**, ch 3, dc in same st, dc in next st, (2 dc in next st, dc in next st) across, turn (36 dc).

NOTE: Work all remaining rnds of Skirt in **back lps** only.

Rnd 3: Working in rnds, ch 3, dc in same st, dc in each of next 2 sts, (2 dc in next st, dc in each of next 2 sts) around, join with sl st in top of ch-3 (48).

Rnd 4: Ch 3, dc in same st, dc in each of next 3 sts, (2 dc in next st, dc in each of next 3 sts) around, join (60).

Rnd 5: Ch 3, dc in same st, dc in next 4 sts, (2 dc in next st, dc in next 4 sts) around, join (72).

Rnd 6: Ch 3, dc in same st, dc in next 5 sts, (2 dc in next st, dc in next 5 sts) around, join (84).

Rnd 7: Ch 3, dc in same st, dc in next 6 sts, (2 dc in next st, dc in next 6 sts) around, join (96).

Rnd 8: Ch 3, dc in same st, dc in next 7 sts, (2 dc in next st, dc in next 7 sts) around, join (108).

Rnd 9: Ch 3, dc in next 7 sts, (2 dc in next st, dc in next 9 sts) around, join (118).

Rnds 10-15: Ch 3, dc in each st around, join. At end of last rnd, fasten off.

Skirt Trim
Row 1: Working in remaining **front lps** of rnd 1 on Skirt, join white with sc in first st, (ch 4, sl st in 3rd ch from hook, ch 1, sc in next st) across, fasten off.

Row 2: Working on row 2 of Skirt, repeat row 1.

Continued on page 125

Lace-Up Afghan

DESIGNED BY DOT DRAKE

SIZE
42" x 58½".

MATERIALS
Worsted-weight yarn — 16 oz. each dk. rose and off-white, 9 oz. rose/teal/off-white variegated, 8 oz. lt. rose; I crochet hook or size needed to obtain gauge.

GAUGE
3 sc sts = 1"; 3 sc rows = 1". Each Strip is 3½" wide with loops pulled straight.

SKILL LEVEL
★★ Average

STRIP A (make 4 dk. rose and 3 lt. rose)
Row 1: (Ch 11, sc in 11th ch from hook) 96 times, **do not** turn (96 loops).

Row 2: Working along straight edge of loops, ch 1, (sc around side of last sc made, sc in base of next loop) across, **turn** (192 sc).

Row 3: Ch 1, skip first 2 sts, *dc in next st, ch 3, 3 dc over side of dc just made, skip next 2 sts; repeat from * across to last st, dc in last st, turn (63 ch-3 sps, 1 ch-1 sp).

Row 4: Ch 5, sc in top of next ch-3, (ch 2, sc in top of next ch-3) across, dc in last ch-1 sp, turn (63 sc, 62 ch-2 sps, 1 dc, 1 ch-5 sp).

Row 5: Ch 1, sc in each st and in each ch across to last ch-5 sp, sc in each of next 3 chs on last ch-5, turn (191 sc).

Row 6: Ch 10, (sc in each of next 2 sts, ch 10) across, sl st back into last st, fasten off (96 loops).

STRIP B (make 6)
Rows 1-2: With off-white, repeat same rows of Strip A. At end of last row, fasten off.

Row 3: Join variegated with sc in first st, ch 1, dc in same st, *skip next 2 sts, (sc, ch 1, 2 dc) in next st; repeat from * across to last 2 sts, skip next st, (sc, ch 1, dc) in last st, turn (65 sc).

Row 4: Ch 2, dc in same st, (sc, ch 1, 2 dc) in each sc across to last sc, sc in last sc, turn, fasten off (127 dc, 64 sc, 1 ch-2 sp).

Row 5: Join off-white with sc in first sc, sc in each dc and in each sc across to last ch-2 sp, sc in next ch of last ch-2, turn (192 sc).

Row 6: Ch 10, (sc in each of next 2 sts, ch 10) across, sl st back into last st, fasten off (96 loops).

To **join Strips,** with right sides facing you, lay first two Strips (see Strip Assembly Diagram) side by side matching long edges. Draw first loop on first Strip from front to back through first loop on

Continued on page 124

STRIP ASSEMBLY DIAGRAM

Strip A | Strip B | Strip A | Strip B | Strip A | Strip B | Strip A | Strip B | Strip A | Strip B | Strip A | Strip B | Strip A

Lace-Up Afghan

Continued from page 122

other Strip, (draw next loop on second Strip from front to back through same loop on first Strip, draw next loop on first Strip from front to back through same loop on other Strip) across. With separate piece of matching yarn, secure last loop to back side of Strip.

Join all Strips in same manner according to Assembly Diagram.

For each **outer edge,** pull 2nd loop from back to front through first loop, (pull next loop through last loop) across. Secure last loop on wrong side.❖

Green Kitchen Set

Continued from page 118

shell around, join (12 shells).

Rnd 5: Repeat rnd 3 of Coaster.

With tapestry needle and green yarn, working in **back lps** only, sew Hot Pad Sides together.

DISH TOWEL TOPPER

Rnd 1: Ch 4, sl st in first ch to form ring, ch 5, shell in ring, ch 2, dc in ring, ch 2, shell in ring, ch 2, join with sl st in 3rd ch of ch-5 (4 ch-2 sps, 2 shells, 2 dc).

Rnd 2: Ch 4, shell in next ch-2 sp, skip next 2 sts, shell in ch sp of next shell, skip next 2 sts, shell in next ch-2 sp, ch 1, dc in next st, ch 1, shell in next ch-2 sp, skip next 2 sts, shell in ch sp of next shell, skip next 2 sts, shell in last ch-2 sp, ch 1, join with sl st in 3rd ch of ch-4 (6 shells, 2 dc).

Rnd 3: Ch 4, shell in each of next 3 shells, ch 1, skip next 2 sts, skip next ch sp, dc in next st, ch 1, skip next ch sp and next 2 sts, shell in each of next 3 shells, ch 1, skip next 2 sts and last ch sp, join (6 shells, 2 dc).

Rnd 4: Ch 4, *(shell in next shell, skip next 2 sts, shell in next sp between shells, skip next 2 sts) 2 times, shell in next shell, ch 1, skip next 2 sts and next ch sp*, dc in next st, ch 1, skip next ch sp and next 2 sts; repeat between **, join (10 shells, 2 dc).

Rnds 5-6: Ch 4, shell in next 5 shells, ch 1, skip next 2 sts and next ch sp, dc in next st, ch 1, shell in next 5 shells, ch 1, skip next 2 sts and last ch sp, join.

Rnd 7: Ch 1, sc in first st, (sc in next ch, sc in each of next 2 sts, sc in next ch sp, skip next 4 sts, shell in each of next 3 shells, skip next 4 sts, sc in next

ch sp, sc in each of next 2 sts, sc in next ch), sc in next st; repeat between ( ), join with sl st in first sc (18 sc, 6 shells).

Rnd 7: Ch 1, sc in first 7 sts, sc in next ch sp, skip next 4 sts, picot shell in next shell, skip next 4 sts, sc in next ch sp, sc in next 13 sts, sc in next ch sp, skip next 4 sts, picot shell in next shell, skip next 4 sts, sc in next ch sp, sc in last 6 sts, join, fasten off.

Matching picots on last rnd, flatten Topper with single dc sts at each side.

Handle

Row 1: Working on opposite side of rnd 1 on Topper, skipping shells, join with sl st around post of first dc, ch 3, 2 dc around same post, 3 dc around post of last dc, turn (6 dc).

Row 2: Ch 3, skip next 2 sts, shell in next sp between sts, skip next 2 sts, dc in last st, turn (2 dc, 1 shell).

Rows 3-6: Ch 3, shell in ch sp of next shell, dc in last st, turn.

Row 7: Ch 3, picot shell in next shell, dc in last st, fasten off.

Finishing

1: Fold over one end of towel 8"; with sewing needle and thread, gather folded edge to width of opening on flattened Topper.

2: With sewing needle and thread, sew Topper over gathered end of towel.

3: Sew button to rnd 1 of Topper, using space at bottom of picot shell on Handle as buttonhole.❖

Yuletide Hot Pads

Continued from page 115

Rows 2-4: Ch 1, sc in each st across, turn.

Rows 5-28: Ch 1, sc in each st across changing colors according to Package Hot Pad Graph on page 115, turn.

Rows 29-30: Ch 1, sc in each st across, turn. At end of last row, fasten off.

Back

With red, work same as Stocking Hot Pad Back on page 115.

Edging

Work same as Stocking Hot Pad Edging.❖

Blue Kitchen Set

Continued from page 117

Rnd 4: Repeat rnd 2.

Rnd 5: Repeat rnd 3, **do not** turn.

Rnd 6: Skipping ch-2 sps, (ch 3, hdc) in first cl, skip next cl, *(hdc, ch 1, hdc) in next cl, skip next cl; repeat from * around, join with sl st in 2nd ch of ch-3 (14 hdc).

Rnd 7: Repeat rnd 3 (7 cls).

Rnd 8: Ch 2, (2 hdc in next ch sp, skip next st) around, join with sl st in top of ch-2 (15 hdc).

Row 9: For **hanger,** ch 2, fold rnd 8 in half with ch-2 at edge; matching sts and working through both thicknesses, hdc in next 7 sts, turn (8 hdc).

Rows 10-18: Working in rows, ch 2, hdc in each st across, turn.

Row 19: Ch 1, sc in first st, skip next 2 sts, 7 tr in next st, skip next 2 sts, sc in last st, fasten off.

Finishing

1: Cut dish towel in half. Flatten rnd 1 of Topper. With sewing needle and thread, gather cut end of dish towel to fit inside bottom of Topper, secure. Insert ½" of gathered end into bottom of Topper, sew together.

2: Sew button to rnd 9 of Topper, using space at bottom of 7-tr group on row 19 as buttonhole.❖

Trinket Box

Continued from page 121

Rnd 3: Working in remaining **front lps** of rnd 3 on Skirt, join white with sc in first st, ch 4, sl st in 3rd ch from hook, ch 1, (sc in next st, ch 4, sl st in 3rd ch from hook, ch 1) around, join with sl st in first sc, fasten off.

Rnds 4-14: Working on rnds 4-14 of Skirt, repeat rnd 3.

Finishing

1: Place Dress on doll; sew Bodice back opening closed.

2: Cut two 6" pieces pink; tie one in bow around each Sleeve between rnds 5 and 6. Trim ends to ½".

3: Cut 19" piece ribbon; tie into a bow around waist leaving long ends for streamers.

4: For **hair arrangement,** section hair across top front of head leaving back section down; secure top section loosely with rubber band into a ponytail. Tie remaining 6" piece ribbon into a bow around ponytail.

5: Glue ribbon rose to center front of row 7 on Bodice.

6: Center margarine container lid under doll body; stuffing lightly between doll body and dress as you work, glue Dress to outer edge of lid. Snap lid on bowl.❖

Holiday Happiness

Increase the joy and splendor of the
season when you fill your home with the
delights of handmade treasures.
Each item you fashion from hook and
yarn will carry a touch of creative wonder
into your Christmas celebration.

Holiday Angel

DESIGNED BY ESTELLA WHITFORD

SIZE
9" tall.

MATERIALS
Worsted-weight yarn — 4 oz. off-white, 2 oz. variegated blue, ½ oz. blue, small amount each dk. brown and black; size 10 bedspread cotton — small amount gold; black embroidery floss; 10" blue ¼" satin ribbon; 18" metallic gold 2" wired ribbon; 6" gold metallic wired braid; 12" off-white 1" lace; 18" off-white 2" lace; 1" x 1¼" gold heart charm; brush-on powder blush; 3½" cardboard square; craft glue or hot glue gun; polyester fiberfill; tapestry needle; G crochet hook or size needed to obtain gauge.

GAUGE
4 sc sts = 1"; 4 sc rows = 1".

SKILL LEVEL
★★ Average

HEAD & BODY
NOTE: Do not join rnds unless otherwise stated. Mark first st of each rnd.

Rnd 1: Starting at head, with off-white, ch 2, 6 sc in 2nd ch from hook (6 sc).

Rnd 2: 2 sc in each st around (12).

Rnd 3: (Sc in next st, 2 sc in next st) around (18).

Rnd 4: (Sc in each of next 2 sts, 2 sc in next st) around (24).

Rnds 5-7: Sc in each st around.

Rnd 8: (Sc in each of next 2 sts, sc next 2 sts tog) around (18).

Rnd 9: (Sc next 2 sts tog) around (9).

Rnd 10: 2 sc in each st around (18).

Rnd 11: (Sc in each of next 2 sts, 2 sc in next st) around (24).

Rnds 12-17: Sc in each st around.

Rnd 18: (Sc in each of next 2 sts, sc next 2 sts tog) around (18). Stuff.

Rnd 19: (Sc next 2 sts tog) around (9).

Rnd 20: Sc in next st, (sc next 2 sts tog) around, join with sl st in first sc, fasten off leaving 8" for sewing (5).

ARM (make 2)
Rnd 1: Starting at hand, with off-white, ch 2, 6 sc in 2nd ch from hook (6 sc).

Rnd 2: (Sc in next st, 2 sc in next st) around (9).

Rnds 3-10: Sc in each st around. At end of last rnd, join with sl st in first sc, fasten off leaving 10" for sewing. **Do not** stuff Arms.

Flatten last rnd and sew Arms over rnds 11-13 on each side of Body.

LEG (make 2)
Rnd 1: Starting at foot, with off-white, ch 2, 6 sc in 2nd ch from hook (6 sc).

Rnd 2: (Sc in next st, 2 sc in next st) around (9).

Rnds 3-16: Sc in each st around. At end of last rnd, join with sl st in first sc, fasten off leaving 10" for sewing. Stuff.

Sew Legs to bottom of Body.

For **eyes,** with tapestry needle and black yarn, embroider 2 French Knots (see page 159) ⅜" apart over rnds 4 and 5.

For **eyebrows,** using 6 strands black floss, embroider 2 Straight Stitches (see page 159) above eyes as shown in photo.

For **mouth,** using 6 strands black floss, embroider one Fly Stitch (see page 159) below eyes as shown. Brush blush on cheeks.

DRESS
Row 1: Starting at neckline, with variegated blue, ch 23, sc in 2nd ch from hook, sc in each ch across, turn (22 sc).

Row 2: Ch 1, sc in each st across, turn.

Row 3: Ch 1, sc in first 4 sts; for **armhole,** ch 5, skip next 3 sts; sc in next 8 sts; for **armhole,** ch 5, skip next 3 sts; sc in last 4 sts, turn (16 sc, 10 chs).

Row 4: Ch 1, sc in each st and in each ch across, turn (26 sc).

Row 5: Ch 1, sc in each of first 2 sts, (2 sc in next st, sc in each of next 2 sts) across, turn (34).

Row 6: Ch 3, 2 dc in next st, (dc in next st, 2 dc in next st) across, turn (51 dc).

Rows 7-11: Ch 3, dc in each st across, turn. At end of last row, fasten off.

Sew 1" lace across row 1 and 2" lace across row 11. Tie ¼" ribbon into bow, sew or glue to center front at neckline. Place Dress on Angel, sew ends of rows together in back.

HAIR

For **each section (make 8)**, wrap dk. brown around cardboard 10 times. Tie separate strand dk. brown around all loops at one edge of cardboard. Cut loops at opposite edge.

Glue center knot of each section to Head, beginning above eyebrows and ending at back of Head. Tie 4" piece of blue in small bow around all strands of hair on one side of Head, forming ponytail. Trim ends. Repeat on opposite side of Head.

For **bangs**, cut 9 pieces dk. brown each 1½" long. Tie separate piece dk. brown in knot around center of all strands held together. Glue knot in front of front hair section. Fray ends and trim if necessary.

WING (make 2)

Row 1: With off-white, ch 4, sl st in first ch to form ring, ch 3, 2 dc in ring, ch 2, (3 dc in ring, ch 2) 3 times, join with sl st in top of ch-3, fasten off (12 dc, 4 ch sps).

Rnd 2: Join blue with sl st in any ch sp, ch 3, (2 dc, ch 2, 3 dc) in same sp, ch 1, *(3 dc, ch 2, 3 dc) in next ch sp, ch 1; repeat from * around, join.

Rnd 3: Sl st in each of next 2 sts, sl st in next ch-2 sp, ch 3, (2 dc, ch 2, 3 dc) in same sp, 3 dc in next ch-1 sp, *(3 dc, ch 2, 3 dc) in next ch-2 sp, 3 dc in next ch-1 sp; repeat from * around, join, fasten off (36 dc, 4 ch sps).

Rnd 4: Join off-white with sc in any corner ch sp, *[ch 3, skip next st, (sc in next st, ch 3, skip next st) across to next corner ch sp], sc in next ch sp; repeat from * 2 more times; repeat between [ ], join with sl st in first sc, fasten off.

Fold each Wing in half diagonally; sew fold together from center to bottom. Tack Wings to row 1 on center back of Dress.

For **hanger,** tie desired length of yarn to back of Head above Wings.

Tie heart charm tightly to center of wired ribbon with small piece of gold crochet cotton. With tapestry needle and gold crochet cotton, tack ribbon to rnd 3 of each hand 3½" from ends of ribbon. Shape ribbon as desired; cut upside down 'V' shape in each end.❖

Santa's Suit

DESIGNED BY SANDRA MILLER MAXFIELD

SIZE
Fits 14½" Santa Claus doll.

MATERIALS
Woven acrylic sport yarn — 2½ oz. each red, blue and white; white ¾" pom-pom; 2 gold ½" ribbon roses; 6 small snaps; craft glue or hot glue gun; matching sewing thread and needle; F crochet hook or size needed to obtain gauge.

GAUGE
9 sts = 2"; 3 hdc rows = 1".

SKILL LEVEL
★★ Average

HAT
Rnd 1: With red, ch 3, sl st in first ch to form ring, ch 1, 5 sc in ring, join with sl st in first sc (5 sc).

Rnd 2: Ch 2, hdc in same st, 2 hdc in each st around, join with sl st in top of ch-2 (10 hdc).

NOTE: Ch-2 is used and counted as first hdc.

Rnds 3-5: Ch 2, hdc in each st around, join.

Rnd 6: Ch 2, hdc in same st, hdc in next st, (2 hdc in next st, hdc in next st) around, join (15).

Rnds 7-11: Ch 2, hdc in each st around, join.

Rnd 12: Ch 2, hdc in same st, hdc in each of next 2 sts, (2 hdc in next st, hdc in each of next 2 sts) around, join (20).

Rnds 13-14: Ch 2, hdc in each st around, join.

Rnd 15: Ch 2, hdc in each of next 2 sts, 2 hdc in next st, (hdc in each of next 3 sts, 2 hdc in next st) around, join (25).

Rnd 16: Ch 2, hdc in each of next 2 sts, 2 hdc in next st, (hdc in each of next 3 sts, 2 hdc in next st) around to last st, hdc in last st, join (31).

Rnd 17: Ch 2, hdc in next 3 sts, 2 hdc in next st, (hdc in next 4 sts, 2 hdc in next st) around, to last st, hdc in last st, join (37).

Rnd 18: Ch 2, hdc in next 4 sts, 2 hdc in next st, (hdc in next 5 sts, 2 hdc in next st) around to last st, hdc in last st, join (43).

Rnds 19-26: Ch 2, hdc in same st, hdc in each st around, join. At end of last rnd (51), **turn,** fasten off.

Rnd 27: For **Hat brim,** working in **front lps,** join white with sc in first st, sc in same st, sc in each st around, join with sl st in first sc (52 sc).

Rnds 28-34: Ch 2, hdc in same st, hdc in each st around, join with sl st in top of ch-2. At end of last rnd (58), fasten off.

With sewing thread and needle, sew white pom-pom to tip of hat.

PANTS
Row 1: Starting at **waist,** with blue, ch 61, 2 hdc in 3rd ch from hook, hdc in each of next 3 sts, (2 hdc in next st, hdc in each of next 3 sts) across to last 3 sts, hdc in each of last 3 sts, turn (73 hdc).

Rows 2-7: Ch 2, hdc in each st across, turn.

Rnd 8: Working in rnds, overlap first 3 sts over last 3 sts; working through both thicknesses across overlap, sl st in first st, ch 2, hdc in each st around, join with sl st in top of ch-2, **turn** (70).

Rnds 9-11: Ch 2, hdc in each st around, join.

Rnd 12: For **first leg,** ch 5, skip next 34 sts, sl st in next st, ch 2, hdc in each st around to first ch-5, hdc in next 5 chs, join (40).

Rnds 13-19: Ch 2, hdc in each st around, join.

Rnd 20: Ch 1, hdc first 2 sts tog, (hdc next 2 sts tog) around, join with sl st in first hdc (20).

Rnd 21: Ch 1, sc in each st around, join with sl st in first sc, fasten off (20 sc).

Rnd 22: Join white with sc in first st, sc in next st, (sc next 2 sts tog, sc in next st) around, join (14).

Rnds 23-24: Ch 1, sc in each st around, join. At end of last rnd, fasten off.

Rnd 12: For **second leg,** join blue with sl st in first skipped st on rnd 11, ch 2, hdc in next 33 sts, hdc in next worked st where ch-5 is joined; working on opposite side of ch-5, hdc in next 5 chs, join (40).

Rnds 13-19: Ch 2, hdc in each st around, join.

Rnds 20-24: Repeat same rnds of first leg.

Waistband
Row 1: Working in starting ch on opposite side of row 1, join blue with sc in first ch, sc in each ch acorss, turn (60 sc).

Rows 2-4: Ch 1, sc in each st across, turn. At end of last row, fasten off.

With sewing thread and needle, sew snap to ends of Waistband.

VEST
Row 1: With red, ch 61, hdc in 3rd ch from hook, hdc in each ch across, turn (60 hdc).

Continued on page 150

Advent Tree

DESIGNED BY KATHLEEN STUART

SIZE

22½" x 26".

MATERIALS

Worsted-weight yarn — 4 oz. off-white; worsted-weight glitter yarn — 2 oz. green, 1 oz. each red and green/red/white variegated; tapestry needle; G crochet hook or size needed to obtain gauge.

GAUGE

4 sc sts = 1"; 4 sc rows = 1".

SKILL LEVEL

★★ Average

TREE

Row 1: Starting at **top,** with off-white, ch 2, 2 sc in 2nd ch from hook, turn (2 sc).

Row 2: Ch 1, 2 sc in first st, sc in last st, turn (3).

Rows 3-91: Ch 1, 2 sc in first st, sc in each st across, turn. At end of last row (92 sc), fasten off.

Row 92: For **trunk,** skip first 33 sts, join off-white with sc in next st, sc in next 25 sts leaving remaining sts unworked, turn (26 sc).

Rows 93-117: Ch 1, sc in each st across, turn. At end of last row, fasten off.

For **edging,** working around outer edge, join green with sl st in starting ch on opposite side of row 1 at top, ch 1; working from left to right, **reverse sc** (see page 159) in end of each row and in each st around with 2 reverse sc in each outside corner; for **hanging loop,** (sl st, ch 10, sl

st) in same st as first sl st, join with sl st in first st, fasten off.

HEART (make 9 green, 8 variegated and 8 red)

Rnd 1: Ch 3, sl st in first ch to form ring, ch 1, 11 sc in ring, join with sl st in first sc (11 sc).

Rnd 2: Ch 3, (dc, tr) in same st, 3 tr in next st, dc in next st, hdc in next st, 2 sc in next st, sc in next st, 2 sc in next st, hdc in next st, dc in next st, 3 tr in next st, (tr, dc, ch 3, sl st) in last st, do not join (19 sts, 2 ch-3).

Rnd 3: Sc in each of next 3 chs, 2 hdc in each of next 4 sts, hdc in next 4 sts, (hdc, dc) in next st, dc in next st, (dc, hdc) in next st, hdc in next 4 sts, 2 hdc in each of last 4 sts, sc in each of last 3 chs, join with sl st in first sc, fasten off.

Leaving top edge of each Heart open to form pocket, sew to Tree as shown in photo.

STAR

Rnd 1: With red, ch 2, 5 sc in 2nd ch from hook, join with sl st in first sc (5 sc).

Rnd 2: Ch 3, dc in same st, 2 dc in each st around, join with sl st in top of ch-3 (10 dc).

Rnd 3: Ch 1, sc in first st, (hdc, dc, tr, dc, hdc) in next st, *sc in next st, (hdc, dc, tr, dc, hdc) in next st; repeat from * around, join with sl st in first sc (30 sts).

Rnd 4: Sl st in next 2 sts, (sc, dc, sc) in next st, *sl st in next 5 sts, (sc, dc, sc) in next st; repeat from * around to last 2 sts, sl st in last 2 sts, join with sl st in joining sl st on last rnd, fasten off.

Sew Star to top of Tree. ❧

Littlest Snowman

DESIGNED BY MICHELE WILCOX

SIZE
7½" tall.

MATERIALS
Sport yarn — 3 oz. winter white; worsted-weight yarn — 1 oz. each gold and blue/green/mauve variegated; small amount white size 10 crochet or pearl cotton thread; 2 purple ⅜" round 4-hole buttons; ½" red heart button; 7 black 4-mm beads; 5½" twig; small amount tan raffia straw; polyester fiberfill; large-eye embroidery needle; tapestry needle; F crochet hook or size needed to obtain gauge.

GAUGE
With **sport yarn,** 9 sc sts = 2"; 5 sc rnds = 1".

SKILL LEVEL
★ Easy

SPECIAL NOTE
Do not join rnds unless otherwise stated. Mark first st of each rnd.

SNOWMAN
Head & Body
Rnd 1: Starting at Head, with winter white, ch 2, 6 sc in 2nd ch from hook (6 sc).

Rnd 2: 2 sc in each st around (12).

Rnd 3: (Sc in next st, 2 sc in next st) around (18).

Rnd 4: (Sc in each of next 2 sts, 2 sc in next st) around (24).

Rnd 5: (Sc in each of next 3 sts, 2 sc in next st) around (30).

Rnds 6-13: Sc in each st around.

Rnd 14: (Sc next 2 sts tog) around (15).

Rnd 15: Sc in each st around.

Rnd 16: 2 sc in each st around (30). Stuff. Continue stuffing as you work.

Rnd 17: Sc in each st around.

Rnd 18: (Sc in next 4 sts, 2 sc in next st) around (36).

Rnds 19-26: Sc in each st around.

Rnd 27: (Sc in next st, sc next 2 sts tog) around (24).

Rnd 28: Sc in each st around.

Rnd 29: 2 sc in each st around (48).

Rnds 30-40: Sc in each st around.

Rnd 41: Working in **back lps** only, (sc in next 6 sts, sc next 2 sts tog) around (42).

Rnd 42: (Sc in next 5 sc, sc next 2 sts tog) around (36).

Rnd 43: (Sc in next st, sc next 2 sts tog) around (24).

Rnd 44: (Sc in each of next 2 sts, sc next 2 sts tog) around (18).

Rnd 45: (Sc in next st, sc next 2 sts tog) around (12).

Rnd 46: (Sc next 2 sts tog) around, join with sl st in first sc, fasten off leaving long end for sewing (6). Weave long end through sts of last rnd, pull tightly to gather, secure.

Arm (make 2)
Rnd 1: With winter white, ch 2, 6 sc in 2nd ch from hook (6 sc).

Rnd 2: 2 sc in each st around (12).

Rnds 3-12: Sc in each st around. Stuff lightly.

Rnd 13: (Sc next 2 sts tog) around, join with sl st in first sc, fasten off leaving long end for sewing.

Weave long end through sts of last rnd, pull tightly to gather, secure. Sew rnd 13 of Arm over rnds 16-19 on each side of Body. Bending Arms slightly, sew rnd 1 of Arm over rnds 24-26 on Body.

SCARF
Row 1: With variegated, ch 74, sc in 2nd ch from hook. (ch 1, skip next ch, sc in next ch) across, turn (37 sc, 36 ch-1 sps).

Rows 2-5: Ch 1, sc in first st, (ch 1, skip next ch sp, sc in next st) across, turn. At end of last row, fasten off.

HAT
Rnd 1: With gold, ch 4, sl st in first ch to form ring, ch 3, 11 dc in ring, join with sl st in top of ch-3 (12 dc).

Rnd 2: Ch 3, dc in same st, 2 dc in each st around, join (24).

Rnd 3: Ch 3, 2 dc in next st, (dc in next st, 2 dc in next st) around, join (36).

Rnd 4: Ch 3, dc in each st around, join.

Rnd 5: Ch 1, sc in each st around, join with sl st in first sc (36 sc).

Rnd 6: For **brim,** working in **front lps,** ch 2, hdc in next st, 2 hdc in next st, (hdc in each of next 2 sts, 2 hdc in next st) around, join with sl st in top of ch-2 (48 hdc).

Rnd 7: Ch 2, hdc in each st around, join, fasten off.

FINISHING

1: For **eyes,** with embroidery needle and white crochet cotton, forming X in center of button, sew purple buttons to rnd 8 of Head spaced 1⅜" apart. For **nose,** sew one black bead to rnd 9 centered between eyes; for **mouth,** sew 6 black beads to rnds 11 and 12 as shown in photo. Sew heart button to center front of rnd 21.

2: For **broom,** cut about 30 pieces of raffia straw about 4" long. Holding raffia pieces together around one end of twig, covering about 2", wrap another strand of raffia around twig covering about ½" of strands as shown in photo; secure ends under wraps and trim. Insert twig between Body and right Arm.

3: Rolling brim up, place Hat on Head; tie Scarf around neck.♥

Yuletide Poinsettias

DESIGNED BY ROBERTA MAIER

SIZE
53" x 65" not including Fringe.

MATERIALS
Worsted-weight yarn — 67 oz. white, 12 oz. red and 6 oz. gold; tapestry needle; G afghan and crochet hooks or size needed to obtain gauge.

GAUGE
G crochet hook, 4 sc sts = 1"; 4 sc rows = 1".
G afghan hook, 4 afghan sts = 1";
4 afghan st rows = 1".

SKILL LEVEL
★★ Average

PANEL (make 7)
Row 1: Using afghan hook, with white, ch 27, insert hook in 2nd ch from hook, yo, draw up ¼" lp, (insert hook in next ch, yo, draw up ¼" lp) across leaving all loops on hook, **do not** turn; to **work lps off hook,** yo, draw through one lp on hook (see illustration A, page 159), (yo, draw through 2 lps on hook) across (see illustration B) leaving one lp at end of row (27 vertical bars).

Row 2: Skip first vertical bar; for **afghan stitch** (afghan st), insert hook under next vertical bar (see illustration C), yo, draw up ¼" lp; afghan st in each vertical bar across to last vertical bar; for **last st,** insert hook under last bar and st directly behind it (see illustration D), yo, draw up ¼" lp; work lps off hook (27 afghan sts).

Rows 3-243: Repeat row 2. At end of last row, fasten off.

With tapestry needle, using Cross-Stitch (see page 159) and colors indicated on graph, embroider first poinsettia centered over Panel beginning on row 6. Skipping 10 rows between each poinsettia, repeat graph 8 more times, having 5 rows left at top of Panel after last poinsettia.

Edging
Row 1: With right side facing you, working in front vertical bar at ends of rows (see illustration) across one long edge, using G crochet hook, join white with sc in first vertical bar of first row, sc in first vertical bar of each row across, turn.

Row 2: Ch 1; working in back vertical bars at end of rows on Panel and in both lps of sc on row 1 at same time, sc in each st across, turn, fasten off.

Repeat Edging on opposite side of Panel.

ASSEMBLY
To **join Panels,** hold 2 Panels wrong sides together, matching sts of Edging and making sure row 1 of Panels are on same end; working through both

Continued on page 154

POINSETTIA GRAPH
Each square on graph equals one Cross-Stitch worked over one Afghan Stitch. Each vertical line on graph equals one vertical bar.

First Vertical Bar ⟶

FRONT AND BACK BARS ILLUSTRATION

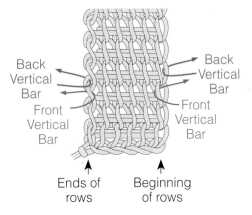

Back Vertical Bar
Front Vertical Bar
Back Vertical Bar
Front Vertical Bar

Ends of rows
Beginning of rows

Joy to the World

DESIGNED BY WILMA BUCKLES

SIZE
30½" x 33½".

MATERIALS
Size 10 bedspread cotton — 2,900 yds. white;
No. 7 steel crochet hook or size
needed to obtain gauge.

GAUGE
7 mesh (see Notes below) = 2"; 7 tr rows = 2".

SKILL LEVEL
★★ Average

WALL HANGING
NOTES: For **mesh,** ch 2, skip next 2 chs or sts, tr in next ch or st.

For **beginning mesh (beg mesh),** ch 6, skip next 2 chs, tr in next st.

For **block,** tr in each of next 3 chs or sts.

Graph is split into quarters. Center gray areas on graphs are to be worked only once. Front of row 1 will be wrong side of work.

Row 1: Ch 321, tr in 9th ch from hook (first mesh made), mesh across, turn (105 mesh).

Row 2: Beg mesh, mesh across, turn.

Row 3: Beginning at right-hand edge on row 3 of Graph A on page 141, beg mesh, mesh, block 51 times; continuing across on Graph B (see page 140, **do not** repeat gray overlap area), block 50 times, mesh 2 times, turn (101 blocks, 4 mesh).

Row 4: Beginning at left-hand edge on row 4 of Graph B, beg mesh, mesh, block, mesh 49 times; continuing on Graph A, mesh 50 times, block, mesh 2 times, turn.

Rows 5-58: Work according to Graphs A and B.

Rows 59-115: Using Graphs C and D on pages 142 and 143, work according to graphs. At end of last row, **do not** turn.

NOTE: For **V-st,** (dc, ch 2, dc) in next st or sp.

Rnd 106: Working around entire outer edge, ch 5, dc in same st, V-st in top of st on end of each row across to next corner, V-st 2 times in next corner; working in starting ch on opposite side of row 1, V-st in base of each tr across to next corner, V-st 2 times in next corner, V-st in top of st on end of each row across to next corner, V-st 2 times in next corner, V-st in each tr across to next corner, V-st in same st as first V-st, ch 2, join with sl st in 3rd ch of ch-5, fasten off.❖

Joy to the World

Instructions on page 139

GRAPH B

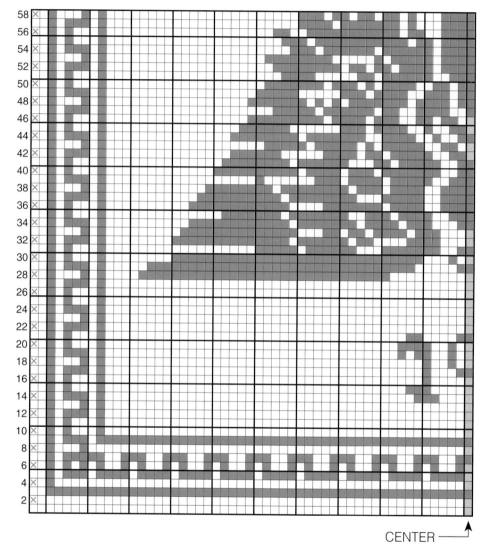

CENTER ———

STITCH KEY
□ = Mesh
■ = Block
⊠ = Beg Block

GRAPH A

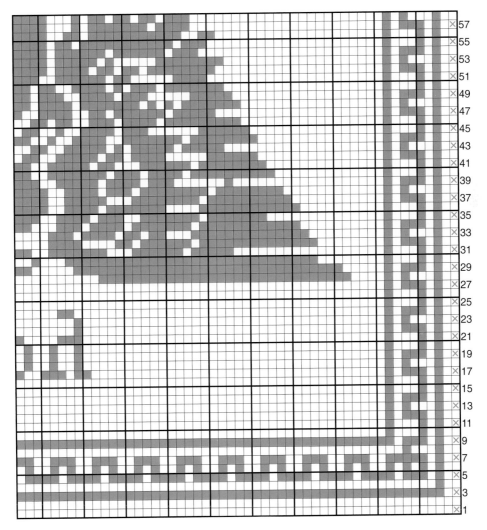

Joy to the World

Instructions on page 139

GRAPH D

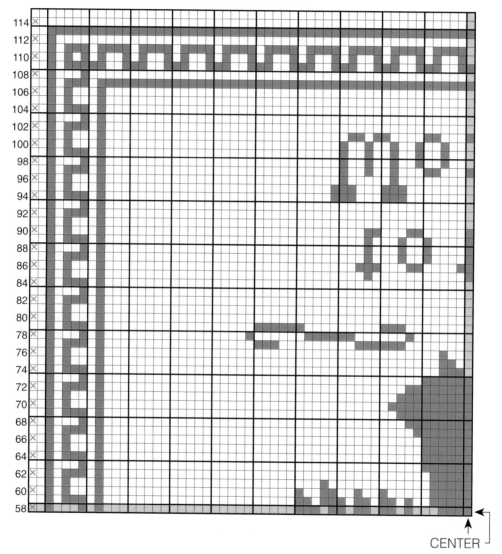

STITCH KEY
☐ = Mesh
■ = Block
⊠ = Beg Block

GRAPH C

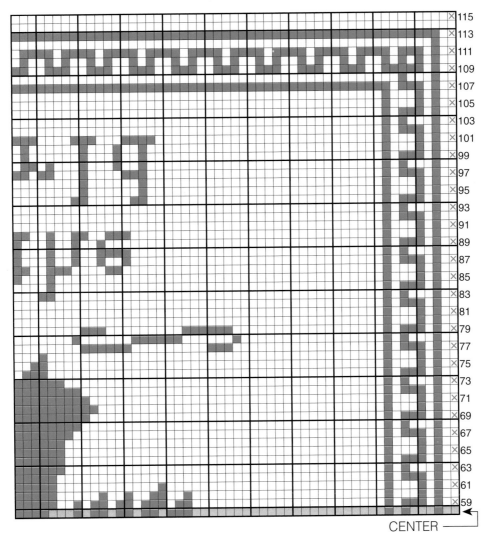

CENTER

Santa Set

DESIGNED BY SANDRA MILLER MAXFIELD

SIZES
Purse is 3¼" x 5¼" without drawstring; Ear Muffs are 3¼" x 16½" without ties; Pocket Appliqué is 3¼" x 6".

MATERIALS FOR SET
Worsted-weight yarn — 2 oz. white, 1 oz. red and small amount lt. peach; 4 pair 12-mm oval wiggle eyes; 4 red ½" pom-poms; craft glue or hot glue gun; tapestry needle; G crochet hook or size needed to obtain gauge.

GAUGE
4 sc sts = 1"; 4 sc rows = 1".

SKILL LEVEL
★★ Average

PURSE
Front
Row 1: Starting at bottom, with white, ch 14, sc in 2nd ch from hook, sc in each ch across, turn (13 sc).

NOTE: For **double loop stitch (dbl lp st),** wrap yarn around one finger 2 times, insert hook in next st and through both lps on finger, yo, draw lp through loops and st, release loops from finger.

Row 2: Ch 1, dbl lp st in each st across, turn.

Row 3: Ch 1, sc in each st across, turn.

Rows 4-6: Repeat rows 2 and 3 alternately, ending with row 2.

NOTE: When changing colors (see page 159), always drop yarn to wrong side of work. Carry yarn loosely across back to next section of same color, catching loose strand every 3 or 4 sts to secure.

Row 7: Ch 1, sc in each of first 3 sts changing to lt. peach in last st made, sc in next 7 sts changing to white in last st made, sc in each of last 3 sts, turn.

Row 8: Ch 1, dbl lp st in each of first 3 sts changing to lt. peach in last st made, sc in next 7 sts changing to white in last st made, dbl lp st in each of last 3 sts, turn.

Rows 9-10: Repeat rows 7 and 8.

Row 11: Repeat row 7, fasten off lt. peach.

Row 12: Ch 1, sc in each st across, turn.

NOTE: For **puff stitch (ps),** (yo, insert hook, yo, draw up ⅜" lp) 3 times in next st, yo, draw through all 7 lps on hook.

Row 13: Ch 1, sc in first st, (ps in next st, sc in next st) across, turn, fasten off.

Row 14: Join red with sc in first st, sc in each st across, turn.

Rows 15-20: Ch 1, sc in each st across, turn.

Row 21: Ch 4, skip next st, dc in next st, (ch 1, skip next st, dc in next st) across, fasten off.

Back
Rows 1-3: Repeat same rows of Front.

Rows 4-10: Repeat rows 2 and 3 alternately, ending with row 2.

Rows 11-12: Ch 1, sc in each st across, turn.

Rows 13-21: Repeat same rows of Front.

With wrong sides held tog, matching colors, sew Front and Back together across sides and bottom leaving top edges open.

For **drawstring (make 2),** with red, ch 70, fasten off. Starting at left side, weave one drawstring through ch sps around top, tie ends together. Starting at right side, weave remaining drawstring through ch sps around top, tie ends together.

For **pom-pom** (make 2), wrap white around 2 fingers 25 times. Slide loops off fingers and tie separate piece white tightly around middle of all loops. Cut loops and trim pom-pom to measure 1½". Tie one pom-pom to each drawstring over tied ends.

For **mustache,** wrap white around 4 fingers 2 times. Tie in center with separate piece white. Glue center of mustache to center of row 7 on Front.

For **nose,** glue red pom-pom to Front above center of mustache. Glue one wiggle eye to each side of nose.

EAR MUFFS
Side (make 2)
Row 1: Starting at tie, with white, ch 71, 2 sc in 2nd ch from hook, turn (2 sc).

Row 2: Ch 1, dbl lp st in each st across, turn.

Row 3: Ch 1, 2 sc in each st across, turn (4).

Row 4: Repeat row 2.

Row 5: Ch 1, 2 sc in first st, sc in each st across with 2 sc in last st, turn (6).

Row 6: Repeat row 2.

Row 7: Ch 1, sc in first st, 2 sc in next st, (sc in next st, 2 sc in next st) across, turn (9).

Row 8: Repeat row 2.

Continued on page 155

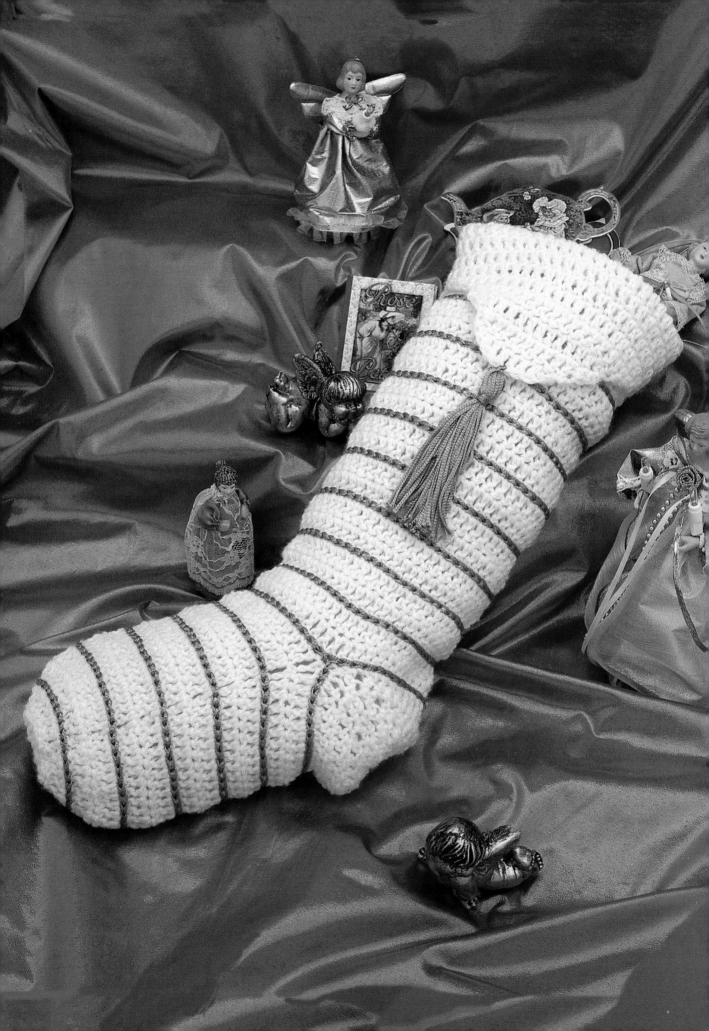

Tassel Stocking

DESIGNED BY FRANCINE MARLIN

SIZE
21" long.

MATERIALS
Worsted-weight yarn — 5 oz. winter white; 50 yds. antique gold ribbon floss; 5" piece cardboard; tapestry needle; H crochet hook or size needed to obtain gauge.

GAUGE
7 sts = 2"; 2 rows = 1".

SKILL LEVEL
★★ Average

STOCKING
NOTE: Back side of sts is right side of work on body of Stocking. Rnds are worked with sts facing out, then Stocking is turned when completed.

Rnd 1: Starting at **top**, with winter white, ch 48, sl st in first ch to form ring, ch 3, dc in each ch around, join with sl st in top of ch-3 (48 dc).

Rnds 2-18: Ch 3, dc in each st around, join.

Rnd 19: For **Heel opening**, ch 24, skip next 23 sts, sl st in next st, ch 3, dc in last 23 sts; working in ch-24, dc in each ch around, join with sl st in top of ch-3 (48 dc).

Rnds 20-28: Ch 3, dc in each st around, join.

Rnd 29: For **toe shaping**, ch 3, dc in next st, dc next 2 sts tog, (dc in each of next 2 sts, dc next 2 sts tog) around, join (36).

Rnd 30: Ch 3, dc next 2 sts tog, (dc in next st, dc next 2 sts tog) around, join (24).

Rnd 31: Ch 3, dc in next st, dc next 2 sts tog, (dc in each of next 2 sts, dc next 2 sts tog) around, join (18).

Rnd 32: Ch 2, dc in next st, (dc next 2 sts tog) around, join with sl st in first dc, fasten off leaving long end for sewing. Weave long end through sts of last rnd, pull tightly to gather, secure.

Heel
Rnd 1: Working around Heel opening, join winter white with sl st in first skipped st on rnd 18, ch 3, (dc next 2 sts tog, dc in next 7 sts) 2 times, (dc next 2 sts tog) 2 times; working on opposite side of ch-24, (dc next 2 chs tog) 2 times, dc in next 7 chs, dc next 2 chs tog, dc in next 7 chs, (dc next 2 chs tog) 2 times, join with sl st in top of ch-3 (38 dc).

Rnd 2: Ch 2, dc in next st, dc next 2 sts tog, dc in next 10 sts, (dc next 2 sts tog) 4 times, dc in next 10 sts, (dc next 2 sts tog) 2 times, join with sl st in top of first dc (30).

Rnd 3: Ch 2, dc in next st, dc next 2 sts tog, *dc in each of next 2 sts, dc next 3 sts tog, dc in each of next 2 sts*, (dc next 2 sts tog) 4 times; repeat between **, (dc next 2 sts tog) 2 times, join (18).

Rnd 4: Ch 2, dc in next st, dc next 2 sts tog, dc in next st, (dc next 2 sts tog) 4 times, dc in next st, (dc next 2 sts tog) 2 times, join, fasten off leaving long end for sewing. Weave long end through sts of last rnd, pull tightly to gather, secure.

Cuff
Rnd 1: Working in starting ch on opposite side of rnd 1, with toe pointing left, join winter white with sl st in first ch, ch 3, dc in each ch around, join with sl st in top of ch-3 (48 dc).

Rnds 2-4: Ch 3, dc in each st around, join. At end of last rnd, fasten off.

Row 5: For **first point**, working in rows, skip first 13 sts, join winter white with sl st in next st, sc in next st, hdc in next st, dc in next 19 sts, hdc in next st, sl st in next st leaving remaining sts unworked, turn (24 sts).

Row 6: Skip sl st, sc in next hdc, hdc in next dc, dc in next 15 sts, hdc in next st, sl st in next st leaving last 4 sts unworked, turn (19 sts).

Row 7: Skip sl st, sc in next hdc, hdc in next dc, dc in next 11 sts, hdc in next st, sl st in next st leaving last 3 sts unworked, turn (15 sts).

Row 8: Skip sl st, sc in next hdc, hdc in next dc, dc in next 8 sts, hdc in next st, sl st in next st leaving last 2 sts unworked, turn (12 sts).

Row 9: Skip sl st, sc in next hdc, hdc in next dc, dc in next 5 sts, hdc in next st, sl st in next st leaving last 2 sts unworked, fasten off.

Rows 5-9: For **second point**, joining in first skipped st on rnd 4 of Cuff, repeat same rows of first point.

Trim
Turn Stocking right side out (so back side of sts is on outside of Stocking).

Continued on page 154

Snow Flowers

DESIGNED BY ELLEN ANDERSON

SIZE
45" across.

MATERIALS
Size 10 bedspread cotton — 2,925 yds. white;
No. 7 steel crochet hook or size needed
to obtain gauge.

GAUGE
Rnds 1-9 = 2" across. Each Hexagon is 5" across.

SKILL LEVEL
★★ Average

HEXAGON (make 60)
Rnd 1: Ch 6, sl st in first ch to form ring, ch 1, 12 sc in ring, join with sl st in first sc (12 sc).

Rnd 2: Ch 1, sc in first st, ch 2, skip next st, (sc in next st, ch 2, skip next st) around, join (6 ch sps).

Rnd 3: Sl st in first ch sp, (ch 3, 3 dc, ch 3, sl st) in same sp, (sl st, ch 3, 3 dc, ch 3, sl st) in each ch sp around, **do not** join (6 small petals).

Rnd 4: Ch 1, sc in first skipped sc on rnd before last, ch 3, skip next small petal, (sc in next skipped sc on rnd before last, ch 3, skip next small petal) around, join with sl st in first sc (6 ch sps).

Rnd 5: Sl st in first ch sp, (ch 3, 5 dc, ch 3, sl st) in same ch sp, (sl st, ch 3, 5 dc, ch 3, sl st) in each ch sp around, **do not** join (6 large petals).

NOTE: Joining hdc on next rnd counts as ch sp.

Rnd 6: Ch 1, sc in first sc on rnd before last, (ch 2, skip next large petal, sc in next sc on rnd before last) around; to **join,** hdc in first sc (6 ch sps).

Rnd 7: Ch 3, dc around joining hdc, (ch 2, 2 dc in next ch sp) around; to **join,** hdc in top of ch-3 (12 dc, 6 ch sps).

Rnd 8: Ch 3, dc around joining hdc, ch 1, *(2 dc, ch 2, 2 dc) in next ch sp, ch 1; repeat from * around, 2 dc around same joining hdc as first 2 sts, join as before (24 dc, 6 ch-2 sps, 6 ch-1 sps).

Rnd 9: Ch 3, dc around joining hdc, ch 1, 2 dc in next ch-1 sp, ch 1, *(2 dc, ch 2, 2 dc) in next ch-2 sp, ch 1, 2 dc in next ch-1 sp; repeat from * around, 2 dc around same joining hdc as first 2 sts, join (36 dc, 12 ch-1 sps, 6 ch-2 sps).

Rnds 10-14: Ch 3, dc around joining hdc, ch 1, (2 dc in next ch-1 sp, ch 1) across to next ch-2 sp, *(2 dc, ch 2, 2 dc) in next ch-2 sp, ch 1, (2 dc in next ch-1 sp, ch 1) across to next ch-2 sp; repeat from * around, 2 dc around same joining hdc as first 2 sts, join, ending with 16 dc and 7 ch-1 sps across each side between ch-2 sps in last rnd.

Rnd 15: Ch 3, dc around joining hdc, dc in each dc and in each ch-1 sp around with (2 dc, ch 2, 2 dc) in each ch-2 sp, 2 dc around same joining hdc as first 2 sts, ch 2, join with sl st in top of ch-3, fasten off (27 dc across each side between ch-2 sps).

To **join Hexagons,** with right sides held tog and working through both thicknesses, join with sc in first ch of any ch-2 sp, sc in each st across to next ch-2 sp, sc in next ch, fasten off. Join Hexagons in rows first, then join rows of Hexagons as shown in Hexagon Assembly Diagram.

HEXAGON ASSEMBLY DIAGRAM

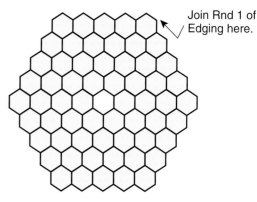

Join Rnd 1 of Edging here.

CENTER TRIM
Rnd 1: Working in chs and sts around opening in center of Tree Skirt, join with sc in any ch sp, ch 2, skip next 2 sts, (sc in next st or ch sp, ch 2, skip next 2 sts or ch sp) around, join with sl st in first sc (58 ch sps).

Rnd 2: Sl st in first ch sp, (ch 3, 3 dc, ch 3, sl st) in same sp, (sl st, ch 3, 3 dc, ch 3, sl st) in each ch sp around, join with sl st in first sl st, fasten off.

EDGING
Rnd 1: Working around entire outer edge, join with sc in ch-2 sp as shown in diagram, ch 3, sc in same sp, [◊ch 3, skip next 3 sts, (sc in next st, ch 3, skip next 3 sts) across to next ch-2 sp, *(sc, ch 3, sc) in next ch-2 sp, ch 3, skip next 3 sts, (sc in next st,

Continued on page 150

Snow Flowers

Continued from page 148

ch 3, skip next 3 sts) across to next seam, sc next 2 ch sps tog skipping seam in between, ch 3, skip next 3 sts, (sc in next st, ch 3, skip next 3 sts) across to next ch-2 sp; repeat from * 3 more times◊, (sc, ch 3, sc) in next ch-2 sp]; repeat between [ ] 4 more times; repeat between ◊◊, join with sl st in first sc.

Rnd 2: Sl st in first ch sp, (ch 3, 5 dc, ch 3, sl st) in same sp, (sl st, ch 3, 5 dc, ch 3, sl st) in each ch sp around, join with sl st in first sl st, fasten off.❖

Santa Suit

Continued from page 130

Rows 2-5: Ch 2, hdc in each st across, turn.

Row 6: For **first front,** ch 2, skip next st, hdc in next 14 sts leaving remaining sts unworked, turn (15).

Rows 7-15: Ch 2, skip next st, hdc in each st across, turn. At end of last row (6), fasten off.

Row 6: For **second front,** skip next 28 unworked sts on row 5, join red with sl st in next st, ch 2, skip next st, hdc in last 14 sts, turn (15).

Rows 7-15: Ch 2, skip next st, hdc in each st across, turn. At end of last row (6), fasten off.

Row 6: For **back,** skip next skipped st on row 5 after first front, join red with sl st in next st, ch 2, hdc in next 25 sts leaving last st unworked, turn (26 hdc).

Rows 7-10: Ch 2, skip next st, hdc in each st across, turn. At end of last row (22).

Row 11: Ch 2, hdc in next 7 sts, sl st in next 6 sts, hdc in last 8 sts, turn.

Row 12: Ch 2, hdc in next 6 sts, sl st in next 8 sts, hdc in last 7 sts, turn.

Rows 13-15: Ch 2, hdc in next 5 sts, sl st in next 10 sts, hdc in last 6 sts, turn. At end of last row, fasten off.

Row 1: For **first front tip,** working on opposite side of starting ch on row 1, join red with sl st in first ch, ch 2, skip next ch, hdc in next 14 chs leaving remaining chs unworked, turn (15 hdc).

Rows 2-4: Ch 2, skip next st, hdc in each st across to last 2 sts, skip next st, hdc in last st, turn (13, 11, 9).

Row 5: Ch 2, skip next st, (hdc next 2 sts tog) 3 times, hdc in last st, turn (5).

Row 6: Ch 2, skip next st, hdc next 2 sts tog, hdc in last st, turn (4).

Row 7: Ch 2, skip next st, hdc next 2 sts tog, fasten off.

Row 1: For **second front tip,** working on opposite side of starting ch on row 1, skip next 28 chs, join red with sl st in next ch, ch 2, skip next ch, hdc in last 14 chs, turn (15 hdc).

Rows 2-7: Repeat same rows on first front tip.

For **shoulder seams,** matching first and last 6 hdc of back to sts on last rows of fronts; working through both thicknesses, join red with sc in first st at armhole edge, sc in next 5 sts; working on back only, sc in next sl st, sl st in next 8 sl sts, sc in last sl st; working through both thicknesses across shoulder, sc in last 6 sts, fasten off.

For **armhole edging,** join red with sc in skipped st at center bottom of underarm; spacing sts evenly so edge lays flat, sc in ends of rows around armhole, join with sl st in first sc, fasten off. Repeat on other armhole.

For **Vest edging,** working in sts and ends of rows around entire outer edge, join red with sc in center back st on next edge; spacing sts evenly so edge lays flat, sc around sides and bottom of Vest, join with sl st in first sc, fasten off.

With sewing thread and needle, sew snaps over rows 2 and 6 at front of Vest. Glue gold ribbon roses over snaps on front as shown in photo.

SHIRT

Row 1: With white, ch 61, sc in 2nd ch from hook, sc in each st across, turn (60 sc).

Rows 2-10: Ch 2, hdc in each st across, turn.

Row 11: For **first front,** ch 2, hdc in next 14 sts leaving remaining sts unworked, turn (15).

Rows 12-17: Ch 2, hdc in each st across, turn. At

end of last row, **do not** turn, fasten off.

Row 11: For **second front,** skip next 30 unworked sts on row 10, join white with sl st in next st on row 10, ch 2, hdc in next 14 sts, turn (15).

Rows 12-17: Repeat same rows of first front.

Row 11: For **back,** skip next 3 unworked sts on row 10, join white with sl st in next st, ch 2, hdc in next 23 sts leaving remaining sts unworked, turn (24).

Rows 12-17: Ch 2, hdc in each st across, turn. At end of last row, fasten off.

For **shoulder seams,** hold right side of last rows on fronts and back together; starting at armhole edge, matching sts and working through both thicknesses, join white with sc in first st, sc in next 7 sts; leaving last 7 sts on first front unworked, sc in next 8 sts on back; skipping first 7 sts on second front, match last 8 sts of seond front to last 8 sts on back; working through both thicknesses, sc in each st across, fasten off.

Collar

Row 1: With wrong side facing you, working across neck edge of Shirt, skip first 4 sts on front, join white with sl st in next st, ch 2, hdc in same st, hdc in each of next 2 sts, hdc in next worked st before seam, hdc in shoulder seam, hdc in next 8 sts, hdc in next seam, hdc in next worked st after seam, hdc in each of next 2 sts, 2 hdc in next st leaving last 4 sts unworked, turn (20 hdc).

Rows 2-4: Ch 2, hdc in same st, hdc in each st across to last st, 2 hdc in last st, turn. At end of last row, **do not** turn.

For **Shirt edging,** working in sts and ends of rows around entire outer edge, spacing sts so edge lays flat, sc around with 3 sc in each outer corner on Shirt and Collar, join with sl st in first sc, fasten off.

With sewing thread and needle, sew 3 snaps evenly spaced down front opening of Shirt.

Sleeves

Rnd 1: Working around one armhole, join white with sc in first skipped st at underarm, sc in each of next 2 sts; working in ends of rows, evenly sp 21 more sc around, join with sl st in first sc (24 sc).

Rnds 2-11: Ch 2, hdc in each st around, join with sl st in top of ch-2 (24 hdc).

Rnd 12: Ch 1, hdc first 2 sts tog, (hdc next 2 sts tog) around, join with sl st in first hdc (12).

Rnds 13-15: Ch 1, sc in each st around, join with sl st in first sc. At end of last rnd, fasten off.

Repeat in other armhole.❖

Holiday Candle

DESIGNED BY BEVERLY MEWHORTER

SIZE
5½" tall.

MATERIALS
Worsted-weight yarn — 1 oz. red, small amount each white, green and yellow; craft glue or hot glue gun; 12-oz. soda can; tapestry needle; G crochet hook or size needed to obtain gauge.

GAUGE
4 sts = 1"; 2 dc rows = 1".

SKILL LEVEL
★ Easy

CANDLE
Rnd 1: With red, ch 4, 9 dc in 4th ch from hook, join with sl st in 3rd ch of ch-4 (10 dc).

Rnd 2: Ch 3, dc in same st, 2 dc in each st around, join with sl st in top of ch-3 (20).

Rnd 3: Ch 3, dc in same st, dc in next st, (2 dc in next st, dc in next st) around, join (30).

Rnd 4: Working in **back lps** only, ch 3, dc in each st around, join.

Rnds 5-12: Ch 3, dc in each st around, join. At end of last rnd, fasten off.

Rnd 13: For **candle holder,** working in **front lps,** join green with sl st in any st, ch 3, 2 dc in same st, 3 dc in each st around, join, fasten off.

Rnd 14: Join white with sc in any st, sc in each st around, join with sl st in first sc, fasten off.

Handle
With white, ch 17, dc in 3rd ch from hook, dc in each ch across to last st, (dc, ch 2, sl st) in last st, fasten off.

Flame
With yellow, ch 10, sl st in 6th ch from hook, fasten off.

Base
Rnds 1-3: Repeat same rnds of Candle. At end of last rnd, fasten off.

FINISHING
1: Sew or glue Flame in center of rnd 1 on Candle.

2: Insert soda can into Candle; working in **back lps** of rnd 12 on Candle and in both lps of rnd 3 on Base, sew Base to Candle.

3: Glue one end of Handle to last rnd on Candle; glue other end to rnd 14 on Candle holder.❖

thicknesses, using G crochet hook, join white with sl st in first st, (ch 1, sl st in next st) across, fasten off.

Repeat until all 7 Panels have been joined.

BORDER

Rnd 1: Working around entire outer edge, with right side facing you, using G crochet hook, join gold with sc in any corner, 2 sc in same sp, sc in each st around with 3 sc in each corner and skipping joining seams, join with sl st in first sc, **turn.**

Rnd 2: Ch 1, sc in each st around with 3 sc in center st of each 3-sc corner, join, **do not** turn, fasten off.

Rnd 3: Join white with sc in center st of any 3-sc corner, sc in each st around with 3 sc in center st of each corner, join, **turn.**

Rnd 4: Repeat rnd 2.

FRINGE

For **each Fringe,** cut 2 strands white each 14" long. Holding both strands tog, fold in half, insert hook in st, draw fold through, draw all loose ends through fold, tighten. Trim ends.

Fringe in each st across short ends of Afghan.❖

Tassel Stocking

Continued from page 147

Beginning and ending at joining seam, using Chain Stitch (see page 159), embroider around top of sts on rnd 1.

Repeat trim around top of each odd-numbered rnd up to rnd 29.

For trim around bottom of heel, beginning and ending where heel and foot join at top of rnd 19, embroider across ch-24 of heel opening as shown in photo.

Tassel

Wrap gold ribbon around 5" piece of cardboard 24 times. Tie separate strand tightly around all loops at one end leaving long ends for tying to Stocking; cut loops at opposite end. Tie another strand around all loops 1" from fold and wrap; secure ends.

Tie Tassel in center of last row on front point of Cuff.❖

Row 9: Repeat row 5 (11).

Row 10: Repeat row 2.

Row 11: Repeat row 5 (13).

Row 12: Repeat row 2.

Row 13: Ch 1, sc in each of first 3 sts changing to lt. peach in last st made, sc in next 7 sts changing to white in last st made, sc in each of last 3 sts, turn.

Row 14: Ch 1, dbl lp st in each of first 3 sts changing to lt. peach in last st made, sc in next 7 sts changing to white in last st made, dbl lp st in each of last 3 sts, turn.

Rows 15-16: Repeat rows 13 and 14.

Row 17: Repeat row 13, fasten off lt. peach.

Row 18: Ch 1, sc in each st across, turn.

Row 19: Ch 1, sc in first st, (puff st in next st, sc in next st) across, turn, fasten off.

Row 20: Join red with sc in first st, sc in each st across, turn.

Rows 21-34: Ch 1, sc in each st across, turn. At end of last row, fasten off.

Sew last row of each Side together.

For **small pom-pom** (make 2), wrap red around 2 fingers 25 times. Slide loops off fingers and tie separate piece red tightly around middle of all loops. Cut loops and trim pom-pom to measure 2". Tie to end of each tie.

For **large pom-pom,** wrap white around 2 fingers 45 times. Slide loops off fingers and tie separate piece white tightly around middle of all loops. Cut loops and trim pom-pom to measure 2". Tie to center top over seam.

For **mustache** (make 2), wrap white around 4 fingers 2 times. Tie in center with separate piece white. Glue center of mustache to center of row 13 on each Side. For **nose,** glue red pom-pom above each mustache. Glue one wiggle eye to each side of nose on both Sides.

POCKET APPLIQUÉ

Rows 1-14: Repeat same rows of Purse Front on page 144.

Rows 15-19: Ch 1, skip first st, sc in each st across to last 2 sts, skip next st, sc in last st, turn, ending with 3 sts in last row.

Row 20: Ch 1, skip first st, sc in next st, sl st in last st, fasten off.

For **pom-pom,** wrap white around 2 fingers 25 times. Slide loops off fingers and tie separate piece white tightly around middle of all loops. Cut loops and trim pom-pom to measure 1¼". Tie to sc on last row.

For **mustache,** wrap white around 4 fingers 2 times. Tie in center with separate piece white. Glue center of mustache to center of row 7.

For **nose,** glue red pom-pom above mustache. Glue one wiggle eye to each side of nose.

With fabric glue, glue side and bottom edges on back of Appliqué to desired garment.❖

Getting Started

Yarn & Hooks

Always use the weight of yarn specified in the pattern so you can be assured of achieving the proper gauge. It is best to purchase extra of each color needed to allow for differences in tension and dyes.

The hook size stated in the pattern is to be used as a guide. Always work a swatch of the stitch pattern with the suggested hook size. If you find your gauge is smaller or larger than what is specified, choose a different size hook.

Gauge

Gauge is measured by counting the number of rows or stitches per inch. Each of the patterns featured in this book will have a gauge listed. Gauge for some small motifs or flowers is given as an overall measurement. Proper gauge must be attained for the project to come out the size stated, and to prevent ruffling and puckering.

Make a swatch in the stitch indicated in the gauge section of the instructions. Lay the swatch flat and measure the stitches. If you have more stitches per inch than specified in the pattern, your gauge is too tight and you need a larger hook. Fewer stitches per inch indicates a gauge that is too loose. In this case, choose a smaller hook size. Next, check the number of rows. If necessary, adjust your row gauge slightly by pulling the loops down a little tighter on your hook, or by pulling the loops up slightly to extend them.

Once you've attained the proper gauge, you're ready to start your project. Remember to check your gauge periodically to avoid problems later.

Pattern Repeat Symbols

Written crochet instructions typically include symbols such as parentheses, asterisks and brackets. In some patterns a diamond or bullet (dot) may be added.

( ) Parentheses enclose instructions which are to be worked again later or the number of times indicated after the parentheses. For example, "(2 dc in next st, skip next st) 5 times" means to follow the instructions within the parentheses a total of five times. If no number appears after the parentheses, you will be instructed when to repeat further into the pattern. Parentheses may also be used to enclose a group of stitches which should be worked in one space or stitch. For example, "(2 dc, ch 2, 2 dc) in next st" means to work all the stitches within the parentheses in the next stitch.

* Asterisks may be used alone or in pairs, usually in combination with parentheses. If used in pairs, the instructions enclosed within asterisks will be followed by instructions for repeating. These repeat instructions may appear later in the pattern or immediately after the last asterisk. For example, "*Dc in next 4 sts, (2 dc, ch 2, 2 dc) in corner sp*, dc in next 4 sts; repeat between ** 2 more times" means to work through the instructions up to the word "repeat," then repeat only the instructions that are enclosed within the asterisks twice.

If used alone an asterisk marks the beginning of instructions which are to be repeated. Work through the instructions from the beginning, then repeat only the portion after the * up to the word "repeat"; then follow any remaining instructions. If a number of times is given, work through the instructions one time, repeat the number of times stated, then follow the remainder of the instructions.

[ ] Brackets, ◊ diamonds and • bullets are used in the same manner as asterisks. Follow the specific instructions given when repeating.

Finishing

Patterns that require assembly will suggest a tapestry needle in the materials. This should be a #16, #18 or #26 blunt-tipped tapestry needle. When stitching pieces together, be careful to keep the seams flat so pieces do not pucker.

Hiding loose ends is never a fun task, but if done correctly, may mean the difference between an item looking great for years or one that quickly shows signs of wear. Always leave 6-8" of yarn when beginning or ending. Thread the loose end into your tapestry needle and carefully weave through the back of several stitches. Then, weave in the opposite direction, going through different strands. Gently pull the end and clip, allowing the end to pull up under the stitches.

If your project needs blocking, a light steam pressing works well. Lay your project on a large table or on the floor, depending on the size, shaping and smoothing by hand as much as possible. Adjust your steam iron to the permanent press setting, then hold slightly above the stitches, allowing the steam to penetrate the thread. Do not rest the iron on the item. Gently pull and smooth the stitches into shape, spray lightly with starch and allow to dry completely.

Stiffening

There are many liquid products on the market made specifically for stiffening doilies and other soft items. For best results, carefully read the manufacturer's instructions on the product you select before beginning.

Forms for shaping can be many things. Styrofoam® shapes and plastic margarine tubs work well for items such as bowls and baskets. Glass or plastic drinking glasses are used for vase-type items. If you cannot find an item with the dimensions given in the pattern to use as a form, any similarly sized item can be shaped by adding layers of plastic wrap. Place the dry crochet piece over the form to check the fit, remembering that it will stretch when wet.

For shaping flat pieces, corrugated cardboard, Styrofoam® or a cutting board designed for sewing may be used. Be sure to cover all surfaces of forms or blocking board with clear plastic wrap, securing with cellophane tape.

If you have not used fabric stiffener before, you may wish to practice on a small swatch before stiffening the actual item. For proper saturation when using conventional stiffeners, work liquid thoroughly into the crochet piece and let stand for about 15 minutes. Then, squeeze out excess stiffener and blot with paper towels. Continue to blot while shaping to remove as much stiffener as possible. Stretch over form, shape and pin with rust-proof pins; allow to dry, then unpin.

Acknowledgments

We would like to extend our sincerest appreciation to the following manufacturers who generously provided their products for use in the projects indicated. Thanks, also, to the individuals and company who provided locations for photography, models, props and other contributions.

AD TECH
Trinket Box	*Crafty Magic Melt Glue*
Santa's Suit	*Crafty Magic Melt Glue*
Santa Set	*Crafty Magic Melt Glue*

BEL-TREE
Santa Set	*Wiggle Eyes*

COATS & CLARK
Butterfly Afghan	*Red Heart Super Saver*
	Red Heart Classic
Oval Pineapples	*J.&P. Coats Old Fashioned*
	Crochet Cotton
Circus Pillow	*Red Heart Classic*
All in White	*Red Heart Baby Yarn*
Garden Blouse	*Knit-Cro-Sheen*
Autumn Wheat	*Red Heart Super Saver*
Pastel Dress	*Knit-Cro-Sheen*
Granny's 9-Patch	*Red Heart Super Saver*
Santa's Suit	*LusterSheen*
Santa Set	*Red Heart Classic*

CARON INTERNATIONAL
Snowballs Sweater	*Sayelle*
Sunny Garden	*Wintuk*
Trinket Box	*Simply Soft*
Yuletide Poinsettias	*Simply Soft*

DMC
Starfire Doily	*Cebelia*

FIBRE-CRAFT
Santa's Suit	*14½" Santa Claus Doll*

KREINIK
Tassel Stocking	*Ribbon Floss*

LION BRAND
Pink Ice Layette	*Jamie & Jamie Baby*
Petite Ripples	*Jamie*
Baby Fans	*Jamie*
Polka-Dot Set	*Wool-Ease*
Tweed Cables	*Wool-Ease*
Fancy Cardigan	*Wool-Ease*

OFFRAY
Trinket Box	*Satin Ribbon*

SPINRITE
Easter Egg Pillow	*Bernat Berella "4"*
Victorian Eyelet	*Bernat Berella "4"*
Littlest Snowman	*Bernat Berella "4"*
Tassel Stocking	*Bernat Berella "4"*

WESTRIM CRAFTS
Polka-Dot Set	*Pom-poms*

Photography locations: Gladys Large Fuller, and Terry & Jill Waggoner, Overton.
Models: Grant Barrage, Courtney Hitt, Michaela Hutchins, Erin Prather, Jill, Hannah & Savannah Waggoner.
Props and Special Help: Dale Miller of Broadway Florist, Big Sandy.

Stitch Guide

Basic Stitches

Front Loop (A)/Back Loop (B)
(front lp/back lp):

Chain *(ch):* Yo, draw hook through lp.

Slip Stitch *(sl st):* Insert hook in st, yo, draw through st and lp on hook.

Single Crochet *(sc):* Insert hook in st (A), yo, draw lp through, yo, draw through both lps on hook (B).

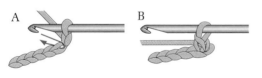

Half Double Crochet *(hdc):* Yo, insert hook in st (A), yo, draw lp through (B), yo, draw through all 3 lps on hook (C).

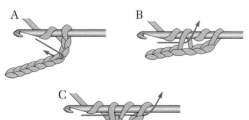

Double Crochet *(dc):* Yo, insert hook in st (A), yo, draw lp through (B), (yo, draw through 2 lps on hook) 2 times (C and D).

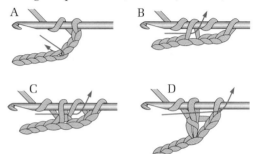

Treble Crochet *(tr):* Yo 2 times, insert hook in st, yo, draw lp through, (yo, draw through 2 lps on hook) 3 times.

Final Step

Double Treble Crochet *(dtr):* Yo 3 times, insert hook in st, yo, draw lp through, (yo, draw through 2 lps on hook) 4 times.

Final Step

Triple Treble Crochet *(ttr):* Yo 4 times, insert hook in st, yo, draw lp through, (yo, draw through 2 lps on hook) 5 times.

Final Step

Special Stitches

Front Post/Back Post Stitches *(fp/bp)*:
Yo, insert hook from front to back (A) or back to front (B) around post of st on indicated row; complete as stated in pattern.

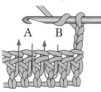

Reverse Single Crochet *(reverse sc)*:
Working from left to right, insert hook in next st to the right (A), yo, draw through st, complete as sc (B).

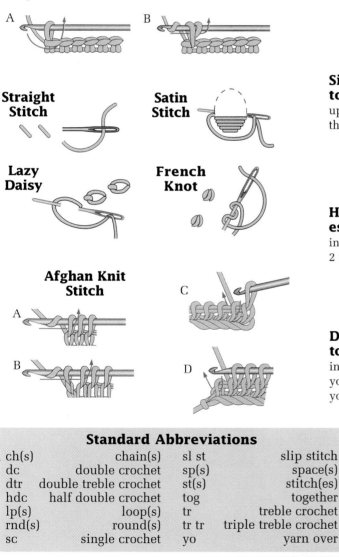

Straight Stitch

Satin Stitch

Lazy Daisy

French Knot

Afghan Knit Stitch

Changing Colors

Single Crochet Color Change
(sc color change): Drop first color; yo with 2nd color, draw through last 2 lps of st.

Double Crochet Color Change
(dc color change): Drop first color; yo with 2nd color, draw through last 2 lps of st.

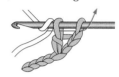

Decreasing

Single Crochet next 2 stitches together *(sc next 2 sts tog)*: Draw up lp in each of next 2 sts, yo, draw through all 3 lps on hook.

Half Double Crochet next 2 stitches together *(hdc next 2 sts tog)*: (Yo, insert hook in next st, yo, draw lp through) 2 times, yo, draw through all 5 lps on hook.

Double Crochet next 2 stitches together *(dc next 2 sts tog)*: (Yo, insert hook in next st, yo, draw lp through, yo, draw through 2 lps on hook) 2 times, yo, draw through all 3 lps on hook.

Standard Abbreviations

ch(s)	chain(s)	sl st	slip stitch
dc	double crochet	sp(s)	space(s)
dtr	double treble crochet	st(s)	stitch(es)
hdc	half double crochet	tog	together
lp(s)	loop(s)	tr	treble crochet
rnd(s)	round(s)	tr tr	triple treble crochet
sc	single crochet	yo	yarn over

Index

For More Information
Sometimes even the most experienced needlecrafters can find themselves having trouble following instructions. If you have difficulty completing your project, write to:

Heavenly Crochet Pleasures Editors
The Needlecraft Shop
23 Old Pecan Road, Big, Sandy, TX 75755